Anarchists Never Surrender

Essays, Polemics, and Correspondence on Anarchism, 1908–1938

Victor Serge

Edited and Translated by Mitchell Abidor

Anarchists Never Surrender: Essays, Polemics, and Correspondence on Anarchism, 1908–1938
Victor Serge. Edited and Translated by Mitchell Abidor.
Foreword by Richard Greeman
This edition copyright © 2015 PM Press

This book has been made possible in part by a generous donation from the Anarchist Archives Project

ISBN: 978-1-62963-031-1

Library of Congress Control Number: 2014908074

Cover by John Yates / Stealworks
Interior design by briandesign

10 9 8 7 6 5 4 3 2 1

PM Press
PO Box 23912
Oakland, CA 94623
www.pmpress.org

Printed in the USA by the Employee Owners of Thomson-Shore in Dexter, Michigan. www.thomsonshore.com

Contents

Meditation on a Maverick
by Richard Greeman

"ANARCHISTS NEVER SURRENDER!" WHAT AN APT TITLE MITCH ABIDOR HAS chosen for his beautifully translated anthology of the anarchist writings of Victor Lvovitch Kibalchich, aka Victor Serge (1890–1947), who up to the age of twenty-eight wrote and agitated under the pseudonym Le Rétif ("Maverick").

The phrase "Anarchists Never Surrender!" comes from a 1909 Maverick article, written at the age of eighteen, and the anarchists in question, like Kibalchich himself, were Russian exiles, resolute bandits who fought to the death against a whole squad of London policemen. Maverick's dramatic declaration foreshadowed his own and his comrades' doom in the 'Tragic Bandits' affair a few years later in Paris. Indeed, Victor Kibalchich may be said to have inherited that fate, as he bore the famous name of N.I. Kibalchich, a distant relative, the People's Will terrorist whose bombs blew up the Czar, executed in 1881 and considered a martyr-hero by Victor's parents.

Victor's whole life was to be one of constant rebellion and constant persecution, and he already had a head start at birth. He spent more than ten of his fifty-seven years in various forms of captivity, generally harsh. He did five years' straight time (1912–17) in a French penitentiary ("anarchist bandit"); survived nearly two years (1917–18) in World War I concentration camp ("Bolshevik suspect"); suffered three months' grueling interrogation in Moscow's notorious GPU Lubianka prison ("Trotskyite spy"); and endured three years' deportation to Central Asia for his declared opposition to Stalin's policies and for refusing to confess to trumped-up espionage charges (1933–36). Small wonder his first novel (written in French) bore the title *Men in Prison*.[1]

---

1   Translated and introduced by Richard Greeman (Oakland: PM Press, 2014).

Born of Russian exile parents camped out in Brussels, Victor was a stateless, undocumented alien from birth, destined to be expelled from nearly every country he ever lived in. He was thus vaccinated against the plague of nationalism and remained immune to the patriotic fever that swept away many socialists and anarchists at the outbreak of World War I in 1914. Young Kibalchich inherited the revolutionary ethos of the Russian intelligentsia, and little else from his penniless parents when they split up, leaving him on his own in Brussels at the age of fifteen. There, he bonded with a gang of teenagers, idealistic underpaid apprentices like himself, "closer than brothers." The Brussels brothers started out as Socialist Young Guards but soon grew impatient with reformism and gravitated to anarchism, impressed with the free life at a short-lived anarchist Commune just outside of Brussels. There they learned the printing trades and eventually put out their own little sheet, *The Rebel*, where Victor first cut his teeth as a writer and adopted the name "Maverick," symbolizing his distance from the tradition of his Russian parents and his embrace of an angry new anarchist identity in the slum streets of Brussels. "Maverick" was the signature on the articles in the first part of this anthology, starting in 1908 and continuing throughout Victor's young manhood to 1917, the year of the Russian Revolution, when Kibalchich started signing "Victor Serge" and decided to go to Russia.

Meanwhile, as "Maverick" he moved to Paris in 1909 and eventually became the editor of the weekly organ of French anarcho-individualism, *l'anarchie*, which preached, among other things, the right of individuals to reappropriate property from the bourgeois bandits who had, after all, stolen it in the first place (Proudhon: property = theft). A perfect theory, until Victor's band of brothers, in total revolt against society and unwilling to be either "masters" or "slaves," began to put it into practice in 1912 through a bloody series of "expropriations" (holdups) in which they pioneered the use of stolen automobiles as getaway cars (the police had only bicycles). Victor/Maverick, although appalled by the bloodshed, defended these "Tragic Bandits of Anarchy" in the pages of *l'anarchie*, declaring, "I am with the wolves!" He was soon arrested. Like the Russian anarchists in London, Maverick's home-boys fought it out to the last, holding off small armies of police, troops, and armed civilians. In 1913, the survivors of what was known as the "Bonnot Gang" were put on trial. Victor's oldest friend got the guillotine, and Maverick was sentenced to five years in solitary in the pen. He managed to survive, and years later wrote a great novel about the experience, *Men in Prison*.[2] That is the context of the early (1908–1913) articles in this collection.

Released in the middle of World War I and expelled from France, Victor ended up in Barcelona, Spain. There he got involved with the local anarcho-syndicalists and participated in the preparation of an insurrectionary general strike in July 1917, itself inspired by the February 1917 Revolution in Russia which seemed to beckon to Victor from across war-torn Europe. He laid to rest his individualist identity of "The Maverick," and began signing himself "Victor Serge," the identity that he would retain for the rest of his life. The Parisian individualist who scorned revolutions as 'illusions,' had now experienced a revolutionary movement in Spain and felt himself drawn to the Russian Revolution as to a flame. Yet we can see in the two articles from 1917 that he was still settling his scores with anarcho-individualism in his mind. And indeed, as "Serge" he retained the essence of his anarchism—the belief in the primacy of the individual, in human freedom—to his dying day.

Arriving in Petrograd,[3] the frozen, starving, besieged capital of Red Russia, Serge made the rounds of the anarchists and socialists before deciding to work with the Bolsheviks as the only practical way to serve the living revolution while hoping to influence it in a libertarian direction once victory was won. The newly founded Communist International immediately put to use Serge's talents as a writer, translator, and printer, and at a crucial moment in the Civil War, when all seemed lost, he joined the Communist Party, the better to serve the cause. In this, he had much in common with other 'Soviet' anarchists, including the Americans Bill Chatov and Big Bill Haywood.

This was the period when Lenin was wooing the "best elements" among the anarchists and anarcho-syndicalists of Europe to the Communist International, and Serge's reports, published in France, were part of that Soviet propaganda campaign. For example Serge's 1920 "The Anarchists and the Russian Revolution,"[4] (like the "Letter from Russia" in this volume) is a passionately argued apology for the Bolshevik monopoly of power, necessitated by the Civil War, and the repression of Russian anarchists, an armed group whose disorganization and irresponsibility spelled a threat to the revolution. Serge concludes

---

2   Translated and introduced by Richard Greeman (Oakland: PM Press, 2014).

3   Later named Leningrad and now again St. Petersburg.

4   Translated by Ian Birchall in Serge, *The Revolution in Danger: Writings from Russia, 1919–1921* (Chicago: Haymarket, 1997).

by calling upon his fellow anarchists to join with the Communists and to "strive to preserve the spirit of liberty."

> They will be the enemies of the ambitious, of budding political careerists and commissars, of formalists, party dogmatists and intriguers, in other words to fight the illusions of power, to foresee and forestall the crystallization of the workers' state as it has emerged from war and revolution, everywhere and always to encourage the initiative of individuals and of the masses, to recall to those who might forget that the dictatorship is a weapon, a means, an expedient, a necessary evil—but never an aim or a final goal.

Thus, on the one hand Serge proved his commitment as a loyal, disciplined, unambitious rank-and-file militant, content to serve the Soviets with all his energy and talent. On the other, he openly maintained his personal criticisms of the regime's abuses and used whatever influence he could muster to correct them. This often included intervening personally with high officials of the Cheka secret police in order to free innocent arrestees, including anarchists and other dissidents, at the risk of his being considered their "confederate" and shot at any moment.

And so, in 1919 Serge chose to steer a precarious course between the Scylla of conformist revolutionary careerism and the Charybdis of impotent isolation among the revolution's embittered critics. Serge struggled to maintain this attitude as long as loyal opposition was tolerated in Russia and even afterward, when he was treated as a pariah. For Serge, as for many others, the crisis came in 1921 with the anarchist-supported revolt of the revolutionary sailors' Soviet at the Kronstadt naval base and its bloody repression by the Soviet government. Serge was involved with the mediation efforts of the American anarchists Emma Goldman and Alexander Berkman but was appalled by the Party's unwillingness to negotiate and by the lies it told about the sailors. Demoralized, he withdrew from politics and joined a short-lived French anarchist agricultural commune near Petrograd, before deciding to accept a Comintern job in Berlin, where he hoped to help bring about a German revolution that would liberate Russia from the constraints of isolation and backwardness.

Two of the articles from Russia in this collection are dated 1921, that is to say *after* the repression of Kronstadt, generally seen as a watershed. The article "New Tendencies in Russian Anarchism" is a catalogue of libertarian groups which, however divided among themselves, all supported the revolutionary dictatorship, while remaining outside of the Party. Only in passing does it mention those anarchists who *did not* support the dictatorship and who thus had no legal publications to analyze, including a vast anarchist-inspired movement under Makhno in Ukraine. And although Serge cites the American anarchists who did join the Communists, he fails to mention Goldman and Berkman, who were, like him, disillusioned by Kronstadt. Sins of omission, to be sure. To my knowledge Serge never fabricates, and his Soviet apologetics, like the highly convincing "Letter from Russia" included here, are not dull propaganda but sharply observed realities presented in passionate argument.

We have not yet come to the end of the litany of arrests, expulsions, and persecutions that punctuated the saga of Serge's life as an irreducible revolutionary maverick. In the hope that a European revolution could relieve the pressure strangling the revolution in Russia, Serge next moved to Berlin as a Communist journalist-cum-secret-agent. During the 1923 crisis, Serge and his family were obliged to flee Germany for their lives after a failed Red coup. In 1925, he returned to Russia to fight Stalin as a member of the Left Opposition. In 1928 he was expelled from the Party and arrested, but then freed thanks to reactions in France, where his revolutionary writings were well known. Arrested again in 1933, he refused to 'confess' after months of pressure and was deported to detention on the Ural.

Serge escaped from the clutches of Stalin's gulag thanks to the protests of his comrades abroad—a "miracle of solidarity" he called it. In April 1936, just before the Great Purges, Stalin finally allowed Serge and his family to leave Russia after his imprisonment had become a *cause célèbre* in Paris, thus saving Serge's life. But Russia then cancelled his passport and deprived him of his Soviet nationality—the only one he ever had. Fleeing the Nazis in 1940–41, again stateless and undocumented, Serge was briefly interned in Marseille as a suspect. After escaping by freighter to Mexico, he was locked up by the Vichy authorities in Martinique, expelled from the Dominican Republic and Haiti, and then jailed by the Cubans.

Thanks to an "invisible international" of comrades, he found asylum in Mexico in 1941, soon after the assassination of Trotsky, but the Communists, on orders from Moscow, prevented him from publishing and physically attacked him when he tried to speak at a public memorial protest for the Italo-American anarchist Carlo Tresca in Mexico.

Exhausted by years of struggle and imprisonment, he died at the age of fifty-seven with three unpublished masterpieces in his desk drawer. Since the Mexican authorities would not admit corpses lacking a nationality into the cemetery, his friends buried him as a citizen of the Spanish Republic—which had ceased to exist upon Franco's victory in 1939.

All the Right Enemies

Victor the Maverick was indeed one of those anarchists who "never surrender." He lived and died an internationalist, an individualist, and an enemy of the state. And although as "Victor Serge" he collaborated with the Bolsheviks from 1919 to 1927, he never surrendered his identity as an anarchist, fighting as best as he could—inside and then outside of the only legal party—for the rights of the individual. As the list of the governments that locked him up or kicked him out indicates, Serge had 'all the right enemies'—both on the Right and the Left.[5] This made his books more or less unpublishable, and his last novels and *Memoirs* only appeared posthumously. As he wrote shortly before his death, "In every publishing house there are three conservatives and at least one Stalinist."

Attacks from the 'Left' began as soon as he arrived in Europe in 1936. The Communist press in France took up the old (1913) bourgeois accusation of 'anarchist bandit' in an attempt to discredit Serge's exposés of the Moscow frame-up trials in Stalin's Russia. Yet he remained under suspicion, and former GPU agents Elsa Reiss and Walter Krivitsky imagined Serge's release from the gulag was a probably a GPU ploy to insinuate an *agent-provocateur* into the European Trotskyist movement. In fact the real Stalinist *agent-provocateur* ("Etienne" aka Marc Borovsky, Trotsky's trusted Paris correspondent) was busy inculcating the Old Man with distrust of Serge, which probably contributed to their eventual break.[6]

Attacks by the Stalinists didn't prevent certain anarchists from chafing Serge for his earlier support of Lenin and Trotsky. But when Serge, who in 1937 was still Trotsky's faithful admirer and French translator, dared raise the issues of Bolshevism's responsibility in the 1918 creation

---

5   *All the Right Enemies* is the title of Dorothy Gallagher's biography of another political maverick, Serge's comrade Carlo Tresca, assassinated in New York by Fascists, Communists, Mafiosi, or all three in 1943. It would have suited Serge's biography just as well.

6   See Richard Greeman, "Victor Serge and Leon Trotsky," in Greeman, *Beware of Capitalist Sharks! Radical Rants and Internationalist Essays (Illustrated)* (Moscow: Praxis Center, 2008).

of the Cheka secret police and the suppression of the 1921 Kronstadt sailors' rebellion, Trotsky excoriated Serge as a "sycophant," "moralist," a dilettante," and a renegade. (See "Once More over Kronstadt" in this collection, 196.)

Back in 1936, Serge, fresh from Stalin's gulag, had joined up with Trotsky's Fourth International and urged them to reach out to the anarchists in Spain, where along with the POUM, they were spearheading the revolution from below and the war against Franco's Fascists (see "Call for an Alliance with the Anarchists in Spain," in this collection, 194). Trotsky was sympathetic to the idea but was then arrested, and his European followers soon turned on Serge for his softness on the POUM. Seventy years later, some Trotskyist epigones still denigrate Serge for not being revolutionary enough, most recently with the unanswerable but specious argument that if he were alive today he "would have become" a neocon.[7] With friends like these, who needs enemies?

Trotsky and his followers also accused Serge—for once with some justice—of attempting to synthesize anarchism and Marxism. Serge, who described his evolution from anarchism to Marxism as "slow and painful," never broke with his anarchist past and, on the contrary, maintained friendly relations with his old anarchist comrades and remained engaged with anarchist ideas throughout his life. Thus, this volume concludes with Serge's very informative 1938 popular study of "Anarchist Thought" and a manuscript essay, "Anarchism," which was found among his posthumous papers in Mexico.[8]

As a novelist too, he was always conscious of the preciousness of the individual, of individual consciousness within the mass. Above all, he saw both Marxism and anarchism as branches of a big, broadly socialist revolutionary movement running through history and attempted to place them both, with their success and failures within that history.

Alas, the sixty years since Serge's death have not softened the resentment of certain French anarchists who cannot pardon the anarcho-individualist who signed his pre-1912 articles "Maverick" for having evolved from individualism to revolutionary syndicalism and thence to Marxism.

---

7   See Richard Greeman, "Victor Serge's Political Testament," *New Politics* 14, no. 3 (Summer 2013), online at http://assets.nybooks.com/media/doc/2012/07/02/Greeman-Serge.pdf.

8   "Anarchism," undated manuscript found among Serge's posthumous paper in Mexico. Victor Serge Papers, box 3, Beinecke Rare Book and Manuscript Library, Yale University.

The year 2011 saw the publication by the anarchist imprint Libertalia of a whole book that attacked Serge not just for betraying anarchism during the period when, like many anarchists eager to fight for the embattled Russian Revolution, he worked with and eventually joined the Bolsheviks, but also portrayed him as fundamentally "duplicitous," a "hardened liar," and a perpetual "schizophrenic" for the crime of changing his views in the course of his—and history's—political evolution. Indeed, the author of *Victor Serge, l'homme double* even sees Serge's turn to fiction-writing as another form of 'lying' (like Plato, who famously banned art from his Republic, as the incarnation of a 'lie.')[9]

Even my old friend Peter Sedgwick—who in 1963 first relaunched Serge with his pioneering translation of *Memoirs of a Revolutionary* and his seminal essays on Serge—ended up blaming Serge for the "inconsistency and even irresponsibility whereby he was constantly drawn close enough to contending alignments of the Left to earn the opprobrium and suspicion of each camp in turn." I suppose that's one way to look at Serge's brand of courageous critical-minded, antisectarian, yet totally committed revolutionary thinking. Sedgwick, a former psychologist, tries to explain Serge's "love-hate oscillation in the embraces of the Bolshevik State" as a psychological aberration, a "bizarre inner need for contrary political identifications."[10]

Yet to me, as to many Serge readers, Serge, whatever his hesitations, uncertainties and inconsistencies, remains an exemplary revolutionary who still provides us with a moral and political compass in times when so many have lost their way. One need not agree with all his political choices; sometimes he steers off course, but never too far or for too long. And that "course" is always "set on hope" as Serge put it in his poem "Constellation of Death Brothers."[11]

---

9   See Jean-Luc Sahagian, *Victor Serge, l'homme double*, preface by Yves Pagès (Paris: Libertalia, 2011), http://www.archyves.net/html/Documents/Serge-HommeDouble-JLSahagian.pdf. (An approximate translation of *l'homme double* is "the duplicitous" or "double-dealing man.")

10 See, for example, Sedgwick's essay "Victor Serge and Socialism" *International Socialism* 14 (Autumn 1963): 17–23; and his fragment "Victor Serge: Unhappy Elitist," posthumously published in *History Workshop Journal* 17 (Spring 1984), http://www.marxists.org/archive/sedgwick/.

11 Serge, *Resistance (Poems)*, translated by James Brook (San Francisco: City Lights, 1989). The original phrase "le cap est de bonne espérance," is a play on the French homonym *cap* meaning both "course" and "cape," and on the Cape of Good Hope.

Double Duty

How did Serge keep his moral and political compass pointing more or less in the right direction through the twists and turns of twentieth-century revolution? The moral key to Serge's behavior is his principle of "double duty," a concept that helps us understand his ethical choices in each of the crises of his political life. Coming out of the anarchist ethical tradition, Serge felt that revolutionaries had a double duty to defend the revolutionary movement, both against its external enemies (the bourgeoisie, the Whites, etc.) and its internal enemies (authoritarianism, brutality, ego-tripping, corruption, stifling of debate, bureaucratization).

Serge first expounded the double duty principle in the 1930 preface to his history of *Year One of the Russian Revolution*, written when the author was living in semicaptivity in Leningrad, a political nonperson subject to arrest at any moment. Although couched in somewhat veiled language, it is a bold statement given the context. Serge exhorts his readers in Russia and the revolutionary workers' movement "to serve the revolution by fighting the [internal] evils which afflict it, by learning to defend it against its own defects, by making every effort toward the ceaseless elaboration and practice of a politics inspired by the higher interests of the world proletariat; externally, to defend the first Workers' Republic." In 1932 Serge again advanced his concept of double duty in his book *Literature and Revolution* as the basis of his critique of conformist, uncritical pro-Soviet writers, but it is implicit in all his writings and essential to understanding his choices.

On the other hand, Serge was also forced to conclude ruefully that "the accomplishment of double duty can place [one] between the hammer and the anvil." The problem with this balancing of internal and external dangers, of which way to bend the proverbial stick, calls for political judgment, and it is not always clear when the exigencies of the external defense should outweigh the dangers from within. Indeed, Serge's political evolution is best understood as his successive responses to changing political circumstances, from the defeat of pre–World War I French anarchism through the victory of the Russian Revolution and its subsequent degeneration into Stalinist totalitarianism.

This concept of double duty helps explain what Serge's critics among both the anarchists and the Trotskyists have called his "inconsistency." For Serge, the violent individual revolts of French anarchism were attempts to escape from 'a world without possible escape' which had ended in absolute defeat: first the Bonnot tragedy and then the overnight conversion of Gustave Hervé and the antimilitarist anarchists into patriots at the outbreak of World War I. In the wake of these defeats, the Russian Revolution offered hope, and as long as he could discern credible hope for serious reform from within he adhered to it—first as a public apologist and private critic, then as an oppositionist, openly attacking bureaucratic tyranny in Russia and counterrevolutionary Comintern policy abroad.

As we have seen, Serge entered the Russian Revolution as an anarchist. He joined the Bolsheviks—all the while vowing to struggle as he could against their dictatorial tendencies—at the very moment when all seemed lost, with the Whites (backed by Poland, Czechoslovakia, France, Great Britain, and Japan) at the very gates of Petrograd. This was hardly an opportunistic move. The external enemy clearly had priority. "The Bolsheviks were certainly wrong on several essential points: their faith in state ownership, their penchant for centralization and administrative measures," wrote Serge. "But if you wanted to struggle against their mistakes with a free spirit and with the spirit of freedom, you had to be among them."

Although appalled by the Cheka secret police and the brutal suppression of the revolt of the sailors at Kronstadt, Serge nonetheless put "the danger from within" on the back burner and continued publicly to write pamphlets for the Reds, all the while privately trying to save political prisoners, anarchists, poets, and intellectuals from the firing squad and warning a few trusted European comrades. As long as he could perceive hope for reform from within and hope for relief abroad, Serge stuck with the Comintern, agitating for revolution in Germany, and writing within the confines of the "line."

In his first interview with Trotsky in 1926, Serge declared, libertarian style, "We must do away with this bureaucracy." "No," replied Trotsky the authoritarian, "we must take it over!"[12] In the words of anarchist historian George Woodcock, "Where Trotsky was always governed in a difficult choice by revolutionary expediency, Serge was moved by a moral insight that preserved the essentially libertarian strain in his thought and

---

12   Author's conversation with Marcel Body, the French anarchist soldier who went over to the Revolution in 1917, worked, like Serge, as a translator of Lenin, headed up the French Communist Group in Moscow, and became the lover and secretary of Alexandra Kollontai. Body was allowed to return to France in 1927, remained briefly in the French CP for a while and ended translating Bakunin's complete works into French. After such a career, it is difficult to understand Body's negative anarchist attitude toward Serge.

nature."[13] Daniel Guérin, the French Marxist turned anarchist, while critical of Serge's silences in the 1920s, concluded: "Victor Serge was certainly too clear-minded to have any illusions about the real nature of the central Soviet power. But this power was still haloed with the prestige of the first victorious proletarian revolution; it was loathed by world counter-revolution; and that was one of the reasons—the most honorable—why Serge and many other revolutionaries put a padlock on their tongues."[14]

Did Serge continue to hope and to hold his tongue too long? In hindsight, perhaps yes. As he himself wrote in 1937 in the introduction to *Russia Twenty Years After*, his powerful, documented exposé of Stalinism: "The past year shows that all the oppositions which, in the last fourteen years, stood up against the bureaucratic regime, underrated its profoundly counterrevolutionary power and, still more, its inhumanity. The judgments formulated hitherto by the Left Opposition to which I belonged, sinned only in indulgence and optimism, because the Opposition stuck to preserving at all costs the last chances, however feeble, of a political recovery, of a great reform which would have brought the Soviet Union back to the road of socialism." Yet in the same Introduction, Serge reveals that many of his friends on the French Left pressured him not to publish his testimony.

Serge's situation reveals that it may be harder to defend the movement against its inner enemies than against its outer ones. Courage to continue fighting the imperialists, capitalists, militarists, reactionaries, and such is rare enough. But such courage wins the praise of one's peers, bonds us to them, and requires only physical sacrifice. It takes a kind of different courage to think for ourselves, to pay attention to our doubts, to carry them to their logical conclusions, to speak out against the internal flaws of our movement: abuses like conformism, the leadership cult, the stifling of debate, the toleration of male-chauvinism and sexism. Rarer is the courage to be in the minority, to stand alone, to reject the pretense that "we" have a monopoly on the truth, which permits us to indulge in Machiavellian deceptions and manipulations. It takes both kinds of courage to follow the rule of double duty, and if you do follow it, you may very well end up like Serge, making "all the right enemies."

What his sectarian critics fail to recognize is that Serge, the lifelong practical revolutionary, saw anarchism and Marxism as currents within

---

13   George Woodcock, "At Once Archaic and Fresh," review of *Birth of Our Power*, *The New Leader* 50, no. 18 (September 4, 1967).

14   Guérin, *Anarchism* (New York: Monthly Review Press, 1970), 97.

the broad historical stream of revolutionary socialism and from that perspective he was at once appreciative and *critical* of both. Summing up at the very end of his life, he noted:

> The anarchists . . . underestimate the necessities of expanding industrial society, the importance of political power in social struggles, the complexity of social development, the impossibility of building a free and equitable society without passing through various transitional phases. Their doctrine is more emotional than scientific. But their denunciation of the role of the State and of coercion, their ceaseless appeal to the creative faculties of man and of the masses constitute important and incontestably fecund contributions to socialist thought.

On the other hand:

> From Marx's day down to our own, the theorists of scientific socialism have often overlooked the significance and importance of anarchism and have at times combatted it with a singularly unintelligent partisanship (Plekhanov). From its very beginnings, Bolshevism, the animator of the Russian Revolution never ceased pursuing the suppression of anarchism which it considered as a manifestation of the "backward-looking mentality of the petty bourgeoisie."[15]

Serge's 'position' was not that we should mechanically make an amalgam of anarchism and Marxism but that revolutionaries coming from the anarchist and Marxist traditions should listen respectfully to each other's criticisms, debate our historical differences openly and honestly, and work together to create a revolutionary socialist theory and practice to meet the challenges of today.[16]

---

15 "Anarchism," Victor Serge Papers, box 3, Beinecke Rare Book and Manuscript Library, Yale University.

16 It was in this Sergian spirit that in the former Soviet Union a group of veteran dissidents from the *perestroika* period—anarchists, syndicalists, critical Marxists and Greens—opened the Victor Serge Library in Moscow, with thousands of donated radical books previously banned under the totalitarian regime. Organized around the Victor Serge Library, the Praxis Center began holding public forums—beginning with the first critical discussion of the Spanish Revolution of 1936 ever held in Russia. Praxis also translates and publishes books by anarchists (for example Volin's history of the Makhnovist movement), critical Marxists (Raya Dunayevskaya, Maximilien Rubel), and of course Serge. For more information, go to http://www.praxiscenter.ru/about_us/english/ and consider attending an annual international conference.

The Old Mole of Individual Freedom

VICTOR SERGE IS BEST KNOWN AS AN OPPONENT OF STALINISM, AN ALLY OF Trotsky who was sent to a Soviet prison camp and who, thanks to a western campaign in his favor, was able to leave the Soviet Union, where he carried on his fight against the Soviet dictator. Far less well known is Serge's anarchist period, which began in an embryonic form in Belgium in 1906 and lasted at least until his departure for the Soviet Union in 1919. The lessons he learned as an anarchist, and more particularly the anarchist defense of individual freedom, would not only play a key part in Serge's thought and action during his directly anarchist period but would also inflect his Bolshevik activity. The continuity in his thought, the way—to paraphrase Marx—the old mole of individual freedom burrowed through his writings in various guises, means that any attempt to analyze Serge's life by giving his openly anarchist years short shrift, as Susan Weissman does in her *Victor Serge: A Political Biography*, misses the core of his political life.

Still known as Victor Kibalchich, Victor began his political activity in the Young Guard of the Belgian Workers' Party (Parti Ouvier Belge, or POB) in his native Brussels in 1905 when he was only fourteen. An immediate indication of the continuity between the socialism of his adolescent years and his later anarchism is that two of his closest friends and comrades were Raymond Callemin and Jean De Boë, both of whom would, like Victor, move to Paris where they would run in the same individualist circles, and both of whom, like Victor, would be defendants in the trial of the Bonnot Gang in 1913. Callemin received the death penalty, De Boë was sent to a penal colony, and Victor, found guilty of complicity, was sentenced to five years.

Though nominally socialist, Victor and his friends, because of their exuberance, were referred to as "anarchists" within the party, and they in fact spent time at an anarchist commune outside Brussels, where Victor not only got a chance to witness a form of anarchy in action but also learned the printing trade that would enable him to earn a living through his hardest times, and where he also began his career as a journalist.

The radicalism of the Young Guard led them to walk out of a Workers Party special conference on the question of the Congo, where the POB supported the annexation of the Congo while the vocally anti-imperialist Young Guard opposed it. The party began a campaign against the anarchists in their midst, and Victor and his friends would eventually leave the POB and establish themselves as the Revolutionary Young Guard of Brussels, changing the name of their newspaper from *Le Communiste* to *Le Révolté*—the rebel. By early 1908, even as the anarchist community he had been part of collapsed, Victor identified himself as an anarchist and wrote in defense of "illegalism," the adoption of theft as a political and economic tactic by anarchists. Though he was still writing articles against imperialism and in support of striking workers in Italy, class struggle anarchism soon disappeared completely from Serge's writings as he became increasingly individualist and increasingly doubtful of working-class activity, calling the Belgian working class a "mass of cowards" in an article published in September 1908.

There would be no turning back for Victor now, and he increasingly marked out a position at the extreme end of anarchist individualism, defending in his article "Anarchists-Bandits" the London illegalists who had killed two people in what became known as the Tottenham Outrage of January 1909 and praising them as exemplars of the revolutionary spirit, men who lived by the motto "Anarchists Never Surrender!"

Among his final activities in Belgium was his defense of the Russian terrorist Hartenstein, tried and found guilty of killing a policeman who had come to arrest him for planting a bomb. Victor served as a character witness at Hartenstein's trial and wrote glowingly about the defendant in his article "A Man" in *Le Révolté*. But the stagnation of the Left in Belgium, dominated by the reformist POB, along with disputes with other anarchists in Brussels led Victor, despairing of any change in Belgium, to move to the heart of anarchist individualism, Paris. There he immediately began writing for, and eventually editing, the movement's principal organ, *l'anarchie* (all letters lowercased to signify that none was more important than any other), founded by the great Albert Libertad in 1905.

As an active journalist at the heart of Francophone anarchism, only occasionally were his writings commentary on news of the day, events like the Liabeuf Affair, the arrest and execution of an *apache* (street tough) for murdering two policemen trying to arrest him, and the early career of the Bonnot Gang. For the most part, instead, his writing revolved around more general themes common to individualist anarchism since the first appearance of the movement in France around 1890.

These themes were antirevolutionism, contempt for the masses, the obligation that individuals make their own revolution immediately, and illegalism. All of these themes are intertwined and flow together naturally: the contemptible masses make a successful revolution impossible, making it necessary for individualists to make the revolution now in whatever way they can, with the most brutal and direct way being illegalism. These were not the only themes current in Victor's individualist milieu, but it is significant that they were the ones for which he showed the greatest concern. The fact that he ignored other common anarchist individualist issues like neo-Malthusianism, diet and general health-faddism, free and plural love, and the extreme biological determinism that played so important a part in the movement, speaks volumes. So strong was this latter current that he would later speak about a split between "scientifics" and "sentimentals"—the latter allowing feelings a role in human activity and development and the former believing that virtually everything was biologically determined. Victor was a "sentimental," while the members of the Bonnot Gang, with whom he was for a period allied, were almost all "scientifics." Herein lies much of the original tension between Victor and his comrades, which would manifest itself at their trial in 1913, when Serge separated himself from the bandits with whom he was on trial. None of these forms of lifestyle anarchism held any particular attraction for Victor, and he didn't expend much energy on them.

When reading his anarchist writings, what is striking is something that is very much a part of the individualist tradition: the lack of references to authorities. If Marxists and, later, Leninists involved themselves in Talmudic disputes over passages in the works of the masters, individualists almost completely eschewed this practice. All of anarchist individualism grew out of Max Stirner's *The Ego and His Own*, which was originally published in France in 1890, but Stirner's name is never used to back up any of Victor's arguments. To do so not only would have meant abdicating his individuality but also would have constituted erecting Stirner into a hero, an idea that was anathema in his circles. While still in Belgium, in an article written on the anniversary of the death of Émile Henry, a man he clearly admired, Victor issued this caveat: "Let them not reproach me for glorifying a man, making him into a banner. We want neither tribunes nor martyrs nor prophets."[1] Instead of relying on specific passages in Stirner's writings, it is his *weltanschauung* that serves as the foundation for almost all of Victor's positions.

A thinker who was clearly of great importance to young Kibalchich was Gustave Le Bon, whose 1895 work "The Psychology of Crowds" demonstrated that crowds subsume the individual and obliterate the identity of the individuals within it, ideas which Victor sometimes credited to Le Bon in his articles and other times simply paraphrased. Just as Stirner was necessary for Victor in establishing the primacy of the One, Le Bon was needed to demonstrate the dangers of the Many.

In this regard another writer, one far less known, influenced Victor: the uncompromisingly pessimistic individualist Georges Palante. Palante posited not just the need for the Self to affirm itself but also established that there was a clear antinomy between the individual and society, that they were eternal enemies. "Individualism," he wrote, "is the sentiment of a profound, irreducible antinomy between the individual and society. The individualist is he who, by virtue of his temperament, is predisposed to feel in a particularly acute fashion the ineluctable disharmonies between his intimate being and his social milieu." If most anarchists, indeed most revolutionaries, contented themselves with viewing the state as the enemy, one that could be defeated because it was a specific entity, for Palante society itself, a far larger and more nebulous foe, was the true adversary, one whose aim was the grinding down of the individual. Indeed, the same pessimism that Victor often expressed concerning the possibilities and even desirability of social change also appeared in the pages of Palante: "In the name of his own experience and his personal sensation of life the individualist feels he has the right to relegate to the rank of utopia any ideal of a future society where the hoped-for harmony between the individual and society will be established. Far from the development of society diminishing evil, it does nothing but intensify it by rendering the life of the individual

---

1   "Émile Henry," *Le Communiste*, May 13, 1908.

more complicated, more laborious and more difficult in the middle of the thousand gears of an increasingly tyrannical social mechanism."

It should be noted that these extracts from Palante's "La Sensbilité Individualiste" were published in 1909, the year Victor Kibalchich arrived in Paris, and appeared in the chapter of the book titled "Anarchism and Individualism." Victor was certainly aware of these writings and quoted or cited Palante on several occasions, including in one of his final articles before leaving for Red Russia in 1919. Palante's influence can be seen up to the end of Victor's spell as editor of *l'anarchie*. A talk he gave on January 28, 1912, at the *Causeries Populaires* lecture series was titled "The Individual against Society," and his notes for the talk show that his opening remarks on the subject were, "It's rather the contrary that should be said: 'society is the enemy of any individuality.'"[2]

The figure of Friedrich Nietzsche floats over Victor's writings as well. Victor settled accounts with the philosopher of the Übermensch in a recently rediscovered essay written in 1917 while he was living in Barcelona, "A Critical Essay on Nietzsche" (in this collection, 135). Nietzsche was one of the tutelary figures of anarchist individualism, and Victor examined Nietzsche's writings in order to establish the ways in which he was at one with or in opposition to the anarchists. Zarathustrian overtones can be found throughout his newspaper writings, with their call to live a free and full life. This is most glaringly clear in his article "By Being Bold," a dithyrambic piece on the Peruvian aviator Jorge Chávez, who died in 1910 while attempting to become the first man to fly over the Alps. Victor wrote that "having reached these heights, gliding over the snowy Alps, he lived minutes that were worth many lives." In a decidedly Nietzschean mode he continued: "Only those who were capable of risking all in vertiginous flights; those who had the strength to conceive the accomplishment of the impossible and to desire it—the thinkers, apostles, and adventurers—were the demolishers of old civilizations and the builders of new lives."

All of these influences, cited or not, fed into the themes that serve as the heart of his anarchist writings.

Contempt for the masses, for the "herd," drips from his writings of the "*l'anarchie*" period from 1909–12, and if there are any Rétifian adjectives they are spineless (*veule*) and cowardly (*lâche*), which recur

---

2   Quoted in Jean Maitron, "De Kibalchiche à Victor Serge," *Le Mouvement Social* 47, 1964.

frequently in his articles. But already in Belgium, at the time of the Hartenstein Affair, he complained of the common run of men, "how ugly they are, how petty, wicked and hypocritical they are toward each other . . . can this be called living? Can these pitiful beings be called men?" Everything the masses enjoy is subject to his scorn. From the time of Libertad individualists had demonstrated ridicule for festivals and anniversaries, and following in Libertad's footsteps Victor would write that "joy on command is unhealthy, grotesque and stupid, like those who savor it," and the festivities the people engage in are "the apotheosis of the stupidity, the illogic, and the cowardice of vast human herds." Mere contact with this gutless mass is repellent to Kibalchich: "The men I rub shoulders with wrong me at every moment. Their limpness, their rapacity, their foolishness prevent me from living."[3]

When France was in an uproar over the first crime of the Bonnot Gang, the robbery and shooting on the Rue Ordener of a messenger for the Société Générale, Victor felt no sympathy, rather contempt and satisfaction at his fate: "This poor wretch, through his submissive weakness and his stupid honesty was the accomplice of criminals of a far higher caliber than the ones they are hunting down."[4]

Despite countless comments similar to these, Victor claimed not to hate the people: "We love you, for we love men." What he hated was not "men" but what they did with their potentially exalted human status: "We deeply detest your vegetative and bestial existence, your pitiful lack of intelligence."[5]

The sources of this misanthropy and elitism are varied. None of Victor's comrades were of the leisure class; none had received university educations, and Victor had received virtually no formal education. To a large extent all were autodidacts, and their feeling that if they were able to rise above their original muck the others could do so as well is clear in the writings of the time. Since all the individual needs do is will something for it to change, the men of the herd were complicit in the continuation of an absurd society and were worthy of scorn, if not worse.

The next logical step in this idea chain is the denial of the possibility of a successful revolution. This idea is entirely consistent with the

3   "La Haine," *l'anarchie*, September 9, 1909. See "Hatred," in this collection, 32.
4   "Les Hauts-Criminels," *l'anarchie*, January 25, 1912. See "The Real Criminals," in this collection, 111.
5   "Par l'audace," *l'anarchie*, October 6, 1910. See "By Being Bold," in this collection, 68.

preceding one, and is far more logical than the revolutionary hopes invested in the masses by syndicalists and socialists. All of these schools acknowledged the degraded state of the worker under the current social system. Only the individualists, and Victor first among them, asked the question: How can we expect people who accept such a fate to be capable of making a revolution, of building a radiant tomorrow?

For Victor this was not a subjective viewpoint but rather an objective fact settled by science: "In all areas impartial science demonstrates to us the inferiority of the working class." What did Victor see before him but "the degenerates, the hereditary slaves, the pitiful mass of working stiffs that we know *de visu* are physiologically incapable of living in harmony." For the *ouvrieristes* the answer to the question of whether or not the workers can change society was "'Yes' (without ever explaining why)"; for Victor, given the degenerate state of the men who make up the working class, "organizing the working class in order to carry out social transformation means wasting time and energy."[6]

Le Rétif proved his case by attacking the most sacred of working-class cows, the Paris Commune of 1871, and in fact did so in two articles entirely dedicated to scathing attacks on its folly. The uprising was pointless, for "crowds are fickle, puerile, credulous. . . . They are capable of heroism, but they can also commit monstrosities. And in all cases they need masters."[7] No, there was no point in ever seizing power, for "to think that impulsive, defective, ignorant crowds will have done with the morbid illogic of capitalist society is a vulgar illusion."[8] Indeed, even though the defeat of the Commune erased all the positive changes it had made, "their victory would have annihilated them, since they'd preserved the essence of the system of social oppression through private property and the law."[9]

Not only did the Commune fail, but all revolutions have failed: "They have neither destroyed what they wanted to destroy nor constructed anything better." Again Victor returns to the root cause of this inevitable failure: "Lacking in education, not used to thinking, not

---

6   "Notre antisyndicalisme," *l'anarchie*, February 24, 1910. See "Our Antisyndicalism," in this collection, 38.

7   "Une Expérience Révolutionnaire," *l'anarchie*, March 30, 1911. See "A Revolutionary Experience," in this collection, 81.

8   "L'Illusion Révolutionnaire," *l'anarchie*, April 28, 1910. See "The Revolutionary Illusion," in this collection, 43.

9   "Une Expéreince Révolutionnaire" ("A Revolutionary Experience").

knowing how to count on themselves . . . could the workers of 1912 do any better?"[10]

None of this, of course, implies that a rebel should sit idly by while the vulgar herd does nothing or foolishly attempts to rise up. There must be a change to the rotten world that created the degenerate humanity that surrounds and inhibits Victor. In answer to the question of who should be counted on, mass action being worthless, "the anarchists will answer with individual revolt."[11]

This will be done in several ways, for "from this day on anarchists liberate minds." Even the lone anarchist living his free life has great revolutionary ramifications, for "all men profit from the act of revolt of one." Unlike those who think the masses will lead the way, like the socialist Jean Jaurès and his anarchist rival Jean Grave, Victor tells us that "there is no more consistent element of progress than individual initiative"[12] and that "in every social grouping the individualist will remain a rebel."[13]

The anarchist, in young Victor's eyes, echoing the Nietzschean notion of the blond beast "is above all a person who challenges. . . . In decadent civilization he is the salutary barbarian, the only one still capable of creating, of erecting his individuality above the pestilence."[14]

In his memoirs, Serge would later write that "Anarchism swept us away completely because it both demanded everything of us and offered us everything,"[15] and during his youth he had written that "we consider anarchism to be, above all, a way of life." Anarchists are creatures of pure will, in this sense again disciples of Nietzsche: "anarchists formulate neither wishes nor vows: they want and immediately act according to their will."[16]

Freedom, individual freedom, is the be all and end all of anarchist individualism, and even in the unlikely event that a mass revolution

10 "Les Fédérés," l'anarchie, March 28, 1912. See "The Communards," in this collection, 120.

11 "Une Expérience Révolutionnaire" ("A Revolutionary Experience").

12 "L'Individualisme facteur du Progrès," Par-delà la Mêlée 16, 1917. See "Individualism, a Factor of Progress," in this collection, 132.

13 "L'Individualiste et la Société," l'anarchie, June 15, 1911. See "The Individualist and Society," in this collection, 78.

14 "Je Nie," l'anarchie, February 17, 1910. See "I Deny!" in this collection, 55.

15 Serge, Memoirs of a Revolutionary, trans. Peter Sedgwick (New York: NYRB Classics, 2012), 23.

16 "Révolutionnaires? Oui, Mais Comment?" l'anarchie, December 14, 1911. See "Revolutionaries? Yes, but in What Way?" in this collection, 101.

were to succeed, that success would do nothing for the free individual since "the hypothesis of a collectivist tomorrow presages a ferocious struggle between the state and the few individuals desirous of preserving their autonomy."[17] Note the use of the word "few," the implicit elitism in the phrase, since the rest will be quite content to accept the new yoke of the new order.

Victor's individualist anarchist is not only one who challenges, he is also and primarily one who fights, and for whom "not to resist means not to exist."[18] Not just the conquering but the preservation of the little freedom allowed the individual today is a duty, and any challenge to it must be reacted to forcefully.

In Belgium, Victor had been extremely vocal in support of the accused anarchist bomb-maker Hartenstein—giving him the highest praise, that of calling him "a man" for having shot down the policemen who'd come to arrest him—and had not only written about him in *Le Révolté* but also served as a character witness at his trial. He had also defended the Russian anarchists who died fighting after the Tottenham Outrage. "The mere act of a policeman putting his hand on your shoulder, because it signifies an attack on the human personality, is sufficient reason to justify any form of revolt," he wrote in defense of Liabeuf.[19]

For Victor and for individualists in general it is not only political rebels who are worthy of support, leading us inevitably to the vexed subject of illegalism, which had been a part of anarchist individualism for years before Victor's arrival on the scene. The belief that anarchists, recognizing no laws, were self-evidently bound by no laws found its justification in the movement's foundational text, Max Stirner's *The Ego and His Own*, where he writes that "since the state is the 'lordship of law' its hierarchy, it follows that the egoist, in all cases where *his* advantage runs against the State's, can satisfy himself only by Crime."[20] Illegalists had been particularly fond of counterfeiting, but a new breed of illegalists was appearing on the scene, a breed far more violent than ever previously seen, their avatar being what came to be known as the Bonnot Gang.

17   "L'Individualiste et la Société" ("The Individualist and Society").
18   "Deux Russes," *l'anarchie*, December 29, 1910. See "Two Russians," in this collection, 72.
19   "Une Tête va Tomber," *l'anarchie*, May 12, 1910. See "A Head Will Fall," in this collection, 58.
20   Max Stirner, *The Ego and His Own*, (New York: Libertarian Book Club, 1963), 238.

At the gang's trial in 1913 Victor denied ever having advocated illegalism; indeed he claimed to have opposed it. There can be no question that he came to oppose it, and that at the time of his trial his condemnation of the "waste" of men and energies it entailed was sincere. What is difficult to pin down is when he became an opponent of illegalism, for no serious reader of his articles on the subject written during the years 1908–12 could find any opposition to this natural outgrowth of the insistence on the primacy of individuals and their will.

Particularly telling is another of his favorite negative epithets: "honest," used as a pejorative against those anarchists opposed to illegalism, those "honest men," and the general use of the adjective against anyone who condemns rebels.[21] Paradoxically, even criminals can be smeared with that brush: "The *apaches* in general don't interest me. They differ too little from honest people."[22]

In some cases he exercised small feats of legerdemain to disguise his support of illegalism. While still in Belgium he claimed that "every revolt is in essence anarchist. And we should stand alongside the economic rebel the same way we stand beside the political, antimilitarist and propagandist rebel."[23] All rebels, thus are equal. He did, however recognize that illegalists "remain far from us, far from our dreams and wishes. But what difference does that make?" If existing means resisting, and crime is a form of revolt, then the illegalists exist "and they aren't part of the herd." The logic of their acts is patent. "An intellectual and moral rebel, it is on fact only logical that the anarchist doesn't fear becoming, whenever the circumstances seem favorable, an economic rebel.[24]

In the immediate aftermath of the first acts of the Bonnot crime wave he praised the bandits for their "daring," which was one of Victor's favored positive characteristics. And if he didn't advocate crime as an anarchist act, he nevertheless said, "I am with the bandits. I find their role to be noble. Sometimes I see in them men," the last word here too being a term of praise in the Rétifian lexicon.[25]

---

21 "Un Honnête Monsieur," *l'anarchie*, June 15, 1911.

22 "Le Bon Example," *l'anarchie*, January 27, 1910. See "A Good Example" in this collection, 51.

23 "Les Illegaux," *Le Communiste*, June 20, 1908. See "The Illegalists," in this collection, 15.

24 "Anarchistes et Malfaiteurs," *l'anarchie*, February 1, 1912. See "Anarchists and Criminals," in this collection, 114.

25 "Les Bandits," *l'anarchie*, January 21, 1912. See "The Bandits" in this collection, 104.

He perhaps came closest to open advocacy of crime in his article "Against Hunger," an article considered important enough to be issued as a pamphlet almost immediately after appearing in *l'anarchie*. In it he declares that "individual re-appropriation—theft—is the logical opposite of the monopolizing of wealth, just as individual revolt is naturally opposed to the arbitrariness of the law and its agents.[26]

Nor should we think that it was only in his writings that Kibalchich defended illegalism and illegalists. In the notes for what must have been his final talk at the *Causeries Populaires* he says of crime that "we think this is logical / ineluctable / necessary," and ended his talk by saying of the illegalist anarchists that "along with us, they are the only men who dare demand life."[27]

Thus we can see that within Victor Serge's anarchist writings there is a natural and consistent flow, that the connections between the four themes common to individualist anarchism are logical, ineluctable, and necessary. Richard Parry, in his excellent and essential book on the Bonnot Gang, comes to the erroneous conclusion that Victor so loudly praised illegalism because "he simply wanted to make a name for himself as the most 'combative' writer in the milieu."[28] As we have seen, far from this being the case, Victor was being utterly sincere and totally consistent when he defended illegalism in the abstract and the Bonnot Gang in particular. His subsequent condemnation of it was the first step along the road to the break that would lead him to abandon anarchism while maintaining its essence, but the process, contrary to the picture painted in his *Memoirs*, was an extremely slow one.

The break appears to have begun during the year he spent in prison between his arrest on January 31, 1912, and the trial of the surviving members of the Bonnot Gang members. His reflections on the folly of illegalism resulted in his refusing to accept responsibility for the acts of the Tragic Bandits, who for their part denied their guilt. He was sincere in saying he didn't support illegalism at the trial, for by that time

---

26   "Contre la Faim," *l'anarchie*, September 21, 1911. See "Against Hunger," in this collection, 92.

27   Quoted in Jean Maitron, "De Kibalchiche à Victor Serge," *Le Mouvement Social* 47, 1964.

28   Richard Parry, *The Bonnot Gang* (London: Rebel Press, 1987), 168.

he appears to have come to condemn it; he went too far in claiming that he had always opposed it.

He spent a further four years in jail, serving a total of five full years, and during that time he began to seriously reflect on his entire belief system up until then. So by February 1917, immediately upon his release from prison, he wrote to Émile Armand that "I no longer believe that the anarchist formula can be contained in one formula alone; I grant much less importance to words than realities, to ideas than to aspirations, to formulas than to sentiments and acts. I am thus ready to collaborate with all those who will show a fraternal goodwill without attributing great importance to secondary divergences in ideas." He continued in the same mode a month later, again in a letter to Armand, stating that he had "lost the sectarian intransigence of the past" and was "capable of working with all those who, animated by the same desire for a better life—one clearer and more intelligent—advance toward their future, even if their paths are different from mine, and even if they give different names I don't know to what in reality is our common goal."[29]

In his exile in Barcelona he worked with syndicalists and participated in a (failed) mass uprising, but in his lengthy settling of accounts with Nietzsche, "A Critical Essay on Nietzsche," he points out the similarities of Nietzsche's ideas to the most reactionary ideas then current, and speaks dismissively of Nietzsche's effect on anarchists. He says that when an anarchist reads Nietzsche, "a kind of puerile pride seizes hold of our comrade and isolates him in a sterile and limited 'cult of the self.'" That cult of the self was the basis for all of Victor's activity until that point.

While in Spain he wrote for the anarchist newspaper *Tierra y Libertad*, and though he later claimed in his *Memoirs* that he had been immediately seized with enthusiasm for the Russian Revolution, his contemporary writings don't bear that out. In the April 4, 1917, issue of the paper he was still saying that "one mustn't expect great results from political revolutions. . . . And so true political power has hardly changed."

After the failure of the July uprising in Barcelona in 1917 he went to France in an effort to join the Russian army and be sent to his parents' homeland. Arrested in October 1917 for violating his expulsion order, he spent over a year in French detention camps but was still able to write occasionally for the anarchist press, where his praise of the Russian

---

29   Maitron, "De Kibalchiche à Victor Serge."

Revolution remained muted. But it was around this time that his anarchism and individualism sought their fulfillment in mass activity, which alone would allow them to flourish. As he wrote in his final article in the anarchist paper *La Mêlée* before his departure, anarchists must "interest ourselves with all our might in the social life that surrounds us and which will finally allow us to more generously, more humanely realize ourselves."[30] Both ideas—individualism and anarchism—continued to play a part in his thought, writings, and activities, but in a radically different way than formerly.

Though this is not the place to discuss Serge's actions in the Soviet Union, his response to Kronstadt and the defeat of the Makhnovists, anarchism continued to play a role in his life and in inflecting his thought. In fact, it served as a leavening to his Bolshevism, serving as a corrective to the harshness of the ideology of the ruling party.

In 1921, two years after his arrival in the USSR, he would write that "I am only a communist—of libertarian philosophy and ethics— because I see no possibility for the future liberation of the individual outside of a communism called on to evolve a great deal (once it has emerged victorious.)"[31] This passage from "New Tendencies in Russian Anarchism" is of enormous importance. The first and most obvious element is Serge's definition of himself as a schismatic communist. That it was allowed to appear in an official Comintern journal, *Bulletin Communiste*, is in itself significant, since dissident works were even then not common, though not as impossible as they would soon become. The Bolsheviks were clearly using Serge as a way of projecting their openness, as a way of attracting support from the anarchists. That he also said that the communism of the Bolsheviks had to evolve greatly is also a bold statement. The parenthetic remark that ends this sentence is significant: he makes it clear that in whatever way Bolshevism will evolve, this evolution can only occur after victory. Until then, he implies, the methods currently in place—harshly repressive ones that do not liberate the individual—can and must continue. His support of the Cheka is here explained.

But this brief passage contains a statement of his new view of the individual, an idea that will henceforth dominate his thought. The

---

30   "Lettre d'un Emmuré," *La Mêlée*, February 1, 1919.

31   "Les Tendances Nouvelles de l'Anarchisme Russe," *Bulletin Communiste* no. 48–49, November 3, 1921. See "New Tendencies in Russian Anarchism," in this collection, 177.

individual here is viewed as a part of society, a part of a movement, someone to be liberated through common action and whose needs are not opposed to society but are an integral part of it. There is no longer an antinomy between the individual and society. For Serge the individual can now only be liberated along with others, not against others. Elsewhere in this article he recognizes the difficulties of handing over the liberation of the individual to the Communists: "What is too often lacking in communist ideology is a philosophy of the individual for the individual's sake." He knows to fear the total subsuming of the individual by the (worker's) state. But he was confident that once victory over the Whites was ensured, the anarchists (who in this same article he insists are not that different from the Bolsheviks) would play a vital role in reshaping society.

His optimism was misplaced. And just as his defense of illegalism played a role in his being considered so dangerous by the French authorities that he was given as harsh a sentence as possible after the Bonnot trial, it is certain that his hopes for the individual under Bolshevism, this time under the form of Trotskyism, would contribute to his fate there. The road from French detention camps to Soviet ones was twisted, but direct.

The Illegalists

(Editor's note: Émile Armand, later to be one of Serge's closest friends, was a central figure of anarchist individualism.)

ARMAND'S CONVICTION IN PARIS FOR COUNTERFEITING HAS BROUGHT BACK the old question of the illegalists.

I don't know Armand or the details of his affair. And so without showing any particular interest in his personality—toward which I only feel that sentiment of fraternity that binds all the militants of the idea—I will simply pose questions of principle.

What should our attitude be toward illegalists (in the economic sense of the word, i.e., people living off illicit labor) and particularly toward the comrades in that category?

The answer seems so clear to me that if I hadn't heard numerous discussions on this subject—and even in our circle—the idea of writing this article would never have occurred to me.

We approve and admire the antimilitarist who either by desertion or by some other means refuses to serve the masters' fatherland, and in so doing puts himself in open combat against society, whose law he violates: that of military service, otherwise known as servitude owed the state.

After this, how can we disavow that other comrade whose temperament bows as little before the regime of the workshop as the antimilitarist bows before that of the barracks and who, by some *illegal* method, puts himself in a state of revolt against the law of the slavery of work?

Every revolt is in essence anarchist. And we should stand alongside the economic rebel (when he is conscious, of course) the same way we stand beside the political, antimilitarist, or propagandist rebel.

All rebels, through their acts, are our people. Anarchism is a principle of struggle: it needs fighters and not servants the way statist socialism does, machines with complicated gears that have only to allow themselves to vegetate in order to live in a bourgeois fashion.

But it seems proper to me to trace a limit. I said above "economic rebel," for if the Duvals and the Pinis,[1] who steal because they can't submit to the oppression of the bosses, are our people, it isn't the same for many so-called anarchists who have paraded through the various criminal courts over the past few years. Theft is often nothing but an act of cowardice and weakness, for the man who commits it has no other goal than to escape work, while at the same time escaping the difficulties of social struggle. Before the jury, instead of being a common criminal the burglar or the counterfeiter declares himself an "anarchist" in the hope of being interesting or looking like a martyr to a cause he knows nothing about. He finds nothing better to respond to the judge who condemns him but the traditional and ever so banal "Vive l'anarchie!" But if this cry in other mouths has taken on a powerful resonance, here it has a flimsy title to our solidarity.

For our part these unfortunates deserve neither sympathy nor antipathy. They aren't rebels but escapists. They have clumsily escaped from the social melee. More clever, more daring, or luckier they would have "arrived" and become bankers, functionaries, or merchants—in a word, honest men. They would have legislated against us like vulgar Clemenceaus and without hesitation would have sent their unlucky brethren to the penal colonies. Such shipwrecks denote so much weakness and powerlessness that they can only inspire pity.

Between them and the militant who steals though *revolt*, the distance is as great as that between a revolutionary terrorist and the highway murderer who kills a shepherd in order to steal ten *sous* from him. One is a rebel of conscience, the other a rebel through powerlessness or bad luck. The act of the former is an act of revolt; the act of the latter is that of a brute too stupid to imagine better.

To stand alongside economic rebels does not in the least mean preaching theft or erecting it into a tactic. This method has so many drawbacks that preaching it would be madness. It is *admissible* and nothing more. Noting this simply means acting as an anarchist who doesn't fear that what he says will be heard, and having the courage to take his reasoning to its limits.

---

1 Clément Duval (1850–1935), French anarchist illegalist, leader of the group called La Panthère des Batignolles; Vittorio Pini (1850–189?), Italian anarchist illegalist active in France.

Admissible, and nothing else. For the anarchist, if he doesn't care about bourgeois legality and honesty, must above all aim at preserving himself as long as possible for action and realizing to the greatest extent possible for himself the life he desires. His work, rather than appearing harmful and destructive, should be a work of life, a long apostolate of stubborn labor, of goodness, of love. In order to partake of this ambiance, the new man, the man of the future must live with goodness, fraternity, and love. In this way, when he will have passed he will have left behind him a trail of sympathy and astonishment that will do more for propaganda than a whole life of petty and shady struggles could have done.

But to work at his labor of life and to preserve himself *all* means are good, for in order to reach the summits of clarity the route is often dark.

(*Le Communiste* 14, June 20, 1908)

Émile Henry

I THINK THAT ACTS OF BRUTAL REVOLT STRIKE THEIR TARGET, FOR THEY awaken the masses, shake them up with the lashing of a whip, and show the real face of the bourgeoisie, still trembling at the moment the rebel climbs the gallows.

To those who say to you that hatred doesn't engender love, answer that it is living love that often engenders hatred.

First, a few words to the comrades.

Let them not reproach me for glorifying a man, making him into a banner. We want neither tribunes nor martyrs nor prophets. But in order to be strong you have to know yourself, and in order to better support the struggles of today you have to know the joys and fears of past hours. And then it is so good, in this world governed by so many crooked interests, among the base masks that surround us, to once again see the clear profiles of those who were able to be honest in a humanity of brutes.

I will also not write an apology for murder of whatever kind. Murders will be the most painful page in our history. And it is certainly one of society's greatest crimes to have forced us, we who want peace and love, to shed blood.

On May 21, 1894, Émile Henry, twenty-one and a half years old, died on the gallows at la Roquette Prison in Paris.

The previous April 28 he had been sentenced to death by the jury of the Seine, having admitted his guilt in a series of terrorist attacks: "The explosion on the Rue des Bons-Enfants, that killed five people and led to the death of a sixth; the explosion at the Café Terminus that killed one person, mortally wounded another, and wounded a number of others; finally, six shots fired at those who pursued him." He had acted with complete lucidity and never once sought to attenuate the terror his acts inspired.

He was twenty-one; it was the springtime of his life; it was the month of May, the spring of nature; and though the death sentence was certain, his tranquil courage, made up of intelligence and enthusiasm, never flagged for a second.

The son of a worker and a worker himself, having worked in a shop. A rational education backed by a remarkable spirit of logic and observation led him to anarchism. At first, simply revolted by the sight of social injustice he became a socialist. "Attracted to socialism for a moment," he said, "it didn't take long for me to move away from the party. I loved freedom too much, had too much respect for individual initiative, too much repugnance for being part of a group to take a number in the matriculated army of the Fourth Estate. In any case, I saw that in the end socialism changes nothing of the current order. It maintains the authoritarian principle and this principle, whatever so-called free-thinkers might say, is nothing but a holdover of faith in a supreme power." His studies showed anarchism to be "a gentle morality in harmony with nature that will regenerate the old world." He became a militant.

The strike in Carmaux had just aborted, killed by politicians, leaving the workers weakened and starving. In the general depression Émile Henry decided to make heard a voice more fearful and virile than that of speechmakers: dynamite. It told the defeated who the real revolutionaries were; it told the victors that outside the speechifiers and the passive crowd that there were men who knew how to act.[1]

Then came the Vaillant Affair (who was guillotined for having thrown a bomb in the Chamber of Deputies). The repression was frightful; in just a few days mass arrests, searches, confiscation of publications, and expulsions decimated the ranks of the propagandists. The rebels were hunted down. Henry responded with an act: the bomb in the Café Terminus.

He was arrested.

At the hearings his calm and tranquility were disconcerting. The newspapers said this was either cynicism or an act. Not at all! It was the satisfied awareness of someone certain of having lived a useful and beautiful life. An actor? It's a strange actor who throws his head to the spectators.

---

1   The bomb Henry placed in the offices of the factories of Carmaux exploded in the commissariat on the rue des Bons-Enfants when the police removed it.

For his judges he had subtle raillery, astounding responses. When the president of the tribunal evoked Henry's bloodstained hands, Henry pointed at his red robe. When the same man reproached him for having abandoned a military career begun at the École Polytechnique, he had this marvelous response: "A beautiful career to be sure. One day they would have ordered me to fire on the unfortunate like Commandant Chapu at Fourmies. Thanks, but I'd rather be here."

Up to the guillotine he remained as good, as brave. And can anyone say that such an end wasn't worth more than the long labor of the submissive and pointless death in a hospice or a park bench? To be sure, there are other struggles that are less bloody and perhaps more useful; to be sure, speech that inspires enthusiasm, the written word, the invincible propagator of ideas, and above all a life spreading examples of love and fraternity are means of combat that are more beautiful. But to end by delivering an axe-blow to the crumbling edifice, to end with the consciousness of having contributed even a bit to the great labor of emancipation, was a hundred times better that the idiotic death of a worker filling the bosses' safes.

On the gallows his dry throat launched at the radiant May sun a cry of hope and bravery that that the sound of the blade couldn't stifle: "Courage, comrades! *Vive l'anarchie!*"

It was a death whose memory will live on. A death which free men will later remember with gratitude. For alongside the people of our century, the arrivistes, crushers, deceivers of all kinds; the immense mass of imbecilic followers and serfs, this young man marching toward death when everything in him wanted to live, this young man dying for the ideal is truly a luminous figure.

His blood was a beautiful seed from which new fighters will be born. And some day soon, when the wind will spread fire and construct barricades, the bourgeois who thought they'd crushed the new idea with bullets and guillotines will see the fatal harvest bloom.

Yes, anarchy is an ideal of peace and happiness. Yes, we love men with an infinite love, and every drop of their blood causes us pain. And it's because we love him, because we want to see him free, good, and happy, that we are merciless toward everything that blocks the road of humanity on its march toward the light!

(*Le Communiste*, May 23, 1908)

Apropos of the Congo

THE CONGO IS ON THE ORDER OF THE DAY. EVERYONE IS TALKING ABOUT IT. There are those who want it and those who don't. I am among the latter.

Those who want it have some good arguments: fatherland, brave Belgium, colonial power, expansion, outlets for trade, civilization . . . I know we need outlets where we can send our spoiled preserves, our cardboard shoes, and the scoundrels we don't know what to do with at home and to whom we confide the great mission of civilizing the blacks. I also know there are peoples guilty of being Negro and who must be inoculated with our genius, syphilis, and religion. I know that gunning down people who don't resemble us is a beautiful and noble task, but I'm a sentimental type and none of this really convinces me.

Those who don't want it talk about millions: it'll cost us this much or this much or that much—zero, zero, comma, zero—and the millions line up in horrific columns. This is what we'd have to pay for the Congo. But since I'm not a millionaire this leaves me cold. Even more because my small nest egg will disappear anyway, either for this or for the fortifications of Antwerp, the basilica of Koekelberg, or some other equally useful institution.

When people talk to me about the Congo, I think about something else. Even if we aren't talking about the proceeding of doubtful honesty that consists in annexing a country and a people over whom we have no right other than that of the stronger; even if aren't talking about the mentality of inferior or so-called inferior peoples the way you and I do of herds of lambs we shear before we eat, thinking about what is called colonization, I see aspects of this that lead me to reflect . . .

There are the peaceful villages decimated by forced labor, our murderous industry suddenly imported and imposed, military expeditions devastating the countryside, spreading terror, hatred, hunger . . .

There is a country flooded with blood by soldiers whose animal instincts are unleashed, with villages set on flame, men executed en masse, women raped . . . What irony: other people's fatherlands are set to the torch and the sword by our patriots.

And that's what will happen to those we civilize. And to us?

It will be our sons, our brothers, and our fathers setting off for there attracted by misleading appearances and returning to us—when they return—burned by fever, degraded, polluted, rotted. It will be the little soldiers we'll send to put down future revolts and who will certainly never return. And even though I don't feel sorry for those who will go there and die working at a task fit for murderers, I think of the void that will be left here by the departed sons and fiancés, intoxicated by big words.

And for we rebels who don't want to don military garb, it will be the penal colony, the famous ones in Africa, and the disciplinary companies where they kill and torture.

Our bourgeoisie will grow fat on all this monetized blood and sweat. The money picked up over there in the mud, in the bloody shade of the forests, will serve to enslave us here and pay the executioners.

And for the unscrupulous, the scoundrels of all kinds, the good-for-nothings for whom the social order isn't able to provide work, it will be an ocean of troubled water where they can fish at their ease.

This is why all the statistics, all the millions they'll throw at us, the reasoning of the deputies of every party, don't convince me of the benefits of colonization.

And those who will speak of the noblest reason, of the duty of the civilized, I'll say that they'd do better to first civilize the native savages of the villages of our bloody Flanders or some corner of Marolles, and that it would seem more useful to me to use my millions to lessen the exploitation of whites!

(*Le Communiste*, May 1, 1908)

Anarchists!

ANARCHY, ANARCHISM, ANARCHIST!!! HORRIFYING WORDS THAT FREEZE WITH fright and make those ignorant of their meaning tremble.

Anarchist!

The bourgeois shudders, a mute anger in his eyes. For him it's the irreducible enemy, the man upon whom neither palliatives, contracts, nor promises have any effect. The bourgeois is stupid: he reads little, doesn't study at all, and less than anything shows any concern for anarchist theory. He only knows of it from the blows delivered by its supporters. When you speak to him of anarchism he recalls violent strikes, expropriations, bombs, Ravachol . . . And he fears for his skin, for his property, for all his happy parasitism that he sees is threatened.

Anarchist!

The worker looks at you flabbergasted and slightly frightened. Ah, yes . . . dynamite, direct action, the implacable war on exploiters, but also the war on the gutless, on the cowardly, on the imbeciles sleeping through their oppression who feel that "things have always been this way and they'll always be this way . . ." The worker is troubled. He fears for his peace of a submissive beast; he is ashamed of his weakness. But above all, he knows nothing about anarchism, and the weak fear what they don't know.

Anarchist!

The socialist has a vague smile of scorn and condescension. "You want to jump over stages. You're going too fast." What a weak argument and how badly it hides all the ignorance and timidity of people who are used to being led and find shepherds necessary. An argument for those who are frightened by action. An argument of those who never heard our ideas . . .

Anarchist!

The scientist and the scholar, those officials of the formulas of knowledge, furrow their brows. For them the anarchist is the heretic who laughs at his dry formulas, logically examines the most age-old gospels. He is the non-indoctrinated, the man outside of every church, even the monist . . .

Anarchy, anarchism, anarchists! Horror!

Oh wretched people, the atrophied and blinded of all classes, poor people who a heredity of slaves has given souls that are senile since childhood, incapable of conceiving a free and young life, powerless to even desire it, how sincerely we pity you!

How our hearts suffer for all of you, men living in the dark, prisoners of old formulas, of absurd conventions, prisoners of your own stupidity!

How powerful is our desire to carry the torch into your darkness, to make a beneficent clarity shine in your minds!

This is why the obscurantism that has taken refuge in you makes us uncompromising enemies. The darkness fears the light.

We love you, for we love men, but we hate your meticulous mercantilism, your hypocritical morality; we deeply detest your vegetative and bestial existence, your pitiful lack of intelligence.

We fight for you as we fight for all men, and it is always you we encounter along the way; it's you we must fight, miserable human herd!

But our love of men, our determination to free them by freeing ourselves gives us the strength to be merciless.

Anarchists, we want a better life for all men, one finally worth living. We want them to be free, equal, brothers in a beautiful and harmonious life from which hatred and anger, injustice, and poverty will be banished.

But for this to occur, for humanity to reach the happiness toward which it has marched for centuries through ravines of blood and tears, all maleficent authorities must be abolished: the state, property, religion, and law.

The state: an impersonal, irresponsible entity that arrogates to itself the absurd right to rule human life.

Property: a criminal institution that arranges things so that a few own what should belong to all, and which permits this few to impose the exploitation of wage labor on the majority of their kind.

Religion: the control of consciences and minds, and whose multiform lies justify every form of injustice.

Laws: ridiculous and vain in their criminal folly of wanting to contain all of life within narrow limits.

When all of this collapses under the triumphant pressure of freed men—anarchists—when tiaras, crowns, codes, and swords will have disappeared, humans will live.

Until then, that is, as long as all of you—O! wretched people, bourgeois, workers, oppressors and oppressed—stubbornly remain in the darkness, we will be your enemy.

Always and in every act of your petty and sad existence you will find confronting you, building over your mud, our insolent life, the anarchist life, continuous rebellion.

(*Le Révolté*, November 28, 1908)

Anarchists—Bandits

(Editor's note; On January 23, 1909, two anarchist illegalists carried out a robbery at a factory on Chestnut Road in Tottenham, in the course of which two people were killed, including a policeman. In the course of their flight, both anarchists shot themselves rather than surrender, one of them fatally. This event—popularly known as the Tottenham Outrage—prefigured the 1911 Siege of Sidney Street and the crime spree of the French Bonnot Gang, where all of the participants were anarchists, and all of them bandits.)

LAST WEEK THE DAILIES RELATED IN DETAIL A TRAGIC INCIDENT OF THE SOCIAL struggle. In the suburbs of London (in Tottenham) two of our Russian comrades attacked the accountant of a factory and, pursued by the crowd and the police, held out in a desperate struggle, the mere recounting of which is enough to make one shiver . . .

After almost two hours of resistance, having exhausted their munitions and wounded twenty-two people, three of them mortally, they reserved their final bullets for themselves. One, our comrade Joseph Lapidus (the brother of the terrorist Stryge, killed in Paris in the Vincennes woods in 1906) killed himself; the other was captured, having been seriously wounded.

Words seem powerless to express admiration or condemnation before their ferocious heroism. Lips are still; the pen isn't strong enough, sonorous enough.

Nevertheless, in our ranks there will be the timorous and the fearful who will disavow their act. But we, for our part, insist on loudly affirming our solidarity.

We are proud to have had among us men like Duval, Pini, and Jacob.[1] Today we insist on saying loudly and clearly: The London "bandits" were our people!

---

1   Marius-Alexander Jacob (1879–1954), head of a band of anarchist illegalists.

Let this be known. Let it be finally understood that in the current society we are the vanguard of a barbarous army. That we have no respect for what constitutes virtue, morality, honesty, that we are outside of laws and regulations. They oppress us, they persecute us, they pursue us. Rebels constantly find themselves before the sad alternative: submit, that is, abolish their will and return to the miserable herd of the exploited, or accept combat against the entire social organism.

We prefer combat. Against us, all arms are good; we are in an enemy camp, surrounded, harassed. The bosses, judges, soldiers, cops unite to bring us down. We defend ourselves—not by all means, for the most peremptory response we can give them is to be better than them—but with a profound contempt for their codes, their morals, their prejudices.

By refusing us the right to free labor society gives us the right to steal. By taking possession of the world's wealth the bourgeois give us the right to take back, however we can, what we need to satisfy our needs. As antiauthoritarians, we have the burning determination to live freely without oppressing anyone, without being oppressed by anyone. Current society, based on the absurd egoism of the strongest, on iniquity and oppression, denies us this. In order not to die of hunger we are forced to resort to various expedients: accept the stupefying and demoralizing existence of the wage earner and work, or the dangerous existence of the illegal and steal and get ourselves out of our mess through means on the margins of the law.

Let this be known! In order to wrest an existence, working—submitting ourselves to the slavery of the workshop—is as much an expedient as stealing. As long as we haven't conquered the ample and great life for which we fight, the various means which the social organization will force us to resort to will be nothing to us but a last resort. And so we choose, in keeping with our temperaments and the circumstances, those that are most appropriate to us.

Your codes, your laws, your "honesty": you can't imagine how we laugh at them!

This is why, in the face of the fuming bourgeoisie, in the face of those who judge, of honest brutes, of the prostitutes of journalism, we insist on proclaiming: "The bandits of London are our people!"

They are also noble bandits, and we can be proud of them. We won't have vain words of regret, vain tears for them. No! But may their deaths be an example and etch in our memories the sublime motto of the Russian comrades: "Anarchists never surrender!"

Anarchists never surrender! No more under policemen's bullets than before the shouts of the crowd or the condemnation of those who judge! Anarchists never surrender!

Resolved to live as rebels and to pitilessly defend themselves to the bitter end, they know, when it's necessary, to accept the epithet of "bandits."

I can guess, dear reader, the sentimental objection that is on your lips: But the twenty-two unfortunates wounded by your comrades' bullets were innocent! Have you no remorse?"

No! For those who pursued them were nothing but "honest" citizens, believers in the state, in authority. Perhaps oppressed, but oppressed who, by their criminal spinelessness, perpetuate oppression. Enemies!

Unthinking, you will answer: Yes, but the ferocious bourgeois is also unthinking. For us the enemy is he who prevents us from living. We are under attack, and we defend ourselves.

And so we don't have words of condemnation for our daring comrades fallen in Tottenham, rather much admiration for their peerless bravery, and much sadness this evening to have thus lost, in the fullness of their vigor, men of an exceptional courage and energy.

(*Le Révolté*, February 6, 1909)

The Athletic Aberration

... A FACE. GRIMACING HORRIBLY. LOOKING LIKE IT'S STRAINED WITH EXCESsive suffering. Pain twists the muscles, deforms the expression. The mouth is writhing, the eyes look mad. Is it some torture victim dying at the hands of a sadistic executioner? Is it a martyr? Some unfortunate suffering the torments of an attack of madness? Is it . . . ?

The monstrous photograph that inspired these questions was found in a prominent place on page one of one of the most popular sporting reviews, *La Vie au Grand Air* (December 19, 1908). It showed a runner making the supreme effort to reach the finish line.

Photos like this one are not at all rare. Who among you hasn't more than once seen in a newspaper the dizzying swerving of autos competing for a trophy? Or a dangerous motorcycle race? Or simply some imbecile (Dorando, for example) fainting after having run forty kilometers? Or a boxing match?

Not counting the innumerable sporting papers dedicated to this kind of brainlessness all newspapers of all parties and all dimensions have taken up the habit of offering their readers, between two sensational crimes, an educational image of this kind, even "l'Humanité" (the organ of the Socialist Party if you please), which in this matter competes in cretinism with the "Petit Journal"—so justly called "Le Petit Idiot"—and "Vélo" and "Auto."

The more we observe it the clearer it is that the love for violent sports seems to be a veritable contemporary malady. The entire younger generation of today is attacked by it, as well as a large part of the others. What newspapers do young people read? What is the reading matter fated to provide what is called the bread of the spirit? *L'Auto, Le Vélo,* etc. They know nothing of the problems of life. They'll passively, sadly, unexceptionally, play their small role, but they know everything about the victories of Jacquelin, Paul Pons, and Jenatzy.

Do they even think of fighting for a better life? Of studying the infinite problems of thought, or even simply of living? You must be kidding! They are burning to equal Farman in the air or to run countless kilometers without a break, or to win the Ardennes Cup. We must renounce putting anything else into noggins stuffed with such foolishness. We must resign ourselves and wait for them to disappear, just as the generations of mediocrities incapable of living must disappear. We must also save the rising ones from the athletic aberration.

For it has all the characteristics of a mental illness. It's an obsession that succeeds in abolishing all reasoning power in its victim. The runner can't control himself. He has lost the little free will that the normal man enjoys. Just as the hysteric doesn't know how to vanquish his pathological desires; just as the alcoholic no longer has the strength to refuse a drink that he knows is fatal; just as the opium smoker or the morphine addict must absorb his poison, the runner doesn't have the force of will to refuse himself a pleasure that everything shows him to be absurd, dangerous, and painful. And at the end there waits the fatal accident, the pitiful death of an exhausted beast collapsing under the sadistic gaze of the hallucinating crowd. What difference does it make? Run! Run! On foot, on a bicycle, in a car, cover kilometers, savor the giddiness of maddening speed, and reach the goal, haggard, your breast collapsed, your eyes bloodshot, with the buzzing of applause in your ears, with your brain drunk on an imbecilic vision of glory.

This man, just like a drunk or an epileptic, is abnormal. Like certain religious madmen (like Hindu fakirs and Christian ascetics) he tortures himself, submits himself to the worst trials because his madness is accompanied by a need for suffering. Something that is also worthy of note: in all branches of intellectual activity the sportsman stands out as an idiot. This sick brain is incapable of thought or study. It is rare that he even has had a primary education.

And so it is that we can contemplate in sporting reviews monstrosities like those that inspired these reflections.

But it would be a mistake to think that only sporting professionals are struck with this mental aberration. What are we to think of the crowds pressed up against the racecourse of the mad machines with the secret hope of seeing a beautiful catastrophe? What can we say about the select public—the journalists, society types, *gens de lettres*—who squeezed into the Alhambra in the past to see brutes pummel each other, break each other's jaws, and give each other black eyes?

Those who enjoy such ignoble spectacles remind me of those primitive peoples for whom animal fights were their greatest joys. They demonstrate a cannibal mentality similar to that of the Romans during their period of decadence presiding over gladiatorial combats. They have preserved the temperament of cannibals.

Like the unfortunate actors of these sad spectacles, the people who find their pleasure in this are worthy of only one name: brutes. And if they didn't have the excuse of unconsciousness we would have to lose hope.

This said, does it follow that, as some have erroneously concluded after an article that appeared in these same columns (see no. 18 of *Le Révolté*) that for fear of the athletic aberration we must renounce sports?

I don't think so. As long as sports aid in the physical development of man they are excellent and can only be encouraged. But from the moment they render people stupid and become a mental illness we must react.

We want a humanity healthy in body and mind. We must fight everything that goes against this goal. Though sports can be a precious factor in the development and maintenance of health, the abusive usage of it renders them harmful.

It is our role to say this.

(*Le Révolté*, January 9, 1909)

Hatred

HATRED HAS FOUND FERVENT APOLOGISTS IN OUR MILIEU.

Since the time of Bakunin, proclaiming the strength and the beauty of the destructive desire, too often, in the daily fight against all forms of oppression, the anarchists have appealed to hatred. It has given rise in our groups to interminable discussions; in our newspapers there are endless polemics. Young people, as enthusiastic as they are impulsive, have called for and ferociously defended it. Even here, in the columns of *l'anarchie* I recall having read a series of articles signed Olivine rehabilitating hatred which, according to Libertad, "alone creates acts of will."

This is a lovely theme for literature, but from the point of view of logic, of reason, and anarchist education, not at all!

We need more than the sonorous assertions of a poetic enthusiasm: we need detailed, exact, and scientific arguments and logical, correct reasoning.

In order to discuss hatred, and it must be discussed for once and for all, we must begin by defining it, and this is precisely what we have neglected to do.

What is hatred?

We can, I think, after impartial analysis, define it in this way:

Hatred is a constant, imperious, *a priori* desire to do evil and to belittle, in order to finally destroy a being or a category of beings.

Is this sentiment in conformity with our vital interests? Is it logical? And in the first place, what is its origin?

Hatred is the child of suffering. It's because we have suffered that we hate the person or persons who were the cause of that suffering. The worker sometimes hates the bourgeois because he sees in him the cause of all his ills. X has a ferocious hatred for Z because the latter caused him prejudice.

In practice, hatred can thus be reduced to a desire to do evil because we have suffered it.

This desire in simple beings—in animals or in men whose mentalities are not well-developed—is entirely understandable and flows from the very principle of the struggle for life. In order to live, the primitive being must be stronger than his adversaries. When he has received a blow he must be able to return two in order for his superiority to be obvious.

Returning two blows for one, striking someone without any immediately useful goal, for no reason but to assert one's strength for a second time and because one was struck oneself—is this not the principle of vengeance, an act of hatred? This act is mechanical, purely reflex.

When a man or a beast, struck a first time, is not able to return the blow and immediately avenge himself, the feeling of permanent danger that the existence of the enemy constitutes gives rise to an uninterrupted desire to do him harm, to destroy him, a sentiment that is a substitute for the instinct of preservation, and which is nothing but hatred.

For the being abandoned to the risks of the brutal struggle for life it is useful. It keeps him on the alert, hounds him, spurs him on during the combat. It has its *raison d'être*.

This theory is confirmed by the observation made many times that the simplest animals, the most primitive men, are those in whom hatred is most developed and the need for vengeance most persistent.

To take examples only from those peoples closest to us, the Italians, the Spaniards, and the Turks—of a temperament much more impulsive and less evolved than that of Northern Europeans—are they not those among our neighbors in whom these feelings are most deeply rooted? On the contrary, the French, the German, the English, and the Scandinavians, with complex and reflective mentalities, are almost totally ignorant of the barbaric custom of the vendetta.

A similar comparison could be made among individuals of a same original temperament. In which category of individuals belonging to the same race is hatred the most developed and its manifestations most frequent? Among the most disinherited, the least educated, unpolished minds submitting to ancestral influences without reacting.

Marc Guyau, in his remarkable study of morality, explains clearly, through a vivid image, the decrease in the feeling of hatred and the desire for vengeance in parallel with the evolution of intelligence: "Irritate a ferocious beast and it will tear you apart. Attack a member of the society world and he will answer with a witty remark. Insult a philosopher and he won't answer you at all."

Conscious man no longer feels the need to respond blow for blow. He knows the inanity of vengeance, and reasoning has abolished in him raging hatred. He will only strike when it is useful and necessary, and until then all he'll do is shrug his shoulders.

As man perfects himself, as the conditions of struggle change, weapons are modified and forces are transformed. Where victory once went to the vigor of fists and muscles, today it goes to clear and perspicacious intelligence. Violence increasingly appears archaic and barbaric.

In the eyes of an impartial logician hatred and vengeance can in no way be justified.

Take vengeance? Why? Can a crime repair the damage caused by anther crime? Is it a reason to commit another? Do we cure evil through evil?

I defend myself. But when my enemy no longer threatens me, whatever the evil he can do me might be, I don't feel the need to do it to him. I strike from necessity and not to do evil, the evil I abhor. Vengeance is absurd and irrational in the light of reason.

To hate! By their unconscious and unharmonious acts the men I rub shoulders with wrong me at every moment. Their limpness, their rapacity, their foolishness prevent me from living. But how can I hate them when I know that their least movements are determined by factors external to their will (heredity, education, prejudices, etc.) and that in the end they are nothing but puppets, worthy only of inspiring pity? The anarchist who would lower himself to hating them would himself cease to be a strong and proud individuality and would become just one more backward plaything of our instincts.

For hatred is impulsive and unreflecting. Hidden away by centuries of warrior-like atavisms in the profound mysteries of our being, in days of struggle it inspires in us senseless desires for blood and murder. Whoever allows himself to act under its impulse allows himself to be determined by ancestral ferocity and abdicates reason, hatred being an *a priori* sentiment.

It can be objected that hatred is a lever that can give rise to individual revolts. Perhaps. In that case it is one of those levers we shouldn't make use of. Like blind anger, like jealousy, like drunkenness, it can give rise to passionate revolts. But revolt only has value insofar as it driven by clear ideas and precise desires. It is only a factor of progress on condition that it is conscious and not passionate.

And when he sees the usefulness of an act the anarchist must find within himself enough energy and will to accomplish it, whatever it might be, coldly, tranquilly, with the precise goal before his eyes and not needing to appeal to the bestial intoxication of hatred in order not to waver.

(*l'anarchie*, September 2, 1909)

The Festival of Lies and Weakness

MEN ARE INAUGURATING THE NEW YEAR WITH AN APOTHEOSIS OF HYPOCRISY and weakness.

The earth begins its life again. It has traced one more circle in luminous space. One cycle of life ends and another begins. The enigmatic future, with its mysteries of joy and suffering, stands before man. And I would like it if man on this day looked life in the face and felt serene, determined, and strong. But no, he lies. He lies and his plaintive weakness is exhaled in timid murmurs.

"Happy New Year, good health, happiness . . ." These wishes are on all lips and fly around the world in the millions of letters written by millions of unconscious and lying hands.

For these men who universally congratulate each other and exchange wishes of happiness and longevity are brutes who will ferociously slaughter each other the next day. And even this evening, murmuring affectionate words, they thought the contrary and smilingly committed acts of hatred, hostility, and evil.

This person wishes long life to parents whose inheritance he impatiently awaits. Another congratulates his hated boss, his abhorred rival, the competitor he sneakily defames.

The hideous faces of bloodthirsty and rapacious beasts hide behind smiles of propriety. Not a single face isn't covered by a mask. Not a mouth that hasn't proffered lies. For a few hours the wolves have disguised themselves as lambs.

And it was the festival of great social hypocrisy, the apotheosis of the stupidity, the illogic, and the cowardice of vast human herds, carrying out together the most inept and insane rites.

The festival of lies is also that of weakness. Those who, servile, humble, and timorous, don't know how to desire; the immense rabble of those who allow themselves to be gagged by life without making the least effort to assert themselves: the spineless have formulated hopes and murmured wishes. Hopes for happiness that the year will convert into hopelessness. Wishes that will be as sterile as the old-fashioned prayers of the devout.

They wish for a prosperous life, happiness, joy. They wish because they don't have the strength to will. After having wished for life, they'll continue to work at death. Serving the authorities, slaves of dogmas and the masters of the moment, they'll waste their existence at evil tasks and will tear each other apart.

You who express wishes for love, you'll bow before convention and the laughter of imbeciles. You who wanted to be free, your weakness will lead you to forge chains for yourself and others. You, who stupid pride makes desire glory, for appearance's sake you will commit base, low acts, infamies.

Wishes of the timid, stammerings of the humble, prayers of those with illusions: all will be in vain. The only wishes that will be fulfilled are those of the strong, whose robust will shall be affirmed in acts. The others, the gray rabble of marionettes will every day see hopes, illusions, and beautiful dreams fade away in smoke . . .

Life doesn't offer itself, it must be conquered. Beautiful and implacable, it reserves its splendors for the strong and virile. They despise conventions and don't deign to lie. They don't formulate wishes, whose pitiful inanity they know, but their peremptory will tames all adversity.

Freed of the hindrances that the weak struggle against, the strong advance without stopping. The mirages of the future don't deceive their minds, avid for immediate life. They don't agree to wait and want to extract a bit of joy from each moment.

Let those who don't know how to want make wishes and allow their dull, monotonous, and foggy lives to evaporate . . . We won't lower ourselves to such puerilities. Not amazed by fabulous hopes, weary of disappointing expectations, anarchists formulate neither wishes nor vows: they want, and immediately act according to their will.

(*l'anarchie*, December 30, 1909)

Our Antisyndicalism

TODAY, IN LIGHT OF THE UPCOMING ANTIPARLIAMENTARY CAMPAIGN, THE anarchists are divided into two apparently irreconcilable groups: the syndicalists and the antisyndicalists.

The comrades on the other side, in a brief declaration that it is only right to recognize has the dual merits of clarity and honesty, have said what they want and who they are. Their antiparliamentary campaign will serve as the basis for syndicalist-revolutionary agitation.

It is thus on this plane that we meet up with them. After Lorulot spelled out our antiparliamentarism I think it is right to spell out what our antisyndicalism should be.

This theme has already been discussed and re-discussed thousands of times among us, and we must recognize that the arguments of both sides have often been of a disconcerting puerility. No later than last week did I not hear friends reproach unions for establishing fixed dues and compare these to taxes? And others defend them by saying that in such and such a professional association they had educational discussions? Ordinarily it is with such futilities that the union movement is attacked and defended. Or else hairs are split over side issues like the functionary-ism of the CGT, the *arrivisme* of the leaders, the authoritarianism of the revolutionary method . . .

These are details that are without a doubt interesting to know and useful to criticize. But our antisyndicalism is based, I believe, on more serious, more profound arguments, and it is important that in the upcoming antiparliamentary battle we have something other than these clichés to oppose to the theoreticians of working-class action.

We shouldn't be declaiming against the demagogues of the Rue de la Grange-aux-Belles, nor should we be involved in endless discussions over whether or not it's advantageous to participate in a corporate association, nor should we be elucidating the question of knowing whether we can make anarchist propaganda there. Yes, there is perhaps an interest in taking part in a trade grouping; yes, we can sometimes carry out good anarchist work. In the same way there is an interest in being a good soldier and a good worker. In the same way it is sometimes possible to spread ideas in a barracks. It's the very principle of syndicalism that should be attacked in order to demonstrate its inanity and dangerous consequences.

Let us first look at what syndicalist theory is and what it rests on. We can sum it up in this way:

Two adverse social classes exist and confront each other: idle owners and working non-owners, the latter being far more numerous. All social evil comes from the fact that the ownership of the means of production permits the minority, called "bourgeois," to pressure and exploit the minority, called "proletarian." There is only one remedy for this state of affairs: that the proletarians group together in corporate associations, in a vast confederation—class associations—and that they battle to every day wrest from the enemy caste a few small advantages until such time as, having become numerous and daring enough, they profit from a war or an economic crisis to decree the insurrectionary general strike and seize the means of production. Once this is accomplished the unions will organize work. It will be the Social Republic. The fundamental "causes" of human suffering having disappeared, humanity will progress in peace, joy, and happiness . . . Here the field remains open to everyone's imagination, permitting the composition at leisure of tableaux of universal happiness that, of course, can only ever be far below reality! This is, with more or less variations, the sales spiels that the syndicalists of all shapes and forms prepare to serve (with, incidentally, much conviction and sincerity) to the good voters. We have to refute this entirely, point by point, omitting nothing. And I say this is quite feasible.

The problem to be solved is this: how do we transform our revolting society in order to finally establish a social milieu that assures every individual the maximum of happiness? This, in summary, is our objective as reformers and is also that of the syndicalists. Let us then pose the question this way: Given this goal, is it logical to count on the working class for this labor of destruction and construction?

Can we reasonably believe it capable of leading such an enterprise to a successful conclusion?

"Yes," say the *ouvrieristes* (without ever explaining why). "No," we answer them, and we will prove it: The working class suffers from the atavism of servitude and exploitation. It is the weaker of the two classes from every point of view. It is above all the less intelligent, and this is the sole cause for its state of subjection. It is within the logic of nature for the stronger to dominate the weaker. By virtue of this law the unconscious and cowardly plebe, the imbecilic masses, credulous and fearful, have always been despoiled by more intelligent, healthier, more daring minorities. At present, after nineteen centuries of oppression, the difference between the two classes has been considerably accentuated. Let us repeat it again: *in all areas* impartial science demonstrates to us the inferiority of the working class. That being so, it is foolish to believe it capable of organizing a rational society. The degenerates, the hereditary slaves, the pitiful mass of working stiffs that we know *de visu* are physiologically incapable of living in harmony.

Consequently, it is a waste of time and energy to organize the working class to carry out social transformation.

Consequently, all the theoretical affirmations flowing from the principle that the working class can and must modify the social regime are false.

Consequently, there is only one urgent, useful, indispensable task, one which, in creating individuals finally worthy of the title of men, gradually improves the society: the task of education and anarchist combat.

This being established through scientific and logical arguments, and the very principle of syndicalism having been demonstrated false, let us now pass to a critical examination of the union movement and see if it confirms our deductions. It fully confirms them.

To begin with, let us note a salient contradiction. With the goal of organizing one class against another, the workers are invited to unite in professional associations. Yet the interests of various corporations are often opposed, which renders class cohesion economically impossible, on this basis at least. And which is the cause of enormous waste . . .

Now let's look at the unions. Examined closely we see that they reproduce to varying degrees the defects and the wounds of the bourgeois society they claim to have a mission to destroy. A union is the old society in miniature. Foolish and complicated administrative gears galore; regulations restrictive of individual initiative; oppression of minorities by feeble majorities; the triumph of the mediocre on condition that they have the gifts of gab and swindling. Everything can be found there, up to and including parasites.

Let us look at their tactics. Far from combating the established social order, it seems that the unions have their sanctioning as a goal. Supposedly antistatists, they never cease battling for this or that law or demanding another one, thus recognizing the entity Law and, as a corollary, the entity State. These antiparliamentarians sign duly legalized contracts and call for this to be voted for and that to be rejected . . .

In their organization they are a perfect copy of the parliamentary farce. Even the clowns aren't missing. Delegation of power, votes, decisions having force of law, as well as half-hidden combinations, personal competition, kitchen squabbles: we can find in the CGT an exact, though reduced, transposition of parliamentary hideousness.

As for the unmistakable incoherence of their blather, they pass from a tragic to a comic character by a series of gradations amusing to observe. It's the smashing—is it not, Clemenceau?—victory of the postal workers transformed a few days later into . . . well, you find the diplomatic word. It's the valiant corporation of construction workers who a few months ago naively allowed themselves to be muzzled by a collective contract that was extremely . . . clever. It's the CGT today building itself up as defenders of bank employees, as if the valets of the financier were not as repugnant as the financier himself. We could write columns on this theme.

Let us look at the results. Today the CGT is combative; in words more than in acts, but combative all the same. With this as a starting point, comrades promise us that in the future its combative force will grow and will end by assuring it the complete triumph of its demands. We saw above what the reasons were that authorize us—let us be modest—to have some doubts on this subject. A glance at our neighboring countries will be instructive in this regard.

At their beginning all parties, all groups (even all individuals) are combative. Age comes, and with it a potbelly and wisdom. This is the story of many men who we are today permitted to admire raised to the top of the social machine, the history of the trade union socialist parties. Very revolutionary during the blessed period of their youth, the English trade unions have become what we know them to be. The same thing happened to many German unions, and is now happening to the Belgian workers' movement, which is losing all its energy as it grows. In certain places in the United States, in Australia, in New Zealand, in England, where the unions have reached their heights, they have only managed to create a caste of privileged, conservative workers, lined up under the protective shield of the state, and are hardly worth more than the more official bourgeois.

Having seen the evolution of the French unions and observed the incoherence of the CGT, I don't think it's possible to foresee a different destiny for it.

We will thus not lack for arguments during the upcoming discussions, for each of these criticisms lends itself to interesting developments and must be backed with proofs drawn from union activity itself—proofs it is not difficult to find cartloads of.

Our critical work thus understood, we still have to define the positive, affirmative part of our propaganda. It is clear and has no need of long developments: the making of anarchists.

In parallel with the tissue of illogic that is syndicalism and the monument of incoherence that is the union, let us show how, by the transformation of men, society is transformed; how as men become more healthy, more noble, more intelligent, more educated, the air becomes breathable and life appears admirable . . .

"Salvation lies within us!" Let us show that the salvation of men is within them and that the route to enlightenment has been laid out for them, if they want to make the effort to free themselves from the old lies . . . Let us show, in all its fertile intransigence, anarchist action!

And I can't end any better than did Lorulot the other week:

"And now . . . to work!"

(*l'anarchie*, February 24, 1910)

The Revolutionary Illusion

"HUMANITY MARCHES ENVELOPED IN A VEIL OF ILLUSIONS," A THINKER—MARC Guyau—said. In fact, it seems that without this veil men aren't capable of marching. Barely has reality torn a blindfold from them than they hasten to put on another, as if their too-weak eyes were afraid to see things as they are. Their intelligence requires the prism of falsehood.

The scandals of Panama, Dreyfus, Syveton, Steinhell, etc; the turpitudes and incapacities of politicians, and the rifle blows of Narbonne, Draveil, and Villeneuve have, for a considerable minority, torn away the veil of the parliamentary illusion.

We hoped for everything from the ballot. We had faith in the good faith and power of the nation's representatives. And that hope, that faith prevented us from seeing the fundamental idiocy of the system, which consists in delegating one to look after the needs of all. But the ballot revealed itself to be a rag of paper. Parliamentarians showed themselves to be ambitious, greedy, corrupt, and, most of all, mediocre . . . Men appeared who were angered by the electoral farce, the comedy of reforms, the reign of republican clowns. A minority was born, which necessarily grows every day and upon which the old illusion has no hold.

Nevertheless, in order to inspire men who are used to being led, in order to stimulate their activity, images are needed . . . and so, replacing the defunct parliamentary illusion, another illusion was forged and encrusted onto brains: the revolutionary illusion.

Yes, laws are powerless to transform society, parliamentary assemblies are pitiful, and there is nothing to expect from governments. But what legislation can't do demonstrations and strikes will do; and union assemblies will keep the promises of their pitiful predecessors, the Chambers. Finally, we can expect everything from the conscious proletariat which . . . and which . . . and that . . .

Once suckers thought that sonorous speeches and official texts written and placarded with solemnity were capable of favorably modifying social life. This time has passed. At present it is thought that in order to do this it suffices to demolish street lamps, burn kiosks, to "knock off" a cop from time to time (on very serious occasions).

Once, popular hopes were concentrated on deputies. These paunchy messieurs were capable of some good morning decreeing marvelous things. Alas! Now that we've seen them slog through the mud the ideal type of the transformer has taken on a different appearance. It's the "comrade secretary," influential member of the CGT, whose voice during meetings unleashes waves of enthusiasm. It's Pataud—his malicious and jovial face, his imperative speech . . . and it's also the long-haired revolutionary, with his hat worn at an angle, and who (his neighbors assert) never goes out without his two automatic pistols . . .

Once the brave voters trusted in parliament—incarnation of the Welfare State—to organize their happiness. Only the "backward masses" today still maintain so foolish a confidence in their representatives. The "advanced," the "conscious," in short: the revolutionaries know what the state and parliament are worth. So they announce to us that after the general strike it will be the CGT that will organize universal felicity and the union committees will deliberate on the measures to be taken for the common welfare. As you can see, this in no way resembles the old parliamentary regime.

Like all errors, it was harmful to become intoxicated with the parliamentary illusion. And it earned for the good citizens of this country the admirable democratic regime, so well illustrated by the Russian alliance, O! Most advantageous of alliances, the great and small Affairs, and, finally the reign of Clemenceau and Briand . . . while waiting for that of Jaurès. M. Viviani—today His Excellency—once said apropos of I don't know which legislature: "There was the Lost Chamber, and there is the Infamous Chamber," and this could equally be said of all the legislatures that have followed, vainly striving to surpass each other in buffooneries. Illusions cost dearly.

And yet, though it's been costly to the poor buggers who have benevolently had their heads shaved, been whipped and shot down, the parliamentary illusion has not done half as much harm as the other illusion can do.

Oh, don't worry. We'll get over this. We'll end up by seeing that the little game of shake-ups doesn't help at all. And we won't see the

 faith we put in them. We'll work for ourselves."

bloody dawn rise that's announced by M. Méric. Illusions don't last forever. But men will have died for the Cause, died stupidly, uselessly. But one or two generations will have wasted their strength in foolish efforts. We would have wasted life—that's all.

We'll get over this. The sun of the great day isn't ready to shine, and probably never will shine, except in the feverish imaginings of its prophets.

And yet, since this dream intoxicates the crowd let's look and see what it presages for us. Let's see what these efforts tend toward, what they will manage to do if an impossible victory was to crown them.

Not too long ago a pamphlet came out that shows us what this will be. Our old friend, Citizen Méric, aka Flax, is the author. It is titled "How We Will Make the Revolution." This pamphlet is serious, like the program of a future party. In certain places it is as enthralling as the novels of Captain Danrit. In its general appearance it recalls the writings of Mark Twain, the phlegmatic and impassive humor of the Americans.

Citizen Méric—who knows what he's about—demonstrates that when all is said and done a revolution is an easy thing. Our Russian friends can have no doubts on this subject. And then, a few words on the organized proletariat. But without a doubt the most interesting chapter is the one that shows us what will happen after the triumphant insurrection. Here it is possible to see just how far minds in the throes of an illusion can be led astray. For if it is possible that Citizen Méric doesn't believe a single word of what he says, it is certain that many people sincerely conceive what he has formulated.

On the day after the great day Citizen Méric when announces the revolutionary dictatorship backed by the Terror, woe to the adversaries of the new social order (read: The Federal Committee). "Violence alone could give us our momentary victory; terror alone can preserve that victory . . . we must not be afraid to be ferocious, We'll talk about justice, goodness and liberty afterward." Well, dear antiauthoritarian pals, we've been warned.

From these lines we can understand the little enthusiasm for M. Méric's revolution on the part of the individualists. The present order crushes us, hunts us down, and kills us. The revolutionary order will crush us, hunt us down, and kill us. The party can count on our assistance.

But Citizen Méric just gets better and better. On page twenty-two we note the existence of two committees, and a revolutionary army and police. The rebels will be executed (*sic, sic, sic*). Isn't this interesting?

The unions "will order everyone to get to work," or else watch out. After this a workers' parliament (*sic*) will be elected, which "will have nothing in common with the odious parliamentarism of today." Yeah, sure. Even more, as we've already noted, this charming little regime will have nothing in common with the abominable bourgeois oppression.

There will also be a permanent labor council. And the comrade ends by saying forthwith: "The current CGT already gives an approximate idea of the future working-class organization." Won't that be lovely!

In order to defend the new fatherland thus constructed, and which will certainly be the gentlest of fatherlands, oh ineffable Méric, militias will be formed. For war is inevitable . . .

And after talking about a "new morality imposing heavy obligations and sacrifices," after having told us of revolutionary prisons and tribunals, in short, of what he himself calls worker tyranny, Citizen Méric tranquilly concludes: "This isn't for today, or for tomorrow." Didn't I tell you he had the impassive humor of the Anglo-Saxons!

Citizen Méric is perhaps a joker or a refined humorist knowing how to push a joke to an extreme. I'd like to think so. But the fact is that there are simple souls who accept these writings as gospel.

The harmful illusion is that of the belief in this redeeming revolution, when there is no other redemption than that of the human personality, when we can build nothing without having made better and stronger men.

The evil illusion is that of waiting for the revolt of the crowd, of the organized, disciplined, regimented masses. In fact, the only fertile acts are those committed by individuals knowing clearly what they want and advancing without let or hindrance, needing neither chiefs nor discipline. In fact, the only good rebellions are the immediate rebellions of individuals refusing to wait any longer and determined to immediately grab their portion of joy.

The imbecilic illusion is that of imagining that by violence alone, by terror, by bombs and rifles we can create the new society. Violence employed by brutes will be absurd and harmful. A society founded on gibbets and maintained by the force of chains will always be ignobly oppressive. The revolution of anger and hatred, the revolution of unionized fanatics can only make flow torrents of blood in vain and prepare the arrival of new filibusterers.

In 1789 Robespierre's dictatorship prepared the way for the Empire. The *guillotinades* were the prelude to the Napoleonic carnage. The

Terror, by decreasing the value of human life, allowed free rein to the bloody folly of the "Little Corsican." This, brutally, is history's response to revolutionary illusions.

To be sure, society does not evolve without bumps, crises, bloody shocks. Often, angry revolts, dictated by sentimental indignation or instilled with faith in the salutary power of violence, break out and are quickly repressed in the horrors of bourgeois reaction. They have their use. They are inevitable. But we should have no illusions as to their fate. Above all, we should not fool ourselves as to the transformative value of force—of the blind force of fanaticized crowds.

In certain circumstances acts of violence can be precious: when they complete the work already accomplished by the revolution in mentalities. And it's a right, a right that sometimes becomes a duty, to rebel by force against the crushing weight of authoritarian institutions. But to deduce from this that the Terror is a panacea is a lamentable error in reasoning.

To think that through disordered shake-ups and with the savage energy of worker cohorts we can abolish a power, establish a bit of harmony, is infantile.

To imagine the ideal actor in the form of an individual quick with the fist—or the gun—is naive.

In order to act fruitfully—in whatever way—it is indispensable to know how to reflect, calculate, appreciate an action, to know how to accomplish it with a vigorous hand. The actor—the individual whose revolt, violent or not, is a factor in progress—must be a strong personality, conscious, clearheaded, and proud, not clouded with hatred or illusions.

To think that impulsive, defective, ignorant crowds will have done with the morbid illogic of capitalist society is a vulgar illusion. It is precisely the defects of these crowds that must be destroyed so that life can be ample and good for all. Bestial violence, hatred, the sheep-like spirit of leaders, the credulity of the crowds, these are what must be annihilated in order to transform society. Improving individuals, purifying them, making them strong, making them ardently love and desire life, making them capable of salutary revolts: these are the only ways out. There is no salvation outside the renewal of man!

(*l'anarchie*, April 28, 1910)

The Religious or the Secular?

AFTER THE OBSCURANTISTS OF THE CHURCH, HERE COME THE STUPEFYING charlatans of the secular.

What we see going on around kids is an ignoble dispute between parties and sects. They hold the future in their frail little hands, and people are afraid they don't want to keep to the straight and narrow road and stay within the routine.

And everyone attacks them in a dispute to see who will mold their nascent intelligent to his profit, so that tomorrow they'll be the sustaining herd, the docile herd of slaves to be sheared and killed.

In the end this is nothing but a fight to exploit this source of wealth. Who will these children be the slaves of? Which dogma, which party will exploit them? Who will they expend their strength and energy for, who will they spill their blood for in the impending slaughterhouses? This is the question.

Will it be in the name of God, for those who dominate by faith, mystical terrors, and inquisitions? Will it be in the name of great fantastic principles, for those who dominate by corruption?

The fight is a bitter one, like all clashes of interests, and will not end soon. For the moment, in a more immediate way, it's a matter of an electoral campaign, skillfully begun with pro-Ferrer agitation and skillfully continued by the defense of the secular. Isn't it touching to see anarchists, syndicalists, and parliamentarians fraternizing on the stage? Everyone for the secular! The old farce of the Dreyfus Affair (everyone for the truth!) is beginning once again, showing how true it is that history is a perpetual starting over and that man's naïveté is unlimited. And isn't this understandable, since almost everyone has passed through the secular or the religious? With minds steeped either in God by priests or in the state, the sad farces from which we suffer can begin over and over again. There's no risk that these men will see clearly!

The blindfold that tomorrow's secularists will put over their eyes is more serious than the old-fashioned religion that every day crumbles a bit more. They'll no longer be taught the divine legends and they'll be ignorant of the dream of paradise and the terrors of hell. But they'll venerate the fatherland, expect everything from beneficent reforms and will live in the respect and fear of the Law. Or else—and doubtless a bit later—they'll venerate the collectivity and the State and will work at building geometrical cities. There will no longer be either believers or subjects: we'll all be citizens of the republic or the new socialist order, unified, unionized. And we'll continue to follow the shepherds to the great abattoirs where treasure of life will be swallowed up in passivity, obedience, and resignation.

The secularist will substitute the breviary of the perfect citizen, the rules of the party and the union card for the Roman catechism. The trade is worth all the trouble!

The role of the secular or the religious school is to prepare children for social life, to adapt them to an unhealthy and irrational environment by annihilating their instinct for revolt and their faculties of logic and initiative. Society wants servile automata for its barracks and factories, and the mission of schools is to provide them. The secular school can be nothing but a factory for soldiers, good workers, and good bosses; a damper and a place of rot.

If it's republican, socialist, syndicalist, or even anarchist (for those who, by anarchism, mean a body of established doctrines), any school in service to a party or a sect can only be a marvelous tool of enslavement. It will make believers in this or in that; it will engrave in minds new dogmas in place of the old and prepare people for new enslavements. *It will kill the individual.*

To be member of a sect, to accept a doctrine means thinking as part of a group. Thinking as a gang, with and through others, means no longer thinking for oneself. It is in this way that the individual disappears, drowned in the anonymous crowd of followers, and its passivity perpetuates the murderous oppressions that prevent it from tasting life.

Does the secular teacher, similar in this to the priest, worry himself about creating a determined, strong, independent man? No. In the first place, this isn't his mission. He is paid to teach for the profit of those who pay him. And then, even if he wanted to he couldn't, disciplinary measures cutting short any reforming desires. In any case, even if he were allowed to do so he would collide with insurmountable obstacles: the methods, the very principle of education.

Experienced educators have often said this. Spencer, Letourneau, Laisant have laid bare the profound vices of the methods currently in use, an authoritarian education appealing not to the student's critical faculties and intelligence, but to his memory. The latter need not know; he must admit, believe, and retain. "This is how it is." "Why?" asks the child, eager to understand. "Because this is how it is!" And let him not try to reason by himself. From which flows the certain destruction of his powers of reasoning and understanding. The child enters school with his intelligence growing, alert and wanting to blossom. He leaves it stuffed with *a priori* notions, knowing how to believe but incapable of knowing, stupefied.

All dogmatic methods of education unfailingly arrive at these results. Whatever its label, school will produce dried fruits.

Other factors enter into play that must be mentioned. For example, the defective conditions of hygiene and discipline. These, you might say, can be remedied. But as long as schooling is either secular or religious we cannot prevent the depressing effects of study in herds from occurring. In order to fully develop the child must take up the habit of *thinking alone and for himself.* This should be the sole concern of the educator. How far we are from this.

We are still far from this. But this isn't a reason for us to take sides in the sad quarrel between secular and religious stupefiers. The difference between them is too small for us to have any preferences. And knowing that every transaction is a diminishment, we have no other way of comporting ourselves than as demolishers.

If the handful of comrades who have been made dizzy by the rhetoric of secularist charlatans saw the horrifying labor of death daily carried out by secular and religious schools; if they took the trouble to observe in real life their pitiful products, the prodigious forces annihilated, the countless minds, innovations, and wills destroyed, they would quickly get a grip on themselves. And when in the morning light they'd see children joyfully bearing their energy to the damper, they too will want to shout at them: "Don't go there . . . Flee! . . . Go play, go anywhere, but don't go in there. People are perverted there, castrated, killed!"

(*l'anarchie*, January 20, 1910)

A Good Example

(Editor's note: Jean-Jacques Liabeuf was an apache, *or member of a Parisian street gang, who, upon his release for his unjust imprisonment as a pimp, sought out the policemen responsible for his arrest and killed a policeman attempting to detain him. His became a cause célèbre of the Left. Despite a campaign that involved socialists, syndicalists, and anarchists, Liabeuf was executed on July 2, 1910.)*

THE OTHER DAY A "TERROR" OF THE CITY BARRIERS, WHO THE COPS WERE arresting for some misdeed I don't know a thing about, rightly wiped the floor with four of them. Four cops taken down like that by a guy they were getting ready to quietly rough up—now that's a job well done. It took a few hundred of Ferrer's avengers on the October 13 of glorious memory to take down just one!

For having done his job so well I find this Liabeuf quite sympatico, much more so than certain fearsome revolutionaries who, after having suffered the third degree, vehemently protest . . . journalistically.

And yet, the apaches in general don't interest me very much. They differ too little from honest people. With certain rare (and estimable) exceptions, their mentality and methods are identical. Both recognize authority and make use of it. Both have a view of life that is illogical and lacking in beauty, which is verified by everything they do. Just as the honest citizen considers his wife as his property and denies her any individual will, the pimp sees his hooker as a profit center. Both shamelessly exploit. The honest merchant robs through deception under the protection of the law; the apache operates through violence against the law. Only the way they end differ in any way. While the financier will end peacefully, honored, and decorated, Charlot de Menilmuche or the Bastoche will likely end up in the penal colony, unless a final bit of bad luck acquaints him with the widow-maker.[1]

I would say that nine times out of ten the apaches are nothing but poorly adapted or unlucky bourgeois. But we must render them this justice: they are less cowardly, less spineless than honest people, and because of this resemble men a bit more.

For example, this Liabeuf, arrested two weeks ago on the Rue Aubry-le-Boucher, in wiping the floor with four cops, acted like a man where almost everyone else—including revolutionaries and anarchists—ordinarily act like cowards.

I don't know why they were arresting him, and in any case that seems to me to be secondary. Whatever the official causes the fact remains: in the name of the lawmen pounced on another man because in the struggle for life he had transgressed the rules of the code.

He had transgressed the law! But did he ever subscribe to it? Had he recognized it?

Is it not the height if illogic to accuse an individual of not recognizing the rules he is perhaps ignorant of, to which no one ever asked him to subscribe, and which others unknown to him decreed?

I am ignorant of the law and I repudiate it. In my eyes nothing justifies it. It is imposed on me by brute force. It is only respected and obeyed by the weakest because of phalanxes of prison guards, cops, and soldiers.

For a word, a writing, an act—simply that, for such is the fantasy of a judge or policeman—the abstract power of the law is made real and delivers a blow. Its dogs attack the rebel. Magistrates deliberately cut so many days, months, and years from his life, which he'll pass in the horror of prison. They coldly torture him through solitude, silence, darkness; they turn him into a formless gray thing without any activity of his own.

There is nothing more natural than the fact that, their gilded abjection being threatened by rebels—conscious resistors or not—the masters of the day defend themselves; that they pitilessly suppress the rebel; that they make Brennus's famous word their motto: "Woe on the vanquished!" and that they kill the apache whose knife threatens their bellies, the poet and the thinker who awaken people's consciousness, and the anarchist conquering his life against theirs. Let them kill! The battle

---

[1]   "Widow-maker" was a slang expression for the guillotine.

will be merciless on both sides, but at least we won't know the infamy and torment of jails.

It is logical that in order to live a man should kill another when the latter gets in his way. It is logical that the dispossessed attack the possessors and that the possessors respond with fusillades. It is logical that the apache, the rebel against the prison of labor, kills a *rentier*, and logical when the *rentier* kills him when they have him in their hands.

Kill. That's your right, and ours. But don't torture. That is the true crime, the evil, repugnant act. To deprive a man of air and light, to gag him, tie his arms and legs, take from him all of life's joys and leave him nothing but suffering, that is the crime par excellence.

Existence without freedom becomes the worst of agonies. And every law being one more hindrance to individual freedom, every individual endowed with will is, by definition, a rebel. So every time that a man is attacked in the name of that law—which creates theft, fraud, and falsehood, which stifles and tortures—if there is even the least drop of virile strength left in him he must defend himself, ferociously, desperately.

The right to live implies the right to kill whoever prevents me from living. The will to live imposes on me the duty (the necessity) of killing whoever wants to rob me of freedom, without which there is no life.

But people are so cowardly these days. Accumulated slaveries have made man so flabby and senile that even the primordial instinct of the animal retaliating for a bite with a blow with his claw has fallen asleep in him. If the wolves who the winter exasperates leave the woods, their mouths burning to wrest their nourishing pittance; if every animal fights back against hunger or the yoke, the poor stoically support their poverty, and all men allow themselves to be oppressed, ridiculed, and tortured without rebelling.

These are no longer the days of open carnage when violent and clearly defined forces collided. A weak humanitarianism lulls masters and slave. They want peace—international, social, individual, all possible peace. And hypocritically, their faces veiled in smiles, they fight through use of corruption, betrayal, and deceit. Fear reigns, the fear of blood and effort, the fear of leaving sweet somnolence behind.

This explains the carefree casualness of the privileged, juggling with the fate of the common run of mortals. Insults, vexations, spoliations, and the arbitrary relentlessly whip the individual on. Men exploit with impunity other men who are a hundred times more numerous than they.

Amid so much weakness and cowardice I admire the person who dares to defend himself. It's necessary that there arise more often the figure of the apache in order to teach poltroons and tormentors respect for the individual.

For the cops received a good lesson, and it was a scathing one, as sharp a one as being whipped. And for those—the anarchist rebels—who push their way through mocking the authorities and who the law waits for in ambush at every turning, this apache gave a good lesson.

(*l'anarchie*, January 27, 1910)

I Deny!

ABOVE ALL, THE ANARCHIST CHALLENGES EVERYTHING. EVERYTHING THAT was affirmed and admitted by his predecessors, everything that is believed and held sacred by his contemporaries, he examines and discovering the lies, the nothingness, the childish errors, feeling the weight of universal stupidity on his shoulders, he denies. Nothing resists his criticism, neither ideas nor institutions nor men. No one has been able to answer him, and though certain gloomy individuals are happy to announce every two weeks the bankruptcy of anarchism, none have refuted it, and with every passing day life confirms our thought.

Anarchism is essentially individualist. Properly speaking it isn't a doctrine and all those—and they exist—who wanted to turn it into a dogma collided with the mocking denials of their own friends. And so despite numerous attempts at this, attempts likely given rise to by psychological remembrance of the authoritarian instinct, anarchism has remained a purely individual philosophy and activity.

And if there are many and widely different tendencies among us, they are all in agreement in proclaiming the right of the Individual to live his own life. With this as a starting point, all refuse to subordinate him in any way to what is pre-established. They incite him to ceaselessly criticize and to only admit what he has himself recognized as true. Individualism and antidogmatism: these are the two fundamental principles of anarchist thought.

Richly endowed with the will to live individually, to assert his selfhood in opposition to a hostile environment; by definition recognizing nothing *a priori*, the anarchist is above all a person who challenges. He knows only one response to the injunctions of the voices of the past that guide the present: I deny!

"I deny what is imposed, immutable, absolute; all religious, moral and scientific dogmas.

"I deny God, faith in whom is imposed on the weak by fear of the unknown, on the blind by the fear of light.

"I deny rights and duties, abstract and purely conventional entities whose censure hinders my actions and which can't be justified. As for rights, I only have those conferred by my strength. Life teaches us there are no rights without power, and no rights that can stand up to force. Duties! I only have those created by my will and my force: I will and I can, so I must.

"I deny good and evil. In itself no act is good or bad; it is only so in relation to this or that other thing. My good can be the evil of my neighbor. I call good anything that contribute to maintaining and amplifying my life, and I call the contrary evil. And I am the sole judge of this.

"I deny scientific dogma, which is as absurd and dangerous as religious immobility. It too often occurs that the truth admitted one day is revealed to be an error the next. I accept no limit to my inquiring spirit: I want to forever rework all concepts, redo all experiments.

"I deny authorities, laws, conventions. Whoever obeys gives up a fragment of his life, and I don't want to cut off any part of mine. I am greedy with every second of life, jealous to take advantage of every precious minute. Because they restrict my activity, because they deform my personality, because they block my road with their guards, I deny authorities. Thirsty for air and light, rich in will, I deny!

"Laws, contracts, conventions: I deny them! I deny! I deny! Laws that others, strong and numerous, made to better strike down rebels; rules issued by majoritarian herds against the boldness of minorities; social contracts whose clauses I never accepted and which even so bind me to beings who are strangers to me; foolish conventions, rites of falsehood, hypocrisy, and ugliness imposing on me a mask with which to smile at the surrounding masks.

"I deny!"

But denying in thought isn't enough, for a thought that isn't realized in action is incomplete, like a word without a thing.

The philosophical attitude of the denier finds practical resolution in combativeness. What the anarchist rejects in himself he also wants to reject in life. He is a destroyer.

Alone, not caring if he's imitated, without any desire to be followed because he's strong, and for the simple pleasure of fighting, the denier is a demolisher.

His penetrating, vigorous, obstinate criticism, his irony, his will spread confusion. And when he passes among them the humble go into a panic, and fanatics are infuriated.

In the old stinking cities where filth and dust reign, among the shapeless huts of the past, the schools, prisons, government offices, and brothels, he strolls with his shovel and his torch.

In decadent civilizations he is the salutary barbarian, the only one still capable of creating, of erecting his individuality above the pestilence.

He denies everything in order to better and increasingly affirm himself.

(*l'anarchie*, February 17, 1910)

A Head Will Fall

NOTHING IS MORE REPUGNANT THAN THE MACABRE JUDICIAL COMEDY THAT all too often ends in a new exploit of the guillotine, one which is contrary to vulgar common sense, revolting to feelings and, from the social point of view, as unjust as it is immoral.

Vulgar common sense clearly demonstrates in vain that a wound isn't healed by amputation; that one crime—and a murder coldly decided on and prepared by the official representatives of society is a crime par excellence—doesn't make right another, and in no way prevents the future crimes that contemporary illogic render inevitable. Logic and common sense! Only a few eccentrics—the anarchists—timidly attempt to conform to them.

Revolting? Yes, the death penalty is as revolting as can be. In a few tragic pages of his *Mêlée Sociale* Clemenceau related the horror of executions. He then hurried to forget them (one forgets so many things when one becomes a minister). Fifteen years after he described it, the sinister scene in the gray and red dawn of La Roquette Prison is being replayed. It only revolts dreamers like us.

Unjust, immoral . . . Big words that are laughed at in this twentieth century of all-out civilization. Do we ever see those who rule by the force of injustice seek to be just in their acts? And do we ever see the imbeciles who live under their influence and support them aspire to anything? Come now!! Justice and morality are things to be taught in the stupefying classrooms so that children learn not to rebel later on.

So instead of worrying about this nonsense they judge, they sentence, and they kill. Journalists, speculating on the bloodthirsty hysteria of the mob demands heads; magistrates, symbolically garbed in purple, deliberate, split hairs, discuss before deciding if the wretch who stands before them will through their sinister good humor be sent to Maroni's garden of tortures or put in the hands of their *compère*

Deibler.[1] This depends strictly on these gentlemen's mod. All that's needed is for the grocer who presides over the jury to be a cuckold, for his business to go badly, for him to have a corn on his foot and a man's fate is sealed. The honest people applaud. The most sensitive rejoice when the clemency of the judges has destined a poor bugger to torture instead of sending him straight to his death. But when a head falls most of them are delirious with joy.

To judge, to condemn, to torture or guillotine are all as idiotic as they are useless, not to say harmful. But who cares? Most people understand nothing about this. It's the veritable apotheosis of imbecility: magistrates, judges, executioners, soldiers, none of them understand a thing.

Others, frightened by crimes whose tide is rising and which threaten them, feel themselves to be in danger and strike out blindly. Not understanding that repressive ferocity is pointless and that it is the cause of crime that must be attacked; that from the moment that people are hungry, lack air and sun, and have their health destroyed in factories and barracks, it is inevitable that they will rob and murder. But go talk of correct reasoning, of science, of determinism to people who are confused by fear and are enslaved to petty interests.

This time will be like all the others. The judicial machine has functioned and unless the chubby Fallières has, after attending some truculent banquet, the "humanitarian" idea of sending Liabeuf to the galleys, a head will fall. But this time it's not the head of some unlucky soul or a brute . . .

This was a very simple story. The vice squad cops who are, as Clemenceau so picturesquely said, "official scoundrels," had sated themselves on this victim in order to justify the salary society allocates to them to brutalize prostitutes and hunt down nonmilitary pimps. They thought it less dangerous to arrest an inoffensive passerby. When dealing with an authentic pimp one must always fear being stabbed. With this worker, they thought, impunity was certain. The little young man protested. A waste of time. If all citizens are equal according to the text of the law, in practice no word can counterbalance the words spoken by a cop. "Pimp!" the cops said, just as on other occasions they said "Demonstrator!" That was enough.

Luckily, it happens that the police sometimes choose poorly. They arrest someone who it happens is not completely flabby and less fearful

---

1   The public executioner.

than an official revolutionary. A good bugger who has guarded intact the notion of his individual dignity and whose energy isn't satisfied with jeremiads and has enough determination to move from words to acts, even if this involves a serious risk.

This is a summary of the Liabeuf Affair.

Personally, there's nothing about Liabeuf to interest us. Honest worker or *apache*, it's no difference to us: the distinction is too subtle for anarchist logic to take pleasure in. Certified honest people are often the worst rats, and among those called apaches there can unquestionably be found people of greater individual value. Nevertheless, taken as a whole, one can say that the ones are no better than the others, which flatters neither of them. As concerns Liabeuf, it doesn't mean a thing to us to know what he really was. But we must recognize the energy he demonstrated in a situation where we are used to seeing cowardice.

Viewed on its own, his act is an anarchist act.

He wanted to kill the policemen Maugras and Mors, who had sent him to prison and prohibited his residing in Paris. Outside any purely sentimental considerations—which have their importance—this sentence nonchalantly delivered was of a kind to upset an entire existence.

The "official scoundrels" of morality—ministerial style—caused him to suffer an irreparable humiliation and brutally intervened in his life, whose course they changed. I understand that a man of a vigorous character thought vengeance was absolutely necessary. But was this really vengeance? Wasn't it rather an act of legitimate defense?

They beat him. He defended himself. What isn't normal is that such cases occur so rarely. What is abnormal is the cowardly indifference of the countless unfortunates who suffer without balking the humiliations of the many valets of capital and authority. Clearly the secular school and the barracks have obtained magnificent results: they have created in the overwhelming majority of those whose youth they've ground down the mentality of slaves they can use at will.

Healthy men will never forget that for the individual defending his life is a primordial duty.

As biology teaches us, in a well-constituted organism every attack that places its organism in danger is immediately followed by a vigorous reaction. Sociologists teach us that in the free communities of primitives, where slavery was not yet established, that to each denial of justice committed to the detriment of someone, to every affront, to every threat, the insulted individual responded with an equivalent reaction. For it is an inexorable law of nature that any being incapable of defending itself will disappear.

And this law is rigorously verified in social life. The man who doesn't defend himself, accepting the oppression society places on him without reacting, always disappears. There are those who simply die, murdered by tuberculosis or in service to the fatherland in Madagascar, in Tonkin, or wherever. There are those who peacefully end their days in bed at age sixty, without having lived a single moment of their own. From their first step till their final shudder they never had their own will, they were never individualities. He was Mr. John Doe, Mr. Everyman, whose existence no one bothered with and whose death will pass noticed. He never struck back; he passively accepted the blows that quickly turned him into a gray, unassuming, flabby silhouette: someone shapeless.

The person who wants to live, to grab in the present his share of the sun, of flowers and joy, must affirm himself. Must know how to walk alone, think with his own brain. Act freely; react without truce against the fetters placed by an absurd social organization on the satisfaction of his most elementary needs and most logical wishes. Resisting enslavement is a condition *sine qua non* of the fulfillment of individual life.

In a word: defending oneself. Rendering blow for blow. There are obstacles, there are circumstances where force is the only weapon that can be used.

Liabeuf, though wanting to strike the direct artisans of his misfortune, struck by chance the agents who arrested him.

There is no worse wrong that can be committed against an individual than that of depriving him of his freedom. Even death is less serious, for it is not painful while imprisonment constitutes a continuous, abominable torture. We can call it a "death that is granted consciousness," and even this metaphor is powerless to explain how horrible the abolition of all that characterizes life for him is for a human being.

Rebellion is essential against this ultimate assault. The sole fact of depriving a man of his freedom for an hour justifies the strongest reprisals on his part. What am I saying? The mere act of a policeman putting his hand on your shoulder, because it signifies an attack on the human personality, is sufficient reason on its own to justify any form of revolt.

I will end by citing the words that legend attributed to Duval, one of the first anarchist militants in France. He is supposed to have responded to the cop's sacramental "In the name of the law, I arrest you," by this phrase that followed the shot from his revolver: "In the name of freedom, I eliminate you!"

(*l'anarchie*, May 12, 1910)

Religiosity and Individualism

A METAPHOR TO DESIGNATE THE SOCIALIST PARTY HAS GAINED COMMON USAGE. In opposition to the black church formed by the disciples of the Nazarene Christ, it is called the red church. Ordinarily this term serves only as an image, but, if we think about it a bit it can be taken literally. No metaphor is as exact.

Just as there is a Roman Catholic and Apostolic church, there exist socialist and syndicalist churches. We are here giving the word "church" its exact meaning: an institution perpetuating the rites of a religion.

In truth, the ideas, the formulas, and the routines varied and vary every day. But at the very least, among most mortals the atavistic sentiments and instincts upon which ideas are grafted do not change, or change with an appalling slowness.

If religions fall into desuetude; if the daily growing sum of human knowledge wipes out the absurd beliefs of the past, the religious sentiment that produces fanatics and pontiffs remains alive in people's minds.

G. Le Bon defines it this way in his remarkable *Psychology of Crowds*: the adoration of a supposedly superior being; fear of his power; impossibility of discussing its dogmas; desire to spread them, and a tendency to consider those who don't accept them as enemies.

Well then, these different characteristics of religiosity can be found in the socialist, in the union member, in the reader of *La Guerre Sociale*, and this to as developed a degree as among the flock of the priest of my parish or a follower of the Salvation Army.

For how many brave and sincere members of the unified unions is Karl Marx not the giant, the hero, the divine being who brought light and truth to the base obscurity of this world? And people venerate these priests every bit as profoundly as the priests of any other religion. Doesn't the crackpot of the Revolution await Méric's great uprising with an impatience and a secret apprehension that are truly mystical? Do we dispute the dogma of the immortal Manifesto with the wild Marxist? And is that of expropriation arguable for the revolutionary? And socialists, members of the CGT, etc., don't they consider the believer of the church across the way, and even more those outside of any party, heretics, impenitents—enemies to be reduced if not destroyed.

The Inquisition sets the stake flame to save lost souls in the name of a religion of love and forgiveness. Today the Reds knock out the poor "yellow" unionists who haven't been enlightened by the truths of the Cause and promise firing squads tomorrow in order to establish universal happiness. The blind sectarianism of the hallucinating continues its work of creating suffering among men.

Religiosity is so strong that in many circumstances it is translated with no modification of its externals: the love of amulets and fetishes and the veneration of martyrs.

In the great cities of Belgium I saw imposing socialist demonstrations: flags and banners flapping in the wind, music, song, ritual speeches, nothing was lacking of what can also be seen in Catholic processions. The costumes were less lovely . . . So as not to cross the border to find examples for free-thinkers, do I need to remind people of the idolatrous free-thinkers on their pilgrimage to the statue of poor Chevalier de la Barre in Montmartre?

And can't that statue, like that of Joan of Arc, be likened to the fetishes, the saints in wood or bronze of the churches? Isn't Ferrer a martyr to free thought for whom statues should be erected, songs dedicated, and flowers offered? Cult of the dead, adoration of sacrifices, fetishism, this is what we find if we analyze the psychological motives that make the atheists and revolutionaries of this century of non-belief act.

If I had the time I could give more examples. Who among us, when leaving some talk, hasn't encountered the gentle, inoffensive dreamer whose days are taken up in the hope for a marvelous future society. He is happy to confide in you his hope that has become a certainty. Things will be thus and no other way. Hope!

And there is the one for whom anarchism is contained in this or that pamphlet, this or that slogan. If I don't accept this I am a contemptible idiot, a boor with whom no camaraderie is possible. And there is the scientific pal who has poorly digested the indigestible books of Le Dantec and now swears only by science. But let's stop here.

So even upon anarchists, who are on the alert thanks to their implacable critical spirit and their ferocious antidogmatism, the religious spirit has taken hold.

I would even say that in the history of the French anarchist movement there was a religious phase.

Idealism exaggerated the brave dreamers of the terrorist period, created a state of mind where religiosity dominated. Yes, idealism is necessary, inevitable and salutary, but when exacerbated, saturated, pushed to the absurd by minds preserving the millennial imprint of Christianity, it produced the type of the anarchist believer. It saw the blooming of a peculiar literature and of particular customs that lasted several years.

Literature, aesthetic and documentary, best preserves the reflections of the life of the past. It suffices to consult newspapers and books of an era to find numerous signs of anarchist religiosity.

Here, taken from among hundreds of similar documents, are a few verses that an anonymous comrade placed on Ravachol's tomb:[1]

> Since they made the earth drink
> At the moment of the sun's birth,
> Dew fruitful and salutary,
> The holy drops of your blood…

Note this human blood that sacrifice sanctifies, just as his martyrdom sanctified the flesh of the Lord. And here again is the end of the ballad of Solness, written by Laurent-Tailhade

> O anarchy, bearer of torches:
> Crush the vermin
> And build in the heavens,
> Even if it's with our graves,
> The bright tower that dominates the waters.

"Even if it's with our graves!" There we have in a well-formulated way the desire to sacrifice oneself for the suprahuman anarchy whose luminous tower will dominate the waters.

Without looking too far it would be possible for me to indefinitely prolong this list. I know songs by d'Avray where the religiosity is even

---

1   On this subject consult: Varenne *De Ravachol à Caserio*; Jean Dubis: *Le Peril anarchiste*; M. and A. Leblond: *La société française d'après la littérature contemporaine* [Note by Serge in the original].

more obvious. "The Madmen" proclaim that they'll blow up the old world,

> Knowing that sacrifice has its uses
> I want to be one of the madmen who'll blow you up.

Or again "The Two-penny Girl"

> . . . Confident, she comes to anarchy
> Where the comrade is freed.
> You'll find a heart among us
> Little two-penny girl.

Oh that marvelous anarchy where the disinherited will find the love that repairs all ills. In what way does it differ from the Kingdom of God, from the bosom of faith, the ideal communion with the crucified?

And so the religious spirit is far from being dead, since it drives most of our human acts and carries out its ravages, even among us.

This last fact should not puzzle us. Anarchists inevitably suffer from the same flaws as their era: most of those who come to us have minds already darkened if not by poorly erased beliefs, at least by a still powerful heredity. It requires exceptional circumstances and an uncommon intellectual vigor to produce an irreligious mentality.

But if one thinks—and this is our opinion—that the less religious a man is the better he lives, it is then worthwhile to seek the elements capable of creating a truly irreligious consciousness.

Free examination, some will say. *A posteriori* reasoning with physical knowledge as the starting point. Hmmm . . . Those who have accepted this criterion alone have themselves become more sectarian, more dogmatic than many vulgar dullards. Science for them is an impersonal truth they admit *a priori*, like God.

My reflections have led me to other results. Free examination, *a posteriori* reasoning, to be sure. And yet they aren't sufficient. In order not to create believers, in order to place no fetters on human thought, we must return to the concept of the individual. There could be religious anarchists, but there can't be individualists influenced by the old ghost of faith. (With the exception, of course, of the good people who, because they heard a talk or read a pamphlet, proclaim themselves to be individualists without knowing what an individual is.) The individualist sensibility is uncompromisingly opposed to any religiosity.

Individualism is the doctrine—the word is defective but there is no other to designate a totality of coordinated ideas—according to which every individual is unique, different from his kind, having *his* life to create and live as best he can. Every man being an original whole can only relate to himself in everything. He knows that that which is true for him is, in the end, true *only* for him. Understanding the relativity of concepts and sensations, he can't accept the faith of his neighbor nor impose his concepts on him. In accordance with his character, he conceives of life in this way or that, never forgetting that others with other temperaments must have different concepts. Criticizing himself, trusting only in his own reason and his own initiative, perpetually seeking what is best for him and his truths, we won't see him among the builders of churches or among the followers of prophets.

If at times he is a dreamer and utopian he will enjoy the dream as a form of intellectual relaxation and won't hide the fact that utopia is only a mirage that encourages those who march. Mystical, sensual, or fickle at different times, he will be so without any religiosity or dogmatism, like a dilettante, for the pleasure of living in the places and realms his tastes choose.

(*l'anarchie*, September 15, 1910)

By Being Bold

DANTON'S FAMOUS PHRASE, "BOLDNESS, MORE BOLDNESS, FOREVER BOLD-ness," has lost nothing of its synthetic value. It remains a great truth that we must never lose sight of; it remains the sole motto for those not content to vegetate in the marshes.

I thought of this the past few days upon reading of the tragic death of a young man who yesterday was obscure and part of the mass of young idlers and is today famous because he was bold. An aviator: Chávez.

It was necessary to be strong to conceive the mad dream of traveling through space above the white peaks that only eagles can reach. And how much determination and boldness did the aviator need to attempt this perilous flight? But having reached these heights, gliding over the snowy Alps, he lived minutes that were worth more than many lives. He felt himself to be a man par excellence, valiant, strong, the risk-taker, through the ardent effort by which all human works have been accomplished. For only those who were capable of risking all in vertiginous flights; those who had the strength to conceive the accomplishment of the impossible and to want it—the thinkers, apostles, and adventurers—were the demolishers of old civilizations and builders of new lives.

The boldness of Christopher Columbus and Amerigo Vespucci conquered a continent; the innovative boldness of Stephenson overturned the modern world by creating the machine and the railroad; Edison, gambling his life in his laboratory; others traveling the world despite pursuit and prison to bring routine-ridden cities their bold thoughts and acts; and that young man killed the other day. These men, strong, determined, bold, left their imprint on life, they destroyed, created, lived. The others do nothing; the others, without knowing why, guard and defend the shadowy routine in which they suffocate. The others lack both the force to destroy and the intelligence to build. And they pass right by life, like stumbling blind men, without hopes or desires.

I thought of these things upon learning of the agony and death of the unfortunate Chávez, who paid with his life for the error of having been too daring. But hasn't it always been thus? There can only be two endings to the great struggle that is accepted by men of energy; one of the two things is fatal: since the man takes a risk he will kill himself or be killed. And what difference does it make if before that he tasted all possible joys, known all possible happiness, savored the battle, felt the pleasure of victory?

Or else he will be killed. Laws are made to prevent the strong from living; their mission is to level things in such a way that no one dares be braver or more intelligent than the cowardly and rotten mass which, in any case, hates those who rise above it. For slaves, in fact, the enemy is not the master, it is the untamed. For the crowd the enemy is the individual. For the strong being is above all an individual. Renan said, "The great men of a nation are those it kills." The eternal conflict that bloodies history has no other causes. In Athens, in Alexandria, in Rome, in antiquity as in modern cities, the same struggle tore society apart: the crowd against the individual. The strangling authorities are created and supported by crowds in order to contain individual rebellions. "All against one"—this is the slogan. And yet, progress only occurs thanks to bold individuals.

Intelligence, will, boldness—to understand, to will, to dare—human strength can be summed up in these three words. But those who possess it being dangerous to a social order, whose most solid bases are precisely stupidity, weakness, and poltroonery; and men of a virile allure being, by definition, hated by brutes, it follows that of necessity everything is done to stifle in these minds the triple seed of revolt.

In school they rot the brain of the child who might have resisted—though this is difficult—the family's continuous oppression. The workshop then cheats him and predisposes him for the barracks if he's a male, or marriage and prostitution if she's a female. The brothel and the barracks do the rest. The being comes out of this emptied, castrated, and flabby. If in an outburst of anger he wasn't able to smash the chains in time he is completely lost—to himself and us.

This is the way honest people are made, the perfect citizens, good workers and excellent soldiers. Is intelligence necessary to pay your rent, work peacefully, put on and take off your uniform when you're ordered to, to vote, to get drunk? What use would boldness be? And what could resist the long decay of such a pitiful existence?

It is thus true that most men don't exist. At the very most they are number-fragments of the crowd. And crowds don't think: they believe what others long dead impose on them. They are dominated by the dead. Crowds don't reason; they become irritated, exasperated and enthusiastic depending on the leader; they are dominated by swindlers and megalomaniacs. Crowds don't understand; they admit, and prestige blinds them just as vehemence frightens them. Crowds don't want, they obey. They are fearful, cowardly, happy only in the beatitude of apathy.

At a certain moment every man has to face the same question: either you will have the strength to be a categorical "self" or you will disappear in the innumerable rabble of vague humanity.

Anarchists are those who don't hesitate between the two possibilities. They remain those who have enough strength to resist the assault of the mob and, despite beatings, the law, and what people say, despite the crowd, are true to themselves: unbelievers, outsiders, rebels.

And the quality most needed to emerge victorious is boldness. The effort to be made isn't a small one, but the results are worth it. There are many obstacles along the way. Sinister traps lie in wait for the insolent. Boldness is needed to take the first step. Will is needed to continue. Dare and risk with every step. And ever more boldness. Anarchists must be bold and not set themselves limits.

It's better to be rash than pusillanimous.

The audacious are individualist by temperament. Whoever these rebels against universal weakness might be, no progress will occur without them. And so whenever a man's daring is manifested through any effort of whatever kind I feel hope for amazing feats.

And so there are men who dare!

And so there are those who, for their pleasure, for their own personal satisfaction, risk their lives, like Chávez. And so there are those who, to carry out a task they have dedicated themselves to, accept the greatest risks. There are risk-takers, the bold.

How comforting the sight of them is after the cowardice of the banal. A vision of marvelous hopes. What if the example of these efforts entered into the plebe and gave rise to other and new feats of daring?

If poor wretches, the starving, seeing the Lathams, the Leblancs, the Chávezes, risk everything for the satisfaction of healthy pride said, "The efforts that these bourgeois dedicate to conquering the blue, we can dedicate to some happiness on this lowly planet." What if the wretched who hunger and cold will murder this winter, if the slaves in the penal colonies found in themselves the boldness to risk everything as well?

They would see that there is a way not to be hungry. And he who was an honest imbecile yesterday will tomorrow be a rebel. The good soldier won't wait to be freed to be free. The adolescent will say that we can love without going before the mayor. The boldness to think and, even more, the boldness to act will have revealed to them the splendor of living.

But first, you must dare.

Well then, the task of anarchists is to teach by example how to dare. To show how we can risk, how we can live boldly. Thumb our nose at laws and those who make them; laugh at conventions and live free despite it all.

Each of us must realize himself. Be neither a sect nor a school but clear, original, vigorous individuals living intelligently.

This is what we are bold enough to attempt. This is the boldness we would like to teach the pitiful people who are hampered by their own inertia.

(*l'anarchie*, October 6, 1910)

Two Russians

RUSSIA . . . WE KNOW WHAT IT IS, ENCOMPASSING THE EAST OF EUROPE AND the north of Asia, an immense empire where the killings never stop. It is said that it's a country of limitless plains, which legend affirms are white with eternal snows. People know almost nothing other than this, and yet they talk about the country often. Few subjects of conversation come up as often as does that of Russia and the Slavic character, the famous character that learned gentlemen dissect in just a few words: mystical, religious if not fanatical, as well as cold and impulsive (see the terrorists). None of this holds together very well. Nevertheless, people's opinions are set, and the least occurrence in Russia becomes the theme for commonplaces.

I think it is desirable that at the very least the anarchists take an interest, a more serious one, in the painful life of the Slavic race. Firstly from simple human solidarity toward the valiant minority there that is carrying out the same combat as we here against the triple chain: lack of consciousness, the spinelessness of the crowd, and the ferocity of the masters.

But also because the Slavic race permits us to make precious observations and at times offers us magnificent examples. Younger than the Latin races because it came later to civilization (i.e., refined and artificial life, large-scale industry, intensive production, the reign of money), it was able to perhaps too hastily accept the good parts and attempt to reject the flawed. If letters, the arts, and the sciences have made astonishing strides, if artists and psychologists like Andreev, Kuprin, and Artzybachev, leave our Bourgets far behind them; if Russian intellectualism has greater value than the ridiculous supposed elite constituted here by the fast-living and arriviste youth of the universities, the Slavs have remained backward on other points. They live more simply, less depravedly, less debauched than the Latins. They are less cunning and more honest. And certain old words that in the West are nothing but old words have preserved some meaning there. Sincere individuals assert themselves, numerous and determined despite the horror of punishments. They know how to fight and act the way they think, even if they have to pay dearly for it, to carry things to the bitter end in the life they've chosen. A curious parallel with here, where repression is comparatively less ferocious, though the oppression of the individual is similar, the revolts are less clear, rarer, more incomplete than there, where repression is implacable, unimaginable . . .

Races live and die in the same way as individuals; they have successive periods of weakness and strength; they grow and decline. And perhaps the entire difference can be found there: the Slavs are young while it appears the Latins have already expended the bulk of their effort. The Slavs have both the defects and the qualities of the young. Accepting this is certainly simpler than splitting hairs over the obscure adjectives distributed by the spreaders of ignorance involved in conformist education. Let them explain the extreme logic of revolts by the mysticism they translate into hallucinations but which in reality is nothing but proof of new vigor and will. These are nothing but a few more howlers added to the existing jumble. But we free investigators don't accept this silliness any more than we accept any other. Let us ask the facts, let us ask men to show us how races live, and we will unflinchingly say what we have seen.

Two men died there recently who are two symbols, who were essentially Slavic psychologies and individualities of a rare force. Their lives were two stubborn revolts and they never wavered in the face of the worst dangers. And though they were at opposite poles of thought, they both fell as defeated men worthy of admiration who remained themselves until death: Tolstoy, the new Christian, and I'm tempted to write the new anarchist Christ, though confined in his dream to such a point that he only saw the ideal, and Sazonov, a proud and upright intelligence who accepted reality as it was, who desired struggle in all its magnitude and got it.

They were at antipodes from each other, the apostle of kindness and the terrorist, the resigned man and the rebel. For centuries man has hesitated between these two extremes. Equally remarkable individuals, they lived as they wanted to live. Now that only their memories remain the question they posed is closer to being answered: How can man conquer the happiness of a life that is full and beautiful?

Tolstoy answered with the words of the Gospel that handed over the good, the gentle and the honest to the unscrupulous and the cruel. Tolstoy repeated the parables of the Galilean anarchist with which kings, popes, and inquisitions have been able to lull the deluded crowds: "Love each other . . ."

Love the brute who strikes you without knowing why; love the brute who despoils and beats you; love the base slave and the insolent lord. Ah, what naïveté was needed to affirm the doctrine of love. Alas, life doesn't belong to those whose only weapon is their intact moral beauty. Life is a struggle, and force alone gives a right to it.

"Don't resist the wicked, for resisting means rendering evil for evil . . ."

What a scathing denial life gave you, gentle, artless old man. When they don't defend themselves the good are crucified by the wicked, or silently asphyxiated by constraints. The good and the weak who didn't resist passed before your very eyes to be slaughtered in the mountains of Manchuria. The good and the weak who didn't resist died of hunger around you, and you yourself, because you didn't want to resist, could only offer them the promise of a paradise you had doubts about. Your eyes, which the ideal veiled with a beautiful mirage, didn't see that the life of a man can only be a ceaseless resistance against nature, society, and himself. Passivity and resignation are synonymous with annihilation.

And yet, your great wisdom led you to say: "Salvation is within you . . . Live simply . . . Help yourself . . . Don't judge . . ."

And these were living words that should not be forgotten. Man mustn't expect his salvation from redeemers: he will only find it in his own ill, in his own power.

He will realize one day, when he will count more on himself, the insane lies and hypocrisy that surround him. He will remember that beauty is simple, and that in order to live in beauty he'll live simply.

He will aid his neighbor, finding an advantage in doing so, and also because his effort will be generous. And knowing the complexity of causes he won't have the presumptuousness to judge, and also because he doesn't himself want to be judged.

Tolstoy was a Slav in both the errors and truths of his doctrine, with a willful and bold temperament, stumbling under the hold of religious heredity and an environment of sadness where consolation and love are vital necessities.

But his strength only shows itself in its entirety when revealed in his acts. Being basically skeptical, the civilized don't know how to be intransigent. They are unable to be faithful to their will, being weakened by the intensity of a refined existence. Being noble and rich, in order to renounce nobility and wealth, in order to refuse glory and honors, it was necessary to accept anathema and demand prison, to be one of those extraordinary individualities that only new races produce.

The death of Tolstoy was the death of a man of strength, of an ascetic and a primitive. To die in a final movement of will, breaking the final fetter, the family, is a sign of will. But in this there is also the ascetic's desire for solitude and the primitive's ferocious intransigence.

But the man having died, his doctrine remains. And it denies itself, it condemns itself. The salutary words it contains were stifled under the weight of error, because in confronting brutal life the absolute dream is an error. Tolstoy, who condemned the corrupt and those who govern, received the homage of the French Chamber of Deputies. He, the author of "I Can No Longer Remain Silent," was saluted on his death bed by the Tsar. His determination to be alone was frustrated, and those he disavowed insult him by honoring him. His doctrine of liberation has become a tool of enslavement. Like that of Christ, it is condemned by its results.

The other doctrine is summed up in one word: resist.

Once the petty squabbles of parties, the disputes over tactics are closed, one essential idea remains: resist. It's not a moral doctrine, but a notion that must impregnate the mind. Not to resist means not to exist. Opposing the passive resistance of the Christian to violence is a form of suicide. There is no individual life outside the struggle. Resist: this is the individualist motto par excellence, a program of action more than a doctrine.

While Tolstoy peacefully died, sickened at seeing himself admired against his will, another man was, like him, dying in a final burst of will: Sazonov.

He only counted on his own strength, knowing that force is the final argument. His bravery and desire not being able to accommodate themselves to a peaceful existence, he was active. Around him was the tyranny of the knout and the gallows. And then there were the factories that crushed energy, and oppression by hunger and oppression by the law, the final forms of violence promoted to the level of necessary institutions.

In such an atmosphere a man cannot fold his arms. A strong man can't limit his revolt to simply lightening the weight of his own chains.

With all his virile youth, the man who just poisoned himself in the penal colony of Zarontovy became, in doing so, an enemy of society, but not a moral enemy, thinker, critic, or apostle, but an enemy in act, by his life, which was that of an outlaw, by his private acts and his terrorist attitude.

It is appropriate to contrast such fighters with Tolstoy. Not to praise their personalities. We respect neither the dead nor heroes. But they are symbols. Tolstoy is the man of the past who seeks refuge in God, who believes and is resigned. Sazonov is the modern man, an unbeliever, determined.

On July 15, 1904, he killed Plehve in the middle of St. Petersburg by throwing a bomb under his landau. With a few friends he had spent months preparing this act. He knew he probably wouldn't return from it, but he preferred this to resignation or to an attitude of revolt limited to himself alone. Wounded by the same bomb, tortured on his hospital bed, he somehow survived, and it's inexplicable how he escaped the death sentence. In these times of "moral complicity" the eight years of forced labors the judges gave him seem almost an act of friendship. So Sazonov only had survive two more years in the penal colony when he committed suicide.

Being young and wanting to again take up his unfinished task he wanted to live, but the prison administration of Zarantovy, having several times provoked the anger of the prisoners with persecutory measures and attacks, the political detainees decided to act on a new round of attacks on their dignity. To continue resisting. But they only have two means of protesting and moving public opinion: hunger strikes and mass suicide. Several of them decided on this final method, hunger strikes doing nothing but provoke new harassments. And so, toward the end of November, Sazonov, along with five other revolutionary prisoners, killed himself in protest.

The facts are simple. But such as they are, they are as eloquent as a doctrine.

I wanted to show these two individualists side by side in order to better illustrate the ideological conflict between defunct Christianity and nascent revolt. I wanted to place these two extreme types of a young race, in whose psychology is mixed both the dizziness of an unfathomable past of mysticism and the boldest desire for life that can be formulated. Tolstoy and Sazonov are worth being understood.

We anarchist individualists no longer have anything to choose between. We no longer need to refute the Christian thesis, which its partisans have refuted through their defeat. We only conceive of individualism as a doctrine of revolt. Sazonov is one of us, and though we don't erect statues it pleases us to see such individualities arise from time to time.

(*l'anarchie*, December 29, 1910)

The Individualist and Society

THE WORD "SOCIETY" IS SYNONYMOUS WITH A GROUP. TODAY MOST MEN CON-
stitute an immense grouping that, though subdivided into an infinite
number of subgroups—races, nationalities, social classes, ideological
groups—can nevertheless be considered as a whole. It is this whole,
this formidable collectivity that we designate with the word society.

To consider society as an assemblage of individuals and to deny
this any importance, as some do, is simplistic, too simplistic. It means
failing to understand social psychology, the psychology of crowds and,
what is most surprising, the results of the most elementary observations. In truth, observation shows us and study confirms that from the
fact that they find themselves brought together through interests, aspirations, or similar heredity, men are modified. A new psychology is created, common to all the members of the association. From this point
they constitute a crowd, and that crowd has a mentality, a life, a destiny distinct from the individuals that compose it.

The existence of a society is this ruled by laws as immutable as those
of biology that rule the existence of individuals.

Let us now pose the question: are these laws favorable to the individual? Are they in harmony with his instincts?

In an excellent little *Précis de Sociologie* Monsieur G. Palante wrote:
"A society, once formed, tends to maintain itself," by virtue of which,
"in all domains—economic, political, legal, moral—individual energies
will be narrowly subordinated to common utility. Woe on those energies that do not bow before that discipline. Society breaks or eliminates
them with neither haste nor pity. It brings the most absolute contempt
of the individual to this execution. It acts like a blind instinct, irresistible and implacable. In a terribly concrete form it represents that brutal
force that Schopenhauer described: 'The will to life separated from
the intellect.' Despite all the optimistic utopias, every society is and

will be exploitative, dominating, and tyrannical. It is so not by accident, but by essence."

This is even more the case because we feel the "general law of social preservation," admitted by almost all contemporary sociologists, weighing painfully upon our shoulders.

And if we add the "law of social conformity, which consists in every organized society demanding of its members a certain similarity of conduct, appearance, and even of opinions and ideas," and which "consequently brings with it a law of the elimination of individuals rebellious to this conformism," the conflict between the individual and society appears to us to its full extent.

A glance around us strikingly confirms the conclusion that we arrived at theoretically.

What is more iniquitous in fact than the so-called social contract, in the name of which each is crushed by all? You will be a worker, you will be a soldier, you will be a prostitute, for social necessities demand this, all because a contract that no one ever asked you to agree to forces you be so. You will obey the law, you will be tradition's servant; you will live according to usage and custom. And yet tradition, law, and usage restrict you, hinder your development, make you suffer. Obey, bow, abdicate, otherwise your neighbors will condemn and pursue you. Public opinion will deride you and will call for the worst punishments for your insolence; the law will attack you. Starved, defamed, cursed, dishonored you will be the rebel who they implacably strangle.

Such is the reality. "I" have neither fatherland, nor money nor property to defend. What difference do my interests make to society? It needs soldiers, and so it imposes on me the fatherland, the barracks, a uniform . . .

"I" am no longer the dupe of the outdated morality that rules the life of the crowd. I aspire to love freely . . . But the social body needs love that is respectful of the law, and if I don't marry before the mayor the law and opinion reserve their rigors for me.

I love work. But I want to freely carry it out. The wage system presents me with the alternative of being a slave, a thief, or dying of hunger.

And we shouldn't condemn one form of social organization—authoritarian capitalism—more than other. To be sure, it isn't difficult to conceive of a society incomparably less bad, more logical, more intelligently organized. But aside from the fact that its more or less distant realization is an arguable hypothesis, we shouldn't hide from ourselves that it will always present serious obstacles to the development of the individual.

The hypothesis of a collectivist tomorrow presages a ferocious struggle between the state and the few individuals desirous of preserving their autonomy. Even understood in the broadest sense—that of our anarcho-communist friends—a social grouping will inevitably tend to impose one ideological credo on its members. There will still be the struggle between the individual and society, but instead of disputing his liberty and his material life, it will dispute his intellectual and moral independence. And nothing says that for the men of the future—if that future is ever realized—the course of that struggle will not be every bit as painful as the fight for bread, love, and fresh air is today!

In every social grouping the individualist will remain a rebel.

We shouldn't be thought to be unsociable simply because we take note of the antagonism between the individual and society. And yet on several occasions adversaries have sought to create that confusion.

Life in society has advantages that none among us would think of contesting. But as egoists, desirous of living in accordance with our ideas, we don't want to accept even the unavoidable inconveniences. This is one of the characteristic traits of an individualist: "He doesn't resign himself, even to what is fated."

If by a sociable individual we mean a person who doesn't disturb his neighbor—or disturbs him as little as possible—the individualist is the soul of sociability. This is first and foremost the case through interest: to disturb more often than not opens one to being disturbed. He thus lets others live as they wish, as long as they grant him the same right. He doesn't ignore the advantages of "association freely consented to," a temporary association of good wills, with a practical goal in mind. But he doesn't want to be the dupe of the idol of Solidarity and allow himself to be absorbed by a coterie, a chapel, or a sect.

If he is strong—and we think that it is impossible to affirm oneself without being strong—he is even more sociable.

The strong are generous, being rich enough to be generous: the most energetic rebels, the most indomitable enemies of society have always been big-hearted.

(l'*anarchie* 323, June 15, 1911)

A Revolutionary Experience

JUST FORTY YEARS AGO THE PARIS COMMUNE—EMPHATICALLY BUT ACCURATELY called by Jules Vallès "the great federation of suffering"—was born and died in blood. Forty years and yet we still have to combat the deplorable errors that inspired it; and the same interests, employing the same methods seem to be leading us toward a renewal of that tragedy.

History is a perpetual return of deceptions and butcheries; the one never goes without the other. Today, as in 1869, while secret intrigues are being hatched in chancelleries that will perhaps result in war tomorrow, the people, the sovereign people, infinitely credulous, infinitely naïve, prepare all unawares the arms that will serve to slaughter them. And the generals of the syndicalist and workers' army, foreseeing the war of tomorrow, prepare the Commune of tomorrow. What do the consequences matter to them? By playing this sad game they earn notoriety, money, and glory.

This is the moment to recall the lesson of the past. But just as our preachers of revolution know how not to be hindered by logic, they aren't hindered by cumbersome memories.

So it us up to us to fill in the gaps in their memory. Aren't we the detestable "pure ones?" The burdensome "theoreticians?" The "metaphysical reasoners?" The ones who prevent people from dancing, feasting and yakking?

Forty years ago, Citizens, the Parisians did what you want to do. You know this and yet you continue to push the working-class cattle intoxicated by your fallacious eloquence to a similar butchery.

If the labels have changed since 1871, the chimeras have remained. After the Franco-German War the Republic, which had just been proclaimed, being threatened by a reactionary parliament, the people of Paris rose up in support of it (March 18, 1871). Republic! This sonorous term at the time meant to the ignorant and battered crowd the realization of its dreams, the end of its sufferings. The establishing of a harmonious and just city. And yet it knew that that Republic was armed with laws, was authoritarian and militarist, but it saw in it "good" authority, its laws would be "good" laws, its army a "people's" army. We smile today at such puerilities. We smile, and people attribute the same virtues to another chimera: the Revolution. Yes, its apostles say, the Revolution must be authoritarian, militarist, armed with laws, but the Committee of Public Safety will govern for the good of all, its edicts will be inspired by the great principles of humanitarian morality, and its army will be a workers' army. In the Year of Our Lord 1911 the grand-children of the executed of Satory, Père Lachaise, and the Lobau barracks are the dupes of the illusions for which their grandparents fell. All that's happened is that one word has replaced another, a word as hollow, as misleading, as dangerous as the old one. The Communards were massacred en masse for an ideal republic. What hecatombs will take place in the name of a miraculous revolution?

In a few words, let's sum up the horrific experience of the Commune. Having taken up arms on March 18, the *fédérés* began by naming an insurrectionary government, which was seated at the Hotel de Ville. The first concern of the rebels was thus to give itself leaders and to charge a dozen phrasemongers, a few of whom were even sincere, to keep an eye on everything. This was logical, these republicans' convictions consisting of nothing but grandiloquent phrases.

Naturally the new government could only reflect the general mentality. Issued from a crowd incapable of leading itself without chiefs, not knowing which way to go, lacking in energy, the government was its quintessence. And so there's nothing surprising in the fact that it revealed itself to be as incapable as every other parliament.

The Commune, artificially established, hastened to organize militia and to endow it with a maximum of uniforms. A major concern if ever there was one! Then it decreed the tearing down of the Vendome Column. It posted guards at the Bank of France. There were stormy sittings with a parliamentary appearance, parties formed competing for a shred of power. And during this time poor devils were being killed on the ramparts; provisions were lacking; disaster approached.

Paris needed money; money could perhaps have saved it. These revolutionaries, like their successors in our time, were honest. Until the final moment they mounted guard over the treasure in the Bank of France without daring to touch it. Paris needed examples of generous and brave energy: instead, its chiefs gossiped, accusing each other of treason. The starving and demoralized city defended itself courageously, but what could it hope for at that moment? What could it hope for from an unconscious and unintelligent population, seized with enthusiasm for an imprecise dream? That it be slaughtered and nothing more. This had to be the inevitable epilogue to this very "revolutionary" adventure. And so it was. After two months of resistance the Commune was crushed. The so-called Versaillaise army—republican as well!—entered Paris and the butchery began, the veritable massacre of an infuriated but powerless crowd. Order, "Moral Order" as its defenders cynically called it, was admirably reestablished. During the last week of May nearly thirty thousand Communards perished under the balls of the patriotic military.

The Commune had been a great movement of revolt, "unthinking" like all crowd movements. Thanks to propitious circumstances all individual sufferings had coalesced, aspiring to a vast dream of calm. The "federation of suffering" was born. The race after mirages too often becomes the race to death. The firing squads dissipated the misleading fog of the dream. Too late, as always: thirty thousand lives were idiotically sacrificed for an illusion, for words, for petty interests and ambitions.

And to obtain what? We can answer this question with a brutal word, with one word alone: nothing! The Communards had only wanted and realized deplorably superficial modifications. Their defeat wiped them out. Their victory would have wiped them out as well, since they'd preserved the essence of the system of social oppression through private property and the law. Some say that even defeated insurrections have worldwide repercussions, and this is no doubt true. But does the propaganda for the spirit of revolt they spread compensate for the effects of firing squads and deportations? Do the "worldwide repercussions" and the addition of great dates to the book of history compensate a population for the loss of all its best energies? And finally, the dead and the sacrifices should also count. What compensation is there for those who lost their lives?

An explosion of rage provoked by the accumulation of rancor, sufferings, and dreams; of blood, of desperate bravery; and then disaster, death. The result: zero! Maybe worse. This is how we can sum up the history of the Paris Commune, the history of that of Cartagena, the history of the insurrections of Moscow and Barcelona. Are there any reasons to think this will change?

The clearest result of these movements is that of authorizing commemorations. The blood of the *fédérés* has allowed for the building of many parliamentary fortunes, as well as others. How many solemn speeches at cemeteries, at public meetings, or in the exuberance of banquets for the benefit of these cult-like comedies that have raised intriguers to popularity! How many crooked affairs and how many dupes!

And that costly experiment will probably begin again. There are a number of naïfs and double-dealers who hope for it, await it, propose it . . .

To be sure, acts of revolt, great movements of revolt are necessary. But in order to be fruitful they must above all be driven by clear, reflective minds. Explosions of indignation, of anger and enthusiasm resemble burning straws, as prompt to be extinguished as they flamed up. And so we are deeply skeptical concerning crowd movements, insurrections, general strikes or more peaceful demonstrations. In their ordinary state crowds of whatever kind, without labels or labeled socialist, syndicalist, or who knows what, are retrograde. It is part of their psychology to never clearly know what they want and to fear change. Crowds are fickle, puerile, credulous. They love the prestige of tinsel and the gift of gab. They are enflamed by the sight of flags and the sound of bugles. They are capable of heroism, but they can also commit monstrosities. And in all cases they need masters. We are thus justified in saying that their psychology renders them incapable of establishing a libertarian environment. And so, for us, changing an oppressive regime is a pure waste of time.

War is possible; some even say it's probable and that it will lead to insurrection. We should remember the experiences of the past. Nothing either new or better will come from the anger of suffering crowds.

People will then ask us, what should we count on?

On the sole force capable of usefully acting, on the sole revolts inspired by consciousness and knowledge, by will and not by sentiment. Reasonably, we can only count on individual force and revolts.

Acts of revolt are needed, for the individual cannot live otherwise. Passive, he doesn't count; he only exists through rebellion. It is in this way that individualities desirous of living are led to salutary revolt. Because the social environment can only be transformed through individual effort: education and action. Education, that is, revolt in ideas; action, that is, revolt in life.

And so we won't accept to go to the imminent slaughters at the borders. The anarchists will answer with individual revolt: intelligent, persevering, skillful. This one will obtain results; instead of wasting lives it will save them; it will lead the crowd to think, it will frighten the masters.

War or a hypocritical and no less deadly peace, our path is laid out. Let the revolutionaries dream, and let them march dreaming of future disasters. Our role is to provoke useful revolts. Let our ever-intensified propaganda create men capable of refusing butchery, capable of resisting, of destroying and building. Men who, counting only on themselves, will no longer be victims of chimeras: individualists.

(*l'anarchie*, March 30, 1911)

Impressions of the Holidays

FOR FOUR FULL NIGHTS MY NEIGHBORHOOD, ALAS, WAS AFFLICTED WITH POP-
ular festivals.

For the custom is, on fixed and traditional dates, to organize public
rejoicing. A custom that all parties, without distinction as to class or
aspiration, respectfully accept, so true is it that human cretinism is
located beyond any quarrels among churches. Through solemn drinking bouts, every year believers commemorate the birth, crucifixion,
resurrection and ascension to heaven of the Galilean rebel who their
predecessors murdered. Through fabulous feats of imbibing and the
countless exploits of the procreating beast, the atheist believers in the
idol of the Fatherland commemorate the capture of a Bastille that has
since been more solidly reconstructed. And the proletarians who are
the future of the world—you certainly don't doubt this, do you?—also
wanted their holiday. At the beginning of each spring they get drunk
and knock each other out in chorus in celebration of the dreadful labor
that has turned them into animals.

As if that's not enough, all these charming people choose other, sup-
plementary dates in order to enjoy as a group rutting, stuffing themselves, and drinking themselves into a stupor. The day on which they
must be gay is specified well in advance. On that morning the usually sad cretins wake up happy as larks, ready for bawdy remarks and
overflowing with sociability. Posters have announced the program of
the celebrations. There'll be half a dozen horrible concerts where fat
ladies and clerks dressed in their Sunday best will crush themselves
together. In the evening the horrible concerts will be followed by dances,
a precious occasion for the merchants of love to exploit their seductive
curves. They'll sing until far into the night on the dark streets, and the
hotels preferred for one-night stands will be the theater of much filthi-
ness. Ladies of the streets, ladies of the high class houses popular with

princes, will do excellent business. And the goddess of modern love—syphilis—will be paid a substantial tribute.

To rejoice on a fixed date! It's difficult for me to express something more deliciously idiotic. To be gay because it was decided that everyone would be so from such and such an hour until such and such an hour seems to me to be beyond imbecility. And yet it's logical. Man, being the most perfect of domesticated animals, wants to see his least acts cataloged in advance. Envying each other, men and women only agree to grant each other the supreme delights after having duly notified their friends and acquaintances. Accomplished without the obscene ceremony of marriage, copulation is impure and its fruit cursed. And so on and so forth. Amorous, laborious, somnolent at certain hours that others designate, man wants to be happy under similar conditions. He asks his masters to order him: "You will rejoice on July 14th and 15th. The 16th you will again become the dreary slave you were the 13th." Conscientious, the honest man succeeds in doing this.

I understand that he demands joy. His life is so dull, so pathetic that from time to time he has to find a way to forget himself for a moment and finally know pleasure. And so the need for festivities, so often manifested by the people, proves the ugliness of their existence. And the habit of celebrating in common shows the inability of the individuals who make up the crowd to find joy by themselves and within themselves. Unfortunately, the effort made to artificially create the joy that their gloomy lives lack arrives at poor results. Joy on command is unhealthy, grotesque, and stupid, like those who savor it. We see them happy to become drunk and licentious beasts for a few hours; happy to display bestialities in broad daylight and to make faces that try to look happy, but are only all the more pitiful.

I saw them, these good people, rejoicing four straight days and I'll long maintain an insurmountable feeling of disgust from it. A noisy crowd hurtled down the streets stinking of bad breath and wine. Raspy voices could be heard from among them, singing "exciting" or patriotic refrains (for the vicinity of brothels and barracks perpetuates itself in people's mentalities). Thanks to the crush of people the men's rut was partially satisfied: touching, gestures, words spoke of overexcited and sick sexualities. Every street festival, every festival in a house is in these times of neurotic and insane life a rush of perverted sexes toward pleasures filthy with hypocrisy. And in addition, every festival is an exaltation of conventional falsehoods. Drunks, as well as clerks and students proud to pass for being so though they hadn't drunk a thing, loudly proclaimed their love of the native soil and their respect for established institutions. Here and there people brawled, for far from making morals gentler, the imbecilic gaiety of the celebrating people increases its brutality. But in general it as a time for embraces, effusions, lying protestations of sympathy, for shows of friendship and the filthy faking of love. All of this amid the filth of a sweaty crowd within the unattractive frame of boulevards and streets on which the only ornamentation was cafes overflowing with people. The masses of the twentieth century rejoice in being set loose for a night: their mugs exult, erections spread far and wide, the universal deceit takes on incredible proportions and the merchants of alcoholic and libidinal felicity make a fortune . . .

This week the hospitals will turn people away. And so many hands will reach out for the ideal.

Truly, this people in a state of ignoble jubilation is right to hate and despise us. We dream of other joys; we want other festivals that are hardly compatible with theirs.

Instead of this noisy meanness we would like for the life of every man to be a bold and valiant joy; we would like to work freely, cleanly, joyfully, and outside of pestilential cities. All of my desires are aimed at this dream. But we don't think it necessary to await its realization. Without any further wait, and whatever it might cost, we need the beautiful festivals of life!

(*l'anarchie*, June 29, 1911)

The Mona Lisa Was Stolen

THE PORTRAIT OF MONA LISA WAS STOLEN, THE LADY WITH A PEERLESS SMILE. A crook, perhaps one of those crooks with whom revolutionaries are embarrassed to be confused, dared to put a profaning hand on da Vinci's painting. In the same way someone would take money from a cash register or take shoes from a cobbler, a thief took the Gioconda and fled for an unknown destination. Unanimous and international desolation.

I'm not terribly sorry about this, though I'm not insensitive to the charm of a work of art. But I'm one of those who didn't have the time to go see it very often, and I have more compassion for the living Mona Lisas, whose smiles are withered every day by honest, legal, and honorable thieves who no one is searching for in order to punish.

It's said that it was a great crime to steal this portrait of an enigmatic and beautiful woman. Do people invoke the superior interests of art, of thought, and aesthetic humanity? Well, these are good reasons. But there are better ones that apply to a similar and much more urgent case.

In vast Paris there are many multiform prostitutions; there are so many young, beautiful, enigmatic women—since you love the perfidious enigma of the smile—that have this over Mona Lisa, that they are living, beautiful, and healthy flesh. Why don't the aesthetes dedicate a bit of the ardor they put to pampering the Gioconda to saving from the ineluctable gangrenes those that are alive and want to live?

The beautiful girls of the *faubourgs*, who resignedly follow the road to the red-lit houses, to the hospitals, prisons, and workshops that destroy them, to the boulevards where the rotten brutes wait for them: who cares about them? The cowardly and puerile aesthetes prefer enchanting fiction.

They indolently send living beauty to decay. They buy it, sell it, sully it. They want whores, perverse models, creatures of morbid pleasure.

And then, satisfied, they prostrate themselves before statues and portraits of women, dream of ideal purity, sing of ideal innocence . . .

Listen to them moan. A portrait was stolen from them, a portrait! Let them try to count all the men and women whose happiness and beauty were killed by their cretinism.

They would never think of this. It requires true valor and not hope for vain reward to occupy oneself with life. But they take refuge in dreams, precisely because they need the sweetness of factitious lights and not the living light of the sun; because they are too phlegmatic to taste the delights of the real.

What's more, it is well-bred—elegant—to admire beauty that is painted or carved in marble. In fact, it's a way of admiring oneself, to feel the flattering approval of the humdrum crowd. The vagabond—that brute—stops before a landscape and knows how to admire the beauty of a farm girl; the velvet-jacketed aesthetes, the aesthetes of the academies, the salons, and the brasseries can't share the instinctive admiration of the vagabond. They are too simple and healthy. Give them icons, poisons that make them dream and spiced up pleasures appropriate to their neuroses . . .

The whole silly world remained stupid before the thief's act, which was so simple, so fatal.

But today isn't everything, absolutely everything, merchandise? Dreams are distributed in pill form by discreet pharmacists and in little glasses pretty much everywhere. Realities—tainted, it's true—are offered to possible purchasers before they've even thought to ask for them. What is ordinarily hypocritically stolen from your neighbor while being careful to save appearances, it is only natural that bold men try to steal without putting on airs.

Honest men, you trafficked in love. Despite your money, expect to be frustrated. You have turned art into commerce. Expect men to "sneak off with" your masterpieces.

You will only ever reap what you sow.

What is disconcerting in this adventure is the deflagration of imbecility it has provoked.

As could be expected, no one took the trouble to seek out the original reason for the theft, for all thefts. No one was struck by this flagrant contrast: on one hand the contempt for, the frittering away of, the wasting of life; and on the other the adoration of dead, artificial, and factitious beauty. The journalists who provide the crowd with the bread of the spirit have their minds on other things.

Some have accused Germany of having stolen the Gioconda from us; after the machine gun, what insolence!

Some have cursed the millionaires across the ocean, for whom the theft was most likely carried out.

Others—and they aren't among the most stupid—have accused the Jews of being the cause of it all. The Jews, the Republic, and particularly Dreyfus are the ones solely responsible for all calamities.

Every paper has found a guilty German, American, or Jew in accordance with his taste. And there are people more stupid still than the scribblers of these papers, the good people who were upset about a painting they don't even know.

The portrait of Mona Lisa was stolen, the lady with the peerless smile. In truth these hydrocephalics don't deserve to have it!

(*l'anarchie*, August 31, 1911)

Against Hunger

WHILE WE WAIT FOR WAR, HUNGER HAS ARRIVED.
Hunger comes, insidiously, in no great hurry, settling in among the people like an old friend. It seems impossible that in our time it is able to extend its ravages over the entire population. We were used to seeing it kill a few hundred ragged indigents every winter. This winter hunger, ever bolder, will attack workers and farmers as much as wandering beggars. The price of food continues to rise, to such a point that people are angry.

Hundreds of exasperated women can be found in the markets standing in front of merchants strong in their right to steal, since they pay for a license from the state. Anger blinds the slaves driven to desperation, an anger born in women who are usually opposed to any agitation. And we've seen them press on, protesting, employing force to impose reductions in prices on merchants and, if need be, preventing markets from operating. There were violent brawls. Policemen, gendarmes, soldiers, three varieties of murder tools, were there to defend the order of theft.

The traditional response: "You demand bread? To serve you all we have is the steel of bayonets and lead."

A peremptory response that doesn't suffice. It is sometimes possible to stem subversive propaganda with arrests and saber and rifle blows; it is always impossible to tame hunger.

And so the protest movement against the rise in the cost of food will grow. We will see more bloody demonstrations. Finally, we will see the furious revolt of the poor inevitably smash up against the might of the masters. But what will come out of this? And, in these days of struggle, what will the men who are not the dupes of the revolutionary illusion do, men who know what the insurrection of angered plebes is worth and yet want to conquer a bit more well-being every day: what will the anarchists do?

Yet again, the anarchists will not march with the herd.

For yet again, the working mass demonstrates to us its inability to revolt usefully.

Because the continuous rise in the price of food places them in an untenable situation the poor are rising up. But they haven't thought through their acts, they haven't taken the trouble to study the question even in a summary fashion. They haven't thought anything through. Let's go! Against the high cost of living! Against those who starve us! Kill the grocer!

This protest movement is instinctive and sentimental. Too painfully insulted, the people rise up ready to strike, not quite sure against whom, without foreseeing the consequences of what they'll do.

And so guilty are they of this that they unfailingly commit the same error: they attack the effects and neglect to investigate the causes. The housewives haven't sought to learn why the cost of food rose: that would have been an effort of the intelligence, an act of reason. Instead, they seized the seller. As if by beating up a butcher, by hanging a baker from a lamppost (which, I hasten to recognize, could be agreeable) it would be possible to shorten an economic crisis. Proceedings as absurd as those of judges who, to suppress crime, condemn poor devils.

Too bad, for this light-mindedness will be paid for. Good people will get months of prison time; after they'll have put up a fight for a long time the price of food will decrease slightly. Politicians will proclaim victory and the naïve will be joyful. But six months later they'll have to start all over again.

Apart from seeking the causes of evil, everything is childishness.

To the rare curious individuals who ask the reason for the economic crisis journalists skillfully answer: the rise in the cost of food is caused by the drought.

Yes, my friends, the sun killed fruits and vegetables, roasted harvests. This is good enough reason to sell dearly what's left, n'est-ce pas? But allow us to ask: and the enormous provisions in the department stores? The reserve of cereals and staple goods accumulated in the depots for the needs of commerce? What has become of them? No one answers, since they are intact. There are enough foodstuffs in the hands of the kings and princes of the shops that this winter everyone could eat his fill, despite the summer's drought.

Other scholarly economists—an economist is always a scholar— declare with sorrow that the cause of all evil is that "the land doesn't produce enough to feed people."

They lie. The proof is in the wealth that is accumulated in the hands of a few privileged individuals. The proof is in the daily increasing productiveness of the land. What? Our natural resources are so precarious that we are at the mercy of a drought? And yet we know that every year large-scale merchants toss their overstock into the ocean which, if it were put up for sale, would cause its price to drop. In Brazil last year tons of coffee were wasted in this way. In France it is common usage among fishermen to throw overabundant catches into the sea. And we have heard stories as well of stocks of fabric burned while the poor have nothing to wear.

The truth is that a rational organization of production and consumption would easily ensure the well-being of all. With the present resources we could want for nothing. But this is the dream of a problematic future. And it should be noted that at present everything is a cause for poverty. Did it rain? The rain destroyed the crop. It didn't rain? The sun is guilty. Or else it's unemployment or overproduction. O irony! When the workers have produced too much hunger lies in wait for them because there is no work for them until the existing supply is exhausted.

Now we can answer the "why," certain we are not in error.

Overproduction starves the workers because they don't produce for the profit of all or for their own profit but rather for a small number who own capital and the instruments of production.

Drought is murderous because this small number is only concerned with its own interests. Big and small merchants have an obvious interest in selling dear, and so they grasp at the least pretext to raise prices.

And it is the control of the mines, factories, workshops and construction sites—of everything man needs to live on his labor—that allows this small minority to organize at will famines, crises, and conflicts.

Let us name in passing a few of the procedures financiers usually use: the creation of trusts, vast unions of capitalists monopolizing the production of a country or an industry in order to be its absolute master (for example, the American steel and gas trusts); what is called in stock exchange slang the cornering of a market: the purchase of the totality of a harvest or production, having as a goal the abrupt rise in prices and sometimes an actual artificial famine. And finally, crooked manipulations of the market . . .

Naturally, the men of prey and money apply these proceedings on a more or less large scale everywhere. We frequently even see the thirst for gain of small-scale producers and merchants become a new factor of economic troubles. Witness the cultivators of Amiens whose land, crisscrossed with canals, had not in the least suffered from the drought and who, from simple greed, raised their prices.

Like war, like prostitution, like the horrors of colonization, economic crises—famines—are inevitable because of the monstrous defects of the social organization. They are nothing but evils derived from the primordial evils: the institutions of capital and authority. We have often demonstrated this and we've never been refuted. This is the enemy.

But these institutions destructive of life were created by men and are defended and supported by men who venerate them, respect them, think them useful, or submit to them with indifference. If we want to combat and destroy them, we who see their harmfulness, we know what to attack: we won't waste our time breaking our lances against the institutions themselves; instead we will attack the mindset that finds them necessary. Our action will kill the respect, confidence, and belief in the usefulness of evil idols.

Examined from this point of view, how superficial and sterile the protest agitation of socialists and syndicalists appear.

What do they want to modify? It's true that they promise to totally transform social life later—infinitely later. But what do they do in the meanwhile? Do they attack the mentality of those who organize the crises, those who suffer from them, and those who through cowardly indolence become accomplices? Of course not!

Socialists and syndicalists demand reforms, legal measures against fraud, the abrogation of certain custom duties. And finally the boldest of them, the hotheads of syndicalism, brag of imposing a lowering of prices.

Appealing to the law and modifying regulations is foolish, the law in itself being the cause of suffering and the surest of ramparts behind which the rich take shelter.

To speak of reforms means limiting oneself to wanting to improve the conditions of famine. "When a building is unhealthy, uncomfortable, falling apart you don't repair it, you destroy it." What is absurd in this case remains so in the social realm, and reforms can be accurately compared to small repairs whose goal is to allow a worm-eaten miasma-filled hut to remain standing.

Combating institutions by the brute force of workers' revolts, without as a precondition having carried out the work of education which makes for deliberate, clear-eyed, intelligent rebels, means heading straight to certain defeat.

And yet, socialists and syndicalists do nothing but this, when they don't do even less.

How many times have they idiotically subordinated the interests of man to who-knows-what abstract interests: class, corporation, the workers' cause. Not only is their reformist or violent action always superficial, it is sometimes horribly petty. An example: those who poison the consumers are without a doubt as dangerous as those who starve them, right? And as such, revolutionaries should track them down with equal vigor, right? Well, listen . . .

A little more than a year ago the union of grocers' agents mounted an energetic campaign against the bosses. Suddenly, in the middle of the fight, the unionized citizens remembered that they served poisoners and rascals and they put up posters denouncing a few falsifications and common thefts. They received satisfaction, claimed victory as usual, and considered that they could, after all, poison and mislead the public without any inconvenience for the corporation. I am forced to admit this because once their campaign was over they ceased their denunciations and in this way continued to be the accomplices of crooked merchants.

An action so incoherent, so poorly thought through, and—to use the *mot juste*—so unintelligent, can only arrive at ephemeral and superficial results. Its value for social transformation is more or less nil.

In the face of the coming hunger the anarchists think that there are better things to do. What might that be? Undermine the evil at its foundation: reform man.

This is a profoundly revolutionary work of criticism and education. Of criticism: take advantage of the propitious circumstances to criticize everything, to lay bare the wounds, denounce all the defects. Destroy in people's minds religious and moral faith, obedience, honesty, passivity in the face of misfortune. Of education: make the defeated feel the need to know, to understand and to will. As soon as the slaves have the real desire to be men and no longer believe that slavery is necessary for the good of all they will know how to liberate themselves. This day is too far off for us to count on it. But from this day on, so that the resistance against oppression become every day stronger, so that it be easier for us to live every day, we hope to see the number of men who have left slavery behind increase. Make free men: there is no other way of transforming the social environment.

But this is not all. We must react now against a regime whose consequences we don't want to suffer from. They want to impose hunger on us. Let honest people suffer it if it pleases them. We will know how to respond as anarchists to the attempts to enslave us through hunger. We think that individual revolt is an excellent remedy for the oppressive force of social institutions. They want to sell us at a high price the things we need? In order to have us live like dogs they want to force us to accept the leash of the wage earner? They won't always succeed: we will *take* what we need.

Indeed! In trying to bend men animated by the firm will to be free they will only succeed in creating more ferocious rebels.

Justification of theft and violence, people will say? Perhaps. All of modern life justifies them. Through trade, through commerce, through wage labor, through taxes, it teaches spoliation and theft. Through the example of judges, executioners, and soldiers it teaches us to kill. In order to defend ourselves the least we can do is put to use these teachings.

Individual re-appropriation—theft—is the logical opposite of the monopolizing of wealth, just as individual revolt is naturally opposed to the arbitrariness of the law and its servants.

To famine, as to all the crises engendered by our immense social waste, the anarchists see two remedies: education and individual revolt.

(*l'anarchie*, September 21, 1911)

Demagogy and Anarchist Action

PEOPLE HAD SPOKEN OF AN ACTION GROUP.

Since that evening it was supposed to lay out its principles and through the authorized voices of its six orators say what its action would consist of, we went to see them.

Action is so rare!

We listened to the orators of the Anarchist Communist Club with the greatest attention. They had previously vituperated against the democratic lie and made short work of "pseudo-educational" and "pseudo-psychological" discussions. Having thus destroyed with a flick and a pejorative what we think is one of the most interesting forms of anarchist activity—education in camaraderie—what were they going to construct?

They spoke for almost three hours and said two varieties of things: criticisms of an acerbic irony but of little difficulty addressed at us, and inevitable repetitions of the theories of traditional *ouvrieriste* anarchism. However, in order not to violate a longstanding rule, they spoke of how distressing the decadence of the individualists was, who occupy themselves with the question of hygiene in their lives before the social problem is solved.

They then laid out what they, the founding members of the Anarchist Communist Club, wanted to do: no hygiene for them, and no neo-Malthusianism, one of them specified. But anarchism being forced to rely on the mechanisms of revolt of the working masses, they will work among these masses in the unions and alongside them, following the path traced in the past by the libertarian and federalist socialists of the Jurassienne Federation. They declared themselves in favor of a freely consented-to discipline, and the example was cited of the Italian revolutionaries who executed comrades who'd disobeyed. We were astonished.

It's really worth the trouble to war against socialists in organizations that castrate energy in order to then talk about discipline among anarchists! And to not want collectivist authority and then promise the arbitrariness of vague committees! And to label yourselves anarchist when you adopt the key points of socialism! And it was really worth it to have once condemned those who called for unity for their resorting to slander in order to yourself make use of malevolence against those who don't want to follow you!

Along with the socialists—both the followers of Guesde and the admirers of Hervé[1]—these comrades admit the primacy of the economic over the psychical, considering that the proletariat has a historic mission to fulfill, and they're concerned with society, the class, and humanity along with other foolishness before ever thinking of the individual.

And aren't things sufficiently clear? They accept the disarming of hatred toward the Socialist Party; among them there is only one hatred that is not disarmed: the hatred of the man alone, of the individualist outside of all parties.

There was no mention of any future action by the group. And then again, there was: future meetings were promised. That is, words, avalanches of words . . .

In truth, there is nothing in common between this socialist demagogy—which differs from official socialism only in its negation of parliamentarism—and our ideas, a concept of individual life that we strive to live and spread.

We don't see the use in finding support for this in the working-class movement. Anarchism doesn't only pose the social question and answer it: anarchism embraces all human questions.

They would like to restrict it to communism, a dream of the future whose realization would put an end to social suffering. This is perhaps good, but it's not all. Anarchism frees minds today, and these free minds conceive immediate revolts, thorough and profound, called on to transform men by having them taste a new life, a life of strictly individual thought and action. And yet a revolutionary life, and so much more so than the pitiful action of clubs like the one under discussion. Revolutionary, because all men profit from the act of revolt of one;

---

1   Jules Guesde (1845–1922), socialist leader; Gustave Hervé (1871–1944), left-socialist antimilitarist writer.

for in rising up for my own benefit I contribute to improving the current situation of those around me and I clear the road for those who'll come after me. Revolutionary through the critical and educational propaganda that produces unbelievers and rebels, through the camaraderie that demonstrates mutual assistance better than the most skillful theoreticians, and through the individual violence that must respond to the insolence of the authorities.

These are the characteristics of anarchist action placed in parallel to those of demagogy.

(*l'anarchie*, November 16, 1911)

Revolutionaries? Yes, but in What Way?

DISCUSSION IS DIFFICULT, DEMANDING KNOWLEDGE AND FORCING YOU INTO argumentation. This is why our usual enemies prefer slandering, mocking, and declaiming to refuting our theses. One of the epithets they like to apply to us without discussion is that of nonrevolutionary, if not antirevolutionary.

To hear them speak, we individualists profess a profound aversion for everything revolutionary. Some so well feign belief in this that, in contrast to us, they have baptized themselves revolutionary anarchists.

Well then, let's talk about this one more time. Do we not have to ceaselessly reexamine these questions so that they are finally clear to a few people of good faith?

Every anarchist is, by definition, revolutionary.

In the realm of philosophy we say we are for free investigation. In these times of faith and dogmatism, is this not already something bold and daring?

In the realm of ethics we have developed a new morality based on life itself as it presents itself to each individual. In these times of convention and legalism, is this not true recklessness?

In the social realm we demand the freedom to work, to tackle issues, to join together with each other or not; we demand individual independence. In these times of enslavement, how can this boldness be described?

But this is not yet the essential thing. If we were to content ourselves with making these demands in speech or writing we wouldn't be overly dangerous. Luckily, no ambiguity is possible. On several occasions we have affirmed our contempt for vain theory. We consider anarchism to be, above all, a way of life.

And so all of our ideas are subversive and irreconcilable with the established order. However strong our desire might be to avoid clashes— and there is none among us who doesn't want to avoid them—sooner or later a moment arrives when we are forced to choose between abdication and the act of revolt.

And the choice is made in advance.

We are revolutionaries because of our ultimate goal.

But one can be so in two ways.

By admitting the hypothesis of a revolution.

By not admitting it.

For one can be in permanent rebellion against the authoritarian environment without believing that a day will inevitably come when, the revolt having become generalized, it carries off a definitive victory.

Or one can revolt for oneself and one's own people—anarchist for the anarchists—without bothering oneself with the sufferings of lords and serfs.

In both cases the anarchist individualist revolutionizes the environment, carries out a labor of social transformation, "creates new values."

And it is precisely here that the confusion is often created, many people having an interest in creating it: the individualists are revolutionaries but don't believe in the revolution.

Not believing it doesn't mean denying it's possible. That would be absurd. We deny that it is *probable* for a long time to come, and we add that if a revolutionary movement was produced at present, even a victorious one, its reforming value would be miniscule.

And we have no difficulty in proving this.

In writing his beautiful book on "Evolution, Revolution, and the Anarchist Ideal," Élisée Reclus so magisterially proves this that years later we have nothing to add to or subtract from it.

Read this book or pamphlet. From the first pages you'll be struck by the definition Reclus gives the words "evolution" and "revolution."

"It can be said," he writes, "that evolution and revolution are two successive acts of the same phenomenon, evolution preceding revolution and the latter preceding a new evolution. Is it possible for a change to occur without bringing with it sudden displacements in life's equilibrium? Mustn't revolution necessarily succeed evolution in the same way that the act succeeds the will to act? They differ from each other only in the time of their appearance."

Starting from these premises, Reclus develops his ideas: "Before the revolution takes to the streets it must first be made in people's minds" We have never said anything different.

Some have contradicted Reclus, have laughed at him while invoking him, have accommodated his well-defined notions and ideas to who knows what demagogy. It wasn't the individualists who did this, but the leaders of the CGT, "official" revolutionaries, and well-known insurrectionists.

When you've read Reclus's work, open Pataud and Pouget's novel *How We'll Make the Revolution*. Skim Malato's pamphlet on social classes. Be brave and heroically read Victor Méric's pamphlet *How They'll Make . . . etc.*

He speaks there of riots, of shooting, of wireless telegraphy, of dictatorship, of catastrophes. He speaks there of the evolution that is a necessary precondition of every revolution. Au contraire! He has things backward: it's no longer a matter, as the scientists understood it, of a violent social transformation made inevitable by the progress of intelligence; it's actually a matter of a revolution that must first be made so that minds can evolve *afterward*!

It is interesting to place these two concepts alongside each other; all the more interesting in that the demagogues of revolution proclaim themselves to be anarchists.

The scientist demonstrates that revolutions produce themselves. They, for their part, say that they will make the revolution.

The scientist wants to prepare it through intellectual evolution (educational work). For their part, they intend to prepare it buy organizing the masses under the rule of an adventurous minority.

I could continue, but what would be the use?

The revolutionism that we combat is not that of the scientist, it's not that of Reclus. We believe it is true, and it is surely so every time it is supported by history. It is probably so when, informed by the past, it tries to predict the future. We note that the evolution of intelligence that is the precursor of great social upheavals has barely begun. We deduce from this that the revolution is still far off and, thinking that the joys of life are in the present we think it unreasonable to dedicate our efforts to this future.

And moreover, can we do anything better for the future than to fight in the present? Not for an insurrection doomed to failure, but to be anarchists?

(*l'anarchie*, December 14, 1911)

The Bandits

(Editor's note: On December 21, 1911, there was a holdup on the Rue Ordener in Paris, the thieves shooting the messenger carrying the receipts of the Société Générale as well as his bodyguard. They fled in a car, the first time an auto was used in a robbery. It was also the first crime of the anarchists of the Bonnot Gang.)

M. ERNEST LA JEUNESSE, A JOURNALIST WHOSE USUAL SPECIALTY IS THE PRAIS-ing and interring of Academicians, has become alarmed at what he calls his red Christmas presents. In truth, we've had a not very happy end of year for the potbellied gentlemen who have money in their pockets and the bank. Barely had the deplorable story of the stolen postal trunk fallen into discreet oblivion than the same day some wretches, some evil wretches, opened the tomb of Mlle. Lantelme, while other wretches attacked a messenger boy carrying funds on the Rue Ordener.

M. La Jeunesse is not completely wrong in being upset. These things have a meaning. That men should tip carrion into a burial ditch in order to rob it proves that there are living men who are determined to live. That in the middle of the day some men shot down a miserable bank boy proves that men have finally understood the virtues of daring. All of these are lessons that for men of M. La Jeunesse's class are not in the least pleasant.

Nothing is more wicked, it is said, than an enraged poltroon. And so it is that M. La Jeunesse, who under the circumstances does nothing but translate the mood of a social category, shows himself implac-able. In order to respond to bold crime, he says, rapid, inexorable, and decisive justice is necessary: in short, lynch law. As for the bandits: "Kill them anonymously like what they are: mad dogs."

Fortunately, this is soon sooner said than done.

And I hope that M. La Jeunesse experiences the sinister joke of meeting up somewhere with one of these famous bandits he makes so little case of.

Having no reason to fear for my safety, it will be understood that Monsieur's reasons do not touch me at all.

Along with honest M. Caby who, poor man, miserable wage earner, consented to transport fortunes; along with the miserable cowards who, not understanding either boldness or the will to live, vociferate against the outlaws; along with the police dogs, the journalist-squealers, the grocers sweating in fear, and the rich as ferocious in their hatred for the rebel as they would be cowardly in his presence, along with all these people M. La Jeunesse joins the mob respectful of the law.

But these laws they respect, I know they're aimed at garroting the weakest, at sanctioning their enslavement by brute force; I know the honesty they proclaim to be falsehood, hiding the worst turpitudes, permitting, even honoring, theft, fraud, and dupery when they are committed in the shade of the criminal code. I know this so called "respect for human life" they never fail to speak of apropos of every murder is ignobly hypocritical, since they kill in its name by hunger, work, subjection, and prison.

I am on the other side, and I'm not afraid to admit it. I'm with the bandits. I find their role to be noble; sometimes I see in them men. Elsewhere I see only fools and puppets.

The bandits demonstrate strength.

The bandits demonstrate daring.

The bandits demonstrate their firm determination to live.

At the same time "the others" submit to the landlord, the boss and the policeman; they vote, protest against iniquities, and die as they lived: miserably.

Whatever he might be, I prefer a man who fights. Perhaps he'll die younger; he'll know pursuit and the penal colony. Perhaps he'll end his days under the abominable kiss of the "widow."[1] It could be. I love the man who accepts the risks of the great struggle: he is virile.

And anyway, victor or vanquished, is his lot not preferable to the dismal vegetation and infinitely slow agony of the proletarian, who will die stupefied and retired, without having profited from existence?

------

1   Familiar name for the guillotine.

As for the bandit, he gambles. And so he has a chance of winning. And that suffices.

The bandit is virile.

Haven't we seen workers whose demonstrations are broken up by the kicks of policemen? And workers who are kept in place by the boss's shouts? And young men lacking in valor that aren't revolted by the insults of non-coms? And idiotic tramps who, finding full purses, bring them to the mocking policeman? And we've also seen the bourgeois of M. La Jeunesse and Co. trembling on the evenings of strikes or on May Day; we've seen them assemble hundreds of cops to solemnly slaughter Liabeuf.

We have seen displayed the imbecility, the cowardice, the ferocity of these masses and slaves so many times that they have ended up by inspiring in us an insurmountable disgust.

But there are the bandits! A few, standing out from of the crowd, firmly determined to not waste the precious hours of their lives in servitude, have decided to fight. And without ambiguity, they set out in conquest of the money that confers might. They dare. They attack. They often pay. In any event, they live.

They kill.

Without a doubt. Is it their fault? Did they desire the fate that is handed them? Many did no wrong other than that of wanting to be men and not citizens, wage earners or soldiers. Some dreamed of working freely in a world without masters. But the choice they were given was between servitude and crime.

Vigorous and valiant, they chose battle: crime.

No, they won't be pallid hooligans, vague pimps, shady and sneaky rebels: they will be bandits whose fearlessness will disconcert you. They will be the anarchists whose ceaseless activity won't allow you to sleep in peace. They will respect neither the putrefied corpses of high whores nor the imbecilic devotion to his master's money of the wage earner. They will respect nothing!

And it will be in vain that the severest measures will be passed against them, the cruelest penalties. As long as the problem is posed as it is posed, as long as men can only choose between theft and submission, there will be enough brave men who will prefer all of rebellions' risks to passivity.

The bandits won't disarm, for it is impossible that they disarm. Their acts constitute the effects of causes situated beyond their personalities.

These causes will only disappear if the social order is transformed. Until then the rebels—anarchists and bandits—will remain, whatever might be done, the champions of the human will to live.

So let them try to apply lynch law to them, as the excellent M. La Jeunesse recommends. We'll see if it's a solution. We'll see this soon, for the cruel violence of the dominators has only ever succeeded in infuriating the rebels.

(*l'anarchie*, January 4, 1912)

Expedients

A COLLABORATOR OF THE *DÉPÊCHE DE TOULOUSE*, M. EUGÈNE FOURNIÈRE, recently commented on the prose of M. Ernest La Jeunesse and the article in response to it that appeared here. M. Eugene Fournière, analyzing my defense of the "bandits" writes that "the murder of a messenger carrying receipts or the violation of a grave" will not "put a stop to the culpable regime." He adds that if, like me, his sympathies are with "those who fight," he distinguishes between those who fight to satisfy their hunger, like a wolf, and "capital's oppressed and exploited, who are uniting and learning in order to attain to collective leadership."

This is more or less how they answer us every time we legitimize the rebellion of the criminal, that economic rebel.

And M. Eugene Fournière exclaims in conclusion: "And I'm too afraid that the wolves will have babies . . . and that they will devour each other. I prefer to reread the admirable 'Mutual Aid' of the anarcho-socialist Kropotkin."

I understand all this. I too would have preferred, instead of writing in praise of the implacable rebels, instead of justifying antisocial crime against a society based on crime, instead of calling for violent, often cruel, and always painful rebellion, to lay out all the good things I think about "Mutual Aid." But no; I don't have the time to talk about it, for there is a fight going on all around me. I am with the wolves—the wolves they are hunting, that are being starved and tracked, and which bite.

And I am with the outsiders and the bandits precisely because I love mutual aid. These wolves live on the edges of society, precisely because, loving mutual aid, the free life, the free collaboration of generous forces, they detest the production line, the factory, wage labor. M. Eugène Fournière must nevertheless know this: what makes us anarchists rebels is not our laziness, our cruel instincts or our antisocial dreams. Society furnishes the lazy, the cruel and the brutal the means to use their strange aptitudes in the colonies—or in the metropolis—in various uniforms. What makes us rebels is our firm determination to be neither masters nor slaves; it's our aspiration for free labor that leads us to refuse the infamous salaried task; it's our desire for true fraternity that leads us to detest hypocritical and misleading social conventions. But above all, we are wolves because, thinking perhaps in the same way as M. Eugène Fournière, who for his part is an honest man, we want to live in accordance with our ideas.

We have no illusions about the social impact of our revolts; it's simply that we remain logical. For every obstacle met there must correspond an appropriate method of struggle. In order to transform the social environment we have confidence only in an education that reforms minds.

We know that force alone is useful in forcing us to respect arrogant masters. In order to conquer our place among the living, in order not to vegetate until the end alongside the sorrowful enslaved, we know that sometimes force is still necessary.

Our objective is twofold. We have often repeated that waiting for the future wastes the present. Well then, without waiting any longer, we intend to profit from the passing moment. Only then will we worry about transforming the social environment.

Living in the present: what is that? For the anarchist it is, M. Eugène Fournière, working freely, loving freely, every day being able to come to know the beauties of life; to be a man—to be healthy, strong, good; to work, think, be artistic. As you see, we demand everything of life. And do you know what is offered us?

Eleven, twelve, thirteen hours of labor a day so as to obtain the daily pittance. And what labor for such a pittance! Robotic labor under authoritarian direction in humiliating and filthy conditions, through which life is permitted us in the gloom of poor housing tracts.

And so, M. Eugène Fournière, we have to choose: will we be slaves or rebels? Or wolves, as you call it.

Allow me to be indiscreet and ask you what you'd choose?

In principle, we always choose revolt. And yet, in accordance with our possibilities we are wage earners or bandits. We can't do much about this. We find the two things equally unpleasant, equally disagreeable. We don't want to be wolves, as I told you, but men. Alas.

Obviously, if we are workers or thieves, we will not, by this fact, transform the social environment. We know that if leagued together

VICTOR SERGE

in a union we were to seek to improve the conditions of our subjection, or that if through our daring we were to wrest a few advantages, the social effect of our gestures would be minimal. Nevertheless, individually we would have profited, which is enough.

In order to transform society—if this is possible—we know that something else is needed besides reformist collective movements or acts of banditry. But in order to do these other things one must live; and in order to live one must be a wage earner or a bandit.

Individual education, the popularization of scientific knowledge, the diffusion of the critical spirit and the spirit of revolt, these, in our opinion, are the surest methods of seeing individuals evolve and, through this, to transform society. We have never failed to say this. Wage labor and banditry are for us nothing but deplorable expedients we are forced to resort to in order to survive and fulfill our task in an abominable world.

(*l'anarchie*, January 18, 1912)

The Real Criminals

THIS WEEK A MOB LYNCHED TWO CRIMINALS WHO, WHILE FLEEING, HAD FIRED on it.[1] I imagine that after hiding under their counters at the sight of the brandished revolvers the shop owners must have felt a heroic pleasure in lynching the disarmed man. They're brave men who are only brave when the enemy is lying on the ground. Little medals of gold, silver and vermeil were their reward.

This is perfectly normal. But allow me to regret that the criminals were such bad shots. They should teach the courageous citizens how to really earn their amusement.

They are enthusiastic in the hunt for rebels while in the face of the other bandits, the real ones, the perfidious and invincible ones, they are oh so servile. O! You thieves, you who have begun the game, when you lose see to it that they pay for their cowardice!

For there are workers in the mob that ferociously lynches rebels, the kind of workers who protest against the rising cost of living; there are rapacious merchants who can't curse loudly enough the financiers whose speculation ruins them; there are functionaries enslaved by the state; prostitutes of all kinds, the defeated, the crushed . . .

When they pounce on the ashen thief they forget those who starve them, those who shoot them down, those who domesticate them. And yet, aren't these the true and the worst criminals?

Men of the pen—and many others—have shed tears over the messenger who is currently dying in the hospital. This poor wretch through his submissive weakness and his stupid honesty, was the accomplice of criminals of a far higher caliber than the ones they are hunting down. He was the lackey of financiers, businessmen who today replace the brigand barons of the past.

---

1   The first robbery by the Bonnot Gang on December 21, 1911.

The money Caby transported, where did it come from?[2] How many dead men were needed to place in the hands of a few cosseted bourgeois those 300,000 francs? How many?

Remember the wages that the workers of the textile mills and the Jewish hatmakers and certain glaziers live on, or rather, die on. Remember that the number of tuberculars reaches the level of 65 percent in certain industries. Do an accounting of the cost in ruined lives, in lives eliminated, for every thousand-franc note deducted from the thankless labor of these dying men!

The Boneff brothers have written a beautiful book on "The Tragic Life of Workers." Dryly, without any emphasis, they have described how entire populations labor, fight in vain, and inevitably die of alcoholism, overwork, poverty, tuberculosis, of a thousand and one gangrenes. And it is precisely from those who suffer most that capital draws it greatest profits. Naturally.

The money of the Société Générale comes from this. It is, if we must speak in terms that are cruel but precise, the profits derived from the systematic murder of the plebes.

It must be admitted that they don't all come from there. The Rothschilds, like Victor Hugo's sinister Thénardier, made their fortune on the mass graves of Waterloo. One fortune is as good as any other, and money has no smell. The Schneiders, etc. fructified their capital in Morocco, unless it was in Tonkin or Madagascar. It was for them that civilization's drunken soldiers massacred and pillaged to such a point that it disgusted Pierre Loti. Yesterday it was Casablanca, today it's Tripoli and the Congo. These names alone speak of the bloodied palm groves, the peaceful villages machine-gunned, oases overflowing with pestilential corpses. But money has no smell.

The criminals who hatch these profitable massacres last summer nearly provoked a Franco-German war. But it was only postponed, not cancelled. Until then they'll continue to enrich themselves with all they'll take from the proletarian mass.

And yet, in the eyes of all it seems impossible to call the rulers criminals, and it is only the rare dreamer who from time to time dreams of lynching them. The crowd they bully respects them, salutes them, votes for them, demonstrates for them, dedicates itself to them, brings them banknotes that they lose, by chance, on the street . . .

---

2   Ernest Caby was the messenger wounded in the robbery.

It's because the crowd is cowardly and they are strong. They kill sheltered behind the ramparts of the penal code; they execute for the fatherland; they own enormous and solid prisons.

But on the other hand, woe on the poor wretch who, tired of wasting his days at the factory, snatches the purse of a society woman so he can live on what she would use only for her amusement. Woe on the exasperated unemployed worker who takes his bread. Woe on the anarchist rebel who refuses slavery and acts like a rebel. The vanquished pay for the others.

"Catch the thief!" A human beast flees down the street, and from all around cops, workers, and shop owners converge on him. Just a moment ago they were all shaking, ready to faint under the threat of the armed rebel. But he dropped his weapon. Too bad for him, now. Eyes shine, fists are tightened, mouths laugh and shout. Ha! Now he's been knocked down. Ha! The savage dance of honest people trampling the defeated, a hundred against one. They'll be given medals, since medals were given to the soldiers in Morocco. They'll be given medals on the orders of the high bandits, the masters of money.

(*l'anarchie*, January 25, 1912)

Anarchists and Criminals

FOR THE HUNDRED THOUSANDTH TIME THE QUESTION HAS BEEN POSED TO us without any ambiguity by policemen in search of conspiracies, by journalists in need of copy, by judges, by passersby who set themselves up as executioners.

What should the attitude of anarchists be toward criminals? Reserved? Hostile? Sympathetic?

We will attempt to answer.

There are criminals and there are criminals.

There are those who live on the margins of society's laws because their nature is different from that of good citizens. And there are the others, those who didn't become—or who didn't remain—honest men, simply because they were weak or pursued by misfortune.

The former are those who don't fit in: rebels, anarchist temperaments.

The latter often end up going straight and later in life become squealers, pimps, barkeeps, shopkeepers.

The first among these, the thief, thanks to his underhanded tact, to his insinuating agility, to his flair for money, would have been a capable business agent, or an agent of the law quick to execute delicate missions. He would have hooked consciences with a dexterity similar to that he showed in picking locks.

The other one, the assassin, if he hadn't been turned from the straight and narrow path by a romantic adventure, would have been a perfect soldier, one of those select killers that dazzle colonizers. This pallid pimp, if it hadn't been for implacable bad luck, would doubtless be one of M. Guichard's best agents . . . and so on and so forth.

The criminal has a professional psychology whose foundations reside in certain instincts which society knows how to put to good use. The assassin's or the thief's defects, barely modified, become the qualities of a judge, a soldier, or a cop.

But in the midst of social waste all aptitudes aren't able to find the means of being employed. There is wastage. And the skillful find the means to get away with things without breaking with the Criminal Code. But some fail due to accidental circumstances.

Whatever the case, as outlaws they preserve the mentality of honest people. They are rebels against mutual aid, pursue their vulgar interests; they are prideful, lacking in daring, fearful. They are squealers who turn people over to the authorities; low crooks who mutually betray each other, lie, and sell each other out. It would perhaps be more precise to say that they wait for the occasion that will allow them to enter the social category they should never have left. They engage in fraud, but respect property. They go from correctional court to the assize, but think that magistrates are indispensable. They suffer in jails, but never think of the iniquity or the absurdity of jails.

But the others are their neighbors, carrying out the same struggle, enduring the same sufferings, but for other reasons. They are those whose indocile temperaments drove them from workshops, or whose ingeniousness, whose desire for a better life, whose lively intelligence led them to break with the law, or those whose adventurous character couldn't accommodate itself to the monotonous life of the wage earner.

They are outlaws through instinctual vigor, through dignity, through originality. They are outlaws because honesty is a framework too narrow for their lives, because their desire for happiness can't be satisfied while in a state of submission.

And as much as they might want, in their moments of weakness, to go straight, to take their place among the countless beneficiaries of cowardice, they won't succeed. They aren't made for commerce; they find work that can be monetized repugnant. Adventure still has an invincible attraction for them.

They can most often be distinguished from the others by their stature in battle and in misfortune. They are of an extreme, a disconcerting, a courageous daring.

They are bandits.

To be sure, they remain far from us, far from our dreams and wishes. But what difference does that make? The fact is that in the social rot they are a ferment of disaggregation; they aren't part of the herd, rather they're a few ardent individualities, and like us they alone proclaim their will to live at whatever cost!

Well, these criminals interest me, and I have as much sympathy for them as I have contempt for failed honest men—or those who have "arrived."

The anarchist, in any event, will often be their brother. The same risks being run in pursuit of the same goal frequently brings them together.

An intellectual and moral rebel, it is in fact only logical that the anarchist doesn't fear becoming, whenever the circumstances seem favorable, an economic rebel.

(*l'anarchie*, February 1, 1912)

Two Lectures

(Editor's note: These are the outlines of two lectures Serge delivered in the heat of the Bonnot affair, just days before his arrest. The first was given within the framework of the Popular University, the second at the Causeries Populaires founded by Albert Libertad.)

The Individual against Society

January 28, 1912

1) It's rather the contrary that should be said.

2) *Society is the enemy of any individuality*

An association is not a simple adding up of individuals; it has its own psychology and vitality. It thus wants to last, to live.

3) In order to live a society necessarily conforms to two laws

A—Law of social preservation; society preserves what created it

= traditional

= enemy of movement

B—Law of social conformism. It wants all individuals to act in consideration of this goal—be in conformity with a type—which it forges by force. Ex. The subject of monarchies, the citizen of democracies thus=enemy of originality

individual independence.

4) In order to be (originally free)

The individual must thus struggle against society.

A. Against imposed social obligations.

Ex: military service

Wage labor

Respect of laws

Morality and respect of conventions.

B. and what is most difficult:

against the deformations produced in him by the social environment

ex: hypocrisy
proprietary instinct (including sexual)
passivity
servility
authoritarianism, etc. . . .
imposed solidarity
(Le Dantec's book *L'Hypocrisie Indispensable*)
5) This was, this is. Will it always be?
Alas, yes.
The laws that preside over the lives of societies are natural laws.
Let us imagine a communist paradise:
– Where there will not be a state of society; the end of all industry, complete and perpetual war against individuals.
– Where there will be collective religiosity
* Morality
* economy
– Where in this the original will be at the very least frowned upon.
Moral constraint
6) Where then does social progress reside?
In a displacement of the field of struggle
We will perhaps no longer fight for bread
Constraint will no longer be physically violent
Even so!
7) But what is the utility of these conclusions?
A—We should have no illusions about the social future
B—We should be sociable without being the dupes of sociability; no spirit of the coterie.

Bandits
Current events offer us this subject
It's a fact; criminality is on the rise.
People kill, steal, engage in fraud
Let us profit from this occasion to say what we think of this.
2) What do we think of this?
We think this is logical
ineluctable
necessary
The social organization produces crime

Everything is sold, everything is stolen
See how institutions and crimes are coordinated
Property—theft
Authority—rebellion
Law—fraud
Poverty—banditry
Repression—reprisals
On one hand society, on the other a few individuals
3) Among the criminals we distinguish
the unlucky, bourgeois souls
the clumsy, unemployed
and the rebels
draft dodgers, deserters, thieves
because unadapted to slavery
Are distinguished by daring
Resoluteness
As much as I despise the former,
that's how much I love the latter.
4) Along with us, they are the only men who dare demand life.

The Communards

MARCH . . . AND NOW RETURNS THE ANNIVERSARY OF MAD HOPES, OF THE furious impulses and butcheries of the Commune, our last attempt at revolution. Forty-one years after the frightening experience the same illusions give rise in the same people to the same dangerous hopes. For if, as the proverb says, we live on hope, it also happens that we die of it; that for his dreams man gambles with his life—and loses.

One of the hopes most deeply rooted in the popular soil is that in the magic virtues of insurrection. This is only natural. It is derived from the feeling of confidence inspired by force. What is force not capable of? The people, who suffer its rigors, upon whom the privileged and adventuress minorities daily exercise their power, learn in this way the immeasurable value of the solid fist, the saber, and ruse. These are the means by which they are tamed and they count on these things alone to have its day and time. There's nothing surprising in the fact that such a faith should preserve its prestige despite the worst lessons. The belief in revolution is nothing but confidence in the power of brute force, a confidence vulgarized and depicted for the use of the crowd. A defeat presages nothing; it doesn't extinguish the hope for victory in the defeated. The Commune died in 1871 under Gallifet's boot? Well, Long Live the Insurrection!

It isn't the intelligence of the popular crowd that expresses itself in this way, but its instinct, and this is why reasoning has no more success with these believers than the costly experiences of yesterday and the day before.

Have there been more conclusive experiences? Revolutions have never achieved their goals. They have sometimes "succeeded," but in reality they have neither destroyed what they wanted to destroy nor constructed anything new or better. In fact, they've only succeeded when bourgeois liberals and intriguers have joined the insurgent people.

Without the assistance of these forces insurrections invariably fail. It was because at the last moment they were abandoned by the wealthy "moderates" that the rebels of Moscow in 1905 were cut to pieces despite their heroism; and it's because the republican petite bourgeoisie didn't agree to back it that the Barcelona uprising was put down in three days. The revolutionary minority, the working people and the masses, lack not only the organizational qualities and the knowledge necessary for the success of a political—and even more, a social—upheaval, but even more, they are lacking in the resources, men and money. There is no doubt that a revolution can triumph with the cooperation of shop owners, liberal and sympathetic philanthropists, lawyers, and a few per-spicacious bankers. But these messieurs will only intervene if they have good reason to do so; in general, they snatch the movement. And when friends are installed in city hall, the barracks, the town halls promis-ing decisive reforms as is right, the game has been won. But by whom?

Is this not the abridged history the recent Portuguese revolution? The proletarians of Lisbon and Porto, socialist and anarchist, who paid for the republic with their persons, only understood their role four months later when the soldiers of the new government—their sons—fired on them. Exactly like the old one. But why insist? Is this not the synthesis of the history of the most famous revolution, of the Great French Revolution, of which all that is left are some refrains: "Ah, ça ira, ça ira . . ." swiped by a brilliant bandit, by men who were soldiers by chance, and by speechmakers . . .

And yet the Commune was the "Great federation of pain," as Jules Vallès said. And if it didn't have a general staff specialized in organiza-tion and social war to guide it toward a propitious destiny, it had strat-egists, several of whom had gone to the excellent school of Blanqui—the true Imprisoned One—and it came at the right moment, rich in horrors, backed by the anger of a population desolated by war having a disorganized government to fight. It was heroic, stubborn, the feder-ation of pains, and heroically incompetent.

It was typical: humanitarian despite the war and as if war can be made by half; honest, as our revolutionaries brag of being, for whom there is no worse insult than being confused with "crooks"; honest and respectful of the money of others, a thousand times more than the others were of the lives of the Communards; futile, divided by the rivalries of impromptu generals and legislators; divided also by mistrust, though they hadn't yet invented the Revolutionary Security force; heroic, to be sure, and admirably so . . . But can the people do better? Lacking in education, not used to thinking, not knowing how to count on themselves, needing for the least effort to be in groups, led, federated—alas—could the workers and beggars of 1912 do better? They would still have the resource of bravely, unblinkingly having themselves killed for their beautiful dream. They'll have only that resource . . .

Because they aren't the strongest. Because their real enemies are within them; their inconsistency, their sentimentality, their ignorance places them at the mercy of avid soldiers, fierce politicians, and loudmouths. A society is a complex organism that takes centuries to form, to perfect itself and that only succeeds in doing so by absorbing countless energies, competencies, and talents. You would like to remake this work in a few days, you race of "serfs" and "villeins" in whom the religious and authoritarian past left a durable imprint? If you caress this dream other *fédérés* will pass before the wall!

And we will perhaps admire them, but we won't follow them. More than they, because we are more conscious, we have a profound love of life and the invincible desire to take our part of the feasts the sun. But in order to become stronger we have to become more circumspect, and we have placed our goals here and not in the beyond, in the reality of our individual lives and not in the fiction "humanity."

Man must live instead of giving himself, offering himself in a holocaust to the Dream! Let his courage allow finally to become a free man, ardent and noble, instead of succumbing as a vain hero to (perhaps) modify the name of a tyranny. And if he falls, it's better that he do so on his own account. And if he succeeds, his life as a rebel will contribute to the evolution of the social environment at least as much as the deaths of the others.

(*l'anarchie*, March 28, 1912)

Letter to Émile Armand
on the Bonnot Trial

WEDNESDAY, JANUARY 22, 1913

My Dear Armand:

I have before me your letter of . . . and the information I asked you for. I love the frankness with which you discuss our defense. I've never taken offense at any criticism that might be made of me concerning my words and acts as long as they're friendly and cordial, as is the case here.

But how difficult it is to avoid misunderstandings! And how wrong you and the comrades are concerning our sentiments. Of course we want to live again soon, have the passionate desire to see the end of this imbecilic and undeserved nightmare if ever there was one. But it seems to me that everything in our previous attitude must tell you that in order to reach a good end we will do nothing and will not allow anything to be done that is contrary to our sentiments. What do I have to say? I admit that I find all this infinitely disagreeable.

Already, in the previous detailed letters, I laid out our defense to you, for up until now I've been in perfect agreement with Rirette. On the whole it will not be modified. And if you didn't give me your opinion, Philippe, who read my manuscript, found nothing wrong with it. So I think that all your fears and the remarks they lead you to make grow out of misunderstandings about us that are created from without, but without our knowing about it.

Of course the courtroom will be neither the time nor the place to discuss illegalism. And I don't plan on doing that. No, *we* don't plan on doing that. But if the indictment tries to say that I am in solidarity with acts I find repugnant (and this is the *mot juste*) then I will have to explain myself. In that case you can rest assured that I will do it in terms clear enough that they won't be able to use my words against our fellow defendants. I wouldn't have taken the trouble of weighing every word during the investigation for fear of implicating some unfortunate comrade to then provide the attorney general with weapons against them. And if they were to want to make use of some possible slip, I would know how to rectify it. It's not concern for my interests that makes me refuse an imposed solidarity at whatever the cost. If it was only a matter of my interests the defense would be able to get around the difficulty. But no. It's that I am—we are—sickened, saddened to see that comrades, comrades for whom I've had affection since the time of their original and beautiful enthusiasm, were able to commit acts as shameful as the butchery of Thiais. I am saddened to see that the others, all the others, madly threw away and wasted their lives in a sad, dead-end fight that beneath an appearance of courage they are unable to defend with pride.

I will seek to avoid discussing or having discussed by M. Le Breton in the courtroom the question of illegalism, about which these sorrows seem to have given a too obvious conclusion. If I'm not able to I will not say this. I will limit myself to proving that I never advocated or was even a supporter of that theory. I will add that I nevertheless wanted to defend the rebels every time it had to be done.

If I am soon free it goes without saying that I will explain myself on this subject without beating around the bush. I believe it is necessary, after these experiences, to reach a conclusion. I regret not having done this in the past. Perhaps if I'd been firmer Valet would be alive and poor Soudy free. I simply lacked combativeness.

And yet, you write me:

"They can still object after your articles in *l'anarchie*, invoking certain details of your past that . . ."

No they couldn't. If I allowed myself before the jury to judge the acts of comrades who are no longer enemies in their ideas but "the crushed," to use Méric's term, they could certainly object to many things I say.

But if I say that I've never been the supporter of a disastrous method of action, if I say it later, as I count on doing, of if I'm forced to say it to the jury, there can be no objections to what I say because it's true. My articles in *l'anarchie*? Have I ever done anything but defend the illegalists or make use of circumstances to make known our way of reasoning and the legitimacy of all revolts (which doesn't mean I advocate all of them)? Didn't I write in the most combative of them ("The Bandits") that "the bandits are the effects of causes situated beyond them?"

At the Libre-Recherche, at the Causeries Populaires (rue de Clignancourt) in Romainville, in many talks I said how much I dreaded illegalism. I obviously couldn't insist, given that I would have had to back my arguments with documents that have no place in public meetings. I opposed Lorulot on this theme on an evening which the comrades must remember. (And that time I had three opponents, our excellent Fallières— five years, Valet—dead, Jacob—in custody in Mantes.) Don't you remember that at the time of your first visit to Romainville we spoke of illegalism and I told you I had many reasons to be against it? A bit before taking over the editorship of the paper the publication of an article by me on this subject that was very clear, too clear, was refused. And a few days before my arrest I explained to Liénard (of *La Vie Anarchiste*) why paper I didn't want to publish my feelings about illegalism in our paper. He even offered to have Butaud insert in his paper the copy I'd showed him.

You see that nothing either from my articles or my past can "be invoked," This in any case constitutes a chapter about which I will allow no discussion. Without being a supporter of wage labor I have been paid wages. Without being a supporter of theft I might have been forced to make use of it. This concerns only me. If people want to discuss my ideas, I desire it. If they want to discuss my acts, which concern only me, I will not allow it. In other words, I allow people to speak and to speak ill; I don't agree to discuss.

What I remind you of above is only to show you that you shouldn't see any "change in attitude" in our conduct, as you write.

And even if there was a change in attitude this would be understandable. The experiences that we have just been through are made to abolish illusions and to rectify theories. Alas! But in this case it is obvious that I wouldn't have the right to say I never advocated and even fought against such misguided ways and ideas among us. And I would be scrupulous enough toward myself to not allow myself to do so.

If I can eventually speak in this way it's because it is perfectly exact. A number of comrades know this and I think you are among them.

Do me the favor of making this letter known to the comrades with whom you discussed our defense.

As I was ending this I received a note from Rirette where she expresses precisely this opinion, that we should not enter into explanations of this nature unless we are forced to.

Attached are a few copies for *Les Réfractiares*. It does me good to use some of my notes (four short articles). If I'm not too preoccupied—impatience—I will talk to you about your newspaper. Continue sending it to M. Le Breton.

I'll send you a letter for publication after the trial in case I am acquitted: I give myself sixty chances out of a hundred. Not one more.

Yours,
Le R

P.S. Important. Attached are two questions (information) to which an answer is urgent.

Egoism

IT CONSTITUTES THE BASIS OF EVERY ANIMAL MENTALITY. BEING NECESSARY, it is legitimate. "Legitimate"—such picturesque language. In truth, our language is poorly adapted to reality. I mean to say that, primordial and indisputable, it is beyond our good and evil; it *is*. We glimpse it in various forms that can be reduced to two essential forms, and this has allowed us to imagine a conflict between altruism and egoism: egoism of the weak, altruism of the strong.

The weak man is greedy, self-interested, narrow minded. What is a weak man? A being poor in strength. Can the poor man give? Offer himself the luxury of being generous, spendthrift, and prodigal? No. He watches over his every penny, he watches out for every occasion to increase his tiny hoard. He is—and he is doubtless right, retreating constantly into himself and taking advantage of all he can in order to survive—at antipodes from altruism.

The altruist? It is he who gives of himself, exerts himself, is prodigal with himself, which demonstrates that he has the means of being so. Altruism is nothing but the logical form of the egoism of the strong. Goodness, generosity, devotion, abnegation are characteristics of strength and health. It's an egoism of superior joys, for not only do they augment the vitality of the person who feels them, but they also provoke an increase in vitality in others. The word "superior" here has no moral value: it is as superior in relation to life that we should understand this. Is there some merit in the strong being strong? We can only admit this when it's a matter of an individual who has strengthened himself by his own will, and even then the strict determinist can protest. Let us leave him there with his casuistry.

Like the will, it seems that egoism is modified by heredity, education, and specific maladies. We should keep them in mind in order to explain these monstrosities: the individual who is strong and vulgarly egoist, and the other whom we admire: the weak, strengthened by his conviction, becoming altruistic—heroically.

(*Les Réfractaires* 2–3, January 1913)

Letters to Émile Armand

PARIS, FEBRUARY 12, 1917

For insertion[1]

My dear Armand,

I have just left prison. I spent five years there. The comrades know why and under what circumstances. I had to answer for the triple crime of being a foreigner, an anarchist, and not wanting to become a fink. But that's all in the past now. I return to life with the same ideas that formerly guided me. I was harshly struck—unjustly, but does social prosecution ever do otherwise? I was tortured for years. Experience thus confirmed me in our criticisms and resolutions. And yet my concept of our fight has changed quite noticeably. I no longer believe that the anarchist formula can be contained in one formula alone; I grant much less importance to words than realities, to ideas than to aspirations, to formulas than to sentiments and acts. I am thus ready to collaborate with all those who will show a fraternal goodwill without attributing great importance to secondary divergences in ideas.

This is how I would have been happy to cooperate in your work, insofar as it was within my strength, even though I have many and serious criticisms of it. But a moral reason prevents me from doing so. I request that you seriously weigh it and make it known to our friends. Among you current collaborators there is a militant[2] whose strange attitude during the tragic affair of "illegalism" contributed in no small

---

1   Armand refused to publish this letter in *l'anarchie*.
2   André Lorulot.

measure to my being buried alive for years. And perhaps it did more harm to some others.

As soon as it will be possible for me to completely elucidate this affair I will do so. In the meanwhile I cannot agree to collaborate in any way with a man upon whom such serious suspicions weigh and who, in any case, was fickle in the saddest meaning of the term to my companion and me.

I don't name him. I don't want to open a polemic on this subject. Those who know of these affairs that are already ancient for so many will understand. As for the others, unless it's absolutely necessary I don't want to initiate them into these dismal stories. If you can offer me conditions for collaboration that are morally acceptable I would be only too happy to do so.

I take this occasion to thank you for the many services you have rendered me since the first hour of my incarceration. And I shake your hand in friendship.

V.S. Le Rétif

MARCH 19, 1917

My Dear Armand:

I ask that you publish these few lines, which are addressed both to you and the comrades who remembered me and assisted me in the present circumstances. I am infinitely touched by their gesture. I thank them.

You prefer not to publish the letter from Toulouse, where I explained the reasons that prevent me from collaborating in your work, though fully one of you. As you wish. In any case, I don't want to cause a polemic on this troublesome theme. I prefer to completely abstain. Before certain moral situations there is only one thing to do: leave. I'm leaving.

But I want to say to our comrades that it's not due to discouragement nor is it the result of a divergence in ideas. In this time of contrary winds that throw weathervanes into a panic, it's necessary to specify things in this way. I have lost the sectarian intransigence of the past. I now attribute less importance to words than to ideas, to ideas than sentiments, and much less importance to casuistry than to good will. I feel myself capable of working with all those who, animated by the same desire for a better life—one clearer and more intelligent—advance toward their future, even if their paths are different from mine, and even if they give different names I don't know to what in reality is our common goal.

And so I am still one of you, confirmed by harsh personal experi-ence, by my desire for combat and the opinion that our effort, however feeble it might be, is necessary. If I currently abstain from your work it's only for the reasons I already laid out and that I ask you to make known to the friends of *Par-delà la Mêlée*.

Yours,
V.S. Le Rétif

Individualism, a Factor of Progress

INDIVIDUALISM IS A FACTOR OF PROGRESS, AS LONG AS WE TAKE IT TO BE AN improvement for man to obtain new fields of activity that will allow him to identify and diversify his activity. Wherever individual autonomy has assumed its legitimate place there can no longer be stability in institutions: ancient theocracies' dream of social immobility soon loses all its prestige. If there was need of it, history could provide us with a multitude of examples that demonstrate this assertion. In the Egypt of the Pharaohs art reached its apex with the decline of the ancient empire, when tradition had not yet mummified it. And it was in pantheist Greece, broken up into a multitude of barely federated small cities, that the human spirit took wing. The century of Augustus in Rome, which would better be called that of Horace, Virgil, and Lucretius, was a century of dissolution and error, so much so that the wise Imperator had to appeal for the assistance of poets and legislators in order to attempt to give the people-king some of the virtues that had created its unity and political power.

Do I need to demonstrate that art is a realm exclusively the province of the individual, but which he can only fully enjoy when freed of routine? The work of art doesn't interest us as a copy of nature, but through the human interpretation of the universe it transmits to us. It is a form of language, a supremely nuanced and personal form of expression. It gives us the profound emotion of the artist, his effort to interpret his life in accordance with his personality. "Art," Zola somewhere said, "is nature viewed through a temperament." That the artist wants to take the easy way out by bending to sometimes arbitrary rules, that he must conform to the facts derived from knowledge, in no way diminishes the part of fantasy and individual sentiment in all artistic creation.

The artist uses knowledge, he isn't used by it, or if so, only incidentally. It assists him in expressing himself without ruling his talent. In the same way, he is the master of the rules he chooses to conform to, particularly because they are in harmony with his individual sensibility. Whenever this isn't the case the work, when it ceases to be strictly individual, loses its value. Sometimes the exaggerated respect for the rule reduces it to a conventional, hieratic signification; sometimes its impersonal exactitude turns it into a nearly scientific document condemned to leaving us indifferent.

But, taking into consideration the impersonal character of science, ("The principle of communicating vases is the same for a physicist at the Institut and for a candidate for the high school leaving exam. The most illustrious geometrician can't explain the equivalence of triangles any differently from a high school freshman" —P. Bourget), it would be wrong to fail to recognize the importance of intellectual speculation and imagination in scientific research. It is here that the role of the talent of the individual scientist begins, and often the results he obtains will depend on his boldness and the freedom of his mind. Most great scientific discoveries are born of the verification of hypotheses that are frequently erroneous, which is why for a long time man's science was more chimerical than positive. And in the elaboration of philosophical concepts, even if they are only the synthetic coordination of sciences, which diminishes them greatly, one must always leave room for metaphysical speculation, where the individual proceeds according to his particular character. From which flows the many differing points of view among thinkers operating with the same knowledge. We can't but consider this useful, since there is no better stimulant to the continuous pursuit of truth.

Finally, how do societies progress? Tradition strives to maintain its stability, ceaselessly troubled by the innovations of individuals who are emancipated from the prejudices of their era or are impelled by new motives. Precursors, inventors, free spirits who are sometimes chimerical, fight, fall, and get up again. Their example rallies around them a section of youth; collects and wins over self-interested support. Tomorrow that minority, apparently defeated, will have modified the attitudes—if not the existence—of its enemies and friends alike. It has introduced a new usage, popularized a discovery, wrested a new freedom. It crystallizes and becomes in its turn rite and tradition. And so on and so forth. There is no more consistent element of progress than individual initiative.

Man wanted to "master nature." Each step that brought this goal closer made him stronger, prouder, happier. But too often he forgot to master himself, or rather he naively thought he was his own master because he didn't see the hands that guided him. And we have seen him, armed with precious knowledge, abandon himself to the transgressions of his ancestors, accepting their errors, preserving their laws, piously maintaining out-of-date usages. He couldn't want, he can't want as long as he doesn't know. We can only understand the universe when we have seen clearly into ourselves. We can only dominate circumstances and things when we possess ourselves. A man who has no inner life is as insignificant as an apparition. What is needed is suggestive knowledge, the intimate knowledge of the human self. The role of the individualist is to remind us of this.

(*Par-delà la Mêlée* 16, 1917)

A Critical Essay on Nietzsche

1. A Philosopher of Violence and Authority

Dead are all the gods: now do we desire the Superman to live. The State is the death of people. Companions, the creator seeketh not corpses—and not herds or believers either. Humanity's goal can only be reached with the most elevated types. —*Thus Spoke Zarathustra*

It is through these words that this creator became dear to us. We singled him out from among the heroes of life, legend, and dreams, for in conceiving human existence as an endless ascent to a future of freedom and grandeur he showed us the way. Some chose him as teacher, saying that the poet who created Zarathustra could not have served any other ideal than anarchism. An oeuvre based on a love of life viewed as being beyond beliefs, and revealed through the thought of a bold free investigator in whom vibrates such free and liberating thoughts, could not serve another cause.

But is this so? Nietzsche often spoke differently than Zarathustra, in whom we thought we had found a guide. His oeuvre has many facets. Viewed as a whole, it is, because of one of its dominant ideas, essentially the antithesis of the anarchist ideal; it is also the only oeuvre that dared to rise up before us, strong and clear, constructing another ideal, another desire, and containing a subtle, strong, persuasive and at times brilliant argumentation.

Nietzsche was a philosopher of authority and violence who undertook to affirm them without any restraint, promising them an unlimited future.

In truth he was and, since his thought lives, *is* our sole and unique enemy. For our old world is used to opposing to us professors, judges, soldiers, or orators rather than men, ideas, or reasons.

Few oeuvres are as multifaceted as his. It is paradoxical, profound, as heavy as it is light, sprinkled with laughter, invocations, invectives, great shouts and confidential whisperings. It disconcerts us by its excess of life. It might thus seem reckless to want to show some of these essential traits. Is it not the product of an entire existence and a tireless intellectual labor?

Nevertheless, I will speak of it without timidity, following the example of this most energetic of free investigators. But I will resist facilities of language, for such shall be my truth, sought with the sole desire to understand and to ceaselessly progress toward greater clear-sightedness. If I don't know how to guide myself, who will guide me? I thus have the courage to criticize in keeping with my convictions and to propose my results to my fellow-travelers, without vain pride, simply with good will.

I certainly do not pretend to present in these notes a complete critical study of his philosophy. I will leave to the side several important points of the multifaceted ideology he left to us. I will limit myself to presenting the frequently forgotten apostle of an authoritarian and vigorous ideal of life, one not without a certain beauty, but profoundly barbarous and an enemy of the progress for which we are fighting.

Nietzsche's oeuvre has misled us because its dualism. Because of his temperament it contains two antagonistic yet complementary aspects. We usually only see one, the most obvious one, the only one that suits us in the absolute. Nietzsche is a demolisher and a builder. We love in him the destroyer, the man who denies moral dogmatism, the disbeliever, the disrespectful man, the great nihilist armed with a fervent word. We don't take account of the fact that he destroys in order to make room for an ideal probably quite distinct from ours. If he seeks to smash the tablets of current values, it's not in order to substitute for them a new order founded on the free development of every human personality, where the only law will be consciousness's inner law finally sublimated and made glorious by a free life but rather to rejuvenate the old order, which he believes in and wants to be eternal. For he adores the brute force that crushes the vanquished, the decisive gesture of the mighty, the harsh struggle of man against man, the result of which is the slavery of some, and what some dare call the culture of others.

His passion for authoritarian affirmation, for victory and conquest, is so strong that he even sees it as the distinctive mark of life at its highest. The rest is only decadence, twilight, descent into corruption, the penchant for death of the weak.

A philosophy is always founded on a powerful sentiment that inspires and dominates it: it can only be the summit of an ideological structure. In Nietzsche this dominant sentiment is an absolute love of life, perhaps to a certain extent in reaction to the pessimism of Schopenhauer and Hartman.

Let us attempt to broadly outline his ideas. Painful, fallacious, weaved of illusions and errors, life *is*. It is beauty, splendor, force, incessant creation, miracle, and pleasure, pleasure above all. And even in suffering, for every life seems to be eternally forced to scream, there is an element of inexpressible pleasure. There exists a way of suffering that is noble. When one has acquired consciousness of this fact, one fervently consents to every effort, even if it is a torture. It is necessary to love life in its endlessly increased and refined power and to expand it with every step, utilizing all our strength in service to it. Here we find ourselves before Nietzsche's dominant idea: "The greatest force must be placed at the service of the most intense life."

This is what is called his "philosophical reform." Until now, Jules de Gaultier writes, philosophy could be defined as the "indignation of the truth." Nietzsche no longer accepts it as it is. In what way is the truth important? Does the truth exist? "The falsity of an idea for us is not an objection to this idea. We seek to know in what way this idea accelerates and preserves life." The new philosopher is the fervent man who creates new values, who gives life meaning, an original meaning. He is the adventurer who know how to joyfully accept the heroic adventure that is life. This love of life imprinted a positive prejudice on those who were strong and lived abundantly. And Nietzsche admires them all in the same way. The Greeks, both athletes and artists; the Vikings; the humanists and condottieri of the Renaissance; the Huguenots of the sixteenth century: these are the ones he selects from the pages of history who marked life with their will. Above them all rises, situated outside his century like an outsized force, the gigantic statue of Napoleon, "the noble ideal par excellence . . . synthesis of the inhuman and the superhuman."

At this point it is difficult to distinguish between what brings us close to and what separates us from the great philosopher. If anarchism can be defined as "the combat for the most intense life" we are in agreement with him concerning the love of life, the source of all rebellions, the goal of all labors. And we, too, admire force, that is, creative, restorative, transformative, perpetually blooming energy. We have attempted to create new values: individual autonomy, originality, the absolute right of conscience, spontaneous solidarity, morality without dogmas or delusions. In a word, to replace the tyrannical abstractions the past imposes on us as so many obligations or social contracts with a new realty: human individuality simply asserted. And it is thus that, by being beyond the strength of the petty men of the base present, this ideal could also be called the superman, since man is too often an animal . . .

Except, I don't readily subscribe to his praise of Napoleon. Like all of us, I know the grandeur and value of strength. But Nietzsche doesn't seem to understand the evolution it has undergone. He often confused energy and violence, which is only its most savage manifestation. There exists another force aside from that of the conquerors of lands and wealth, another force than that of arms, other values than those of the victory of one man over his kind. Force has grown. In the past it manifested itself in the club and the axe; tomorrow it will be through thought and will. Its victory will dominate the old human beast, so often liberated by works of violence. This will be the victory of man over nature and his own nature. Our "noble ideal par excellence" is the humble and purified man who overcomes the ancestral instincts of the bestial struggle because he desires another struggle, one that demands no less courage or strength, but which is more worthy of him. One needs more courage to smash a sword than to use it; to be free and libertarian than to be an oppressor.

"I teach you the superman," he wrote, "because humanity can only pursue one goal; the creation of a superior man of superior culture." The means at our disposal to do this are struggle and effort. For the individual, this means being harsh with oneself and with others in order to surpass oneself. To be sure, whoever doesn't know how to be as harsh as needed will not know how to be good. For society, slavery is needed.

The superior man is born into a differentiation that benefits from the efforts of all, conducted for the profit of some. In order for one Pascal to think it is necessary that the majority of human creatures live the existence of beasts of burden, working the land, living without hope. This is the natural state of the mediocre, who are the most numerous. Let them serve! Their sufferings matter little, since thanks to their harsh labors virile and refined aristocracies are able to live, cultivating their lovely customs, the arts, the pleasures of war and intellectual research: "dominant races and inferior races."

Nietzsche attempts to demonstrate the positive and scientific aspect of this idea of progress based on the servitude of the mediocre masses.

In order to answer him we shall review the facts. Without any hesitation we can say that we find as much true mediocrity among the established aristocracies as we find potential among the masses. Progress gains nothing if it is necessary to sacrifice for the development of one superior man the existence of another or of others, who could also think and labor nobly. In summary, we maintain this: it is society that will bring together the best living conditions for all men, which will offer the superior man the best terrain for cultivation. The environment created by the antagonism between the aristocrats and the servile masses is unhealthy. The intellectual and moral deformation of the dominant is as profound as that of the dominated. The free man is the only true man, oh, philosopher! The superman, if he had to live attached to the chains of command, which are as heavy as those of obedience, would be truly "too human." And there would then begin anew the lusterless history of the Caesars, who count for so little compared to an Epictetus.

Why did the creator stop at this artistic conception of force? One asks this, one is saddened by this when, after having followed his victorious critique and admired the passionate drive of a powerful mind in quest of the impossible, he arrives at this repetition of man's most ancient errors, i.e., the cult of violence and authority, from which the new, superior men increasingly distance themselves with each passing day.

The latter are found outside social classes and despite them. They constitute, in fact, an aristocracy constituted of nobler minds and hearts. Some have raised themselves from the lower depths, and these are not the least great among them. But all are unanimous in recognizing no supremacy other than that which has as its sole source the intellectual and moral value of individuals.

2. The Two Moralities

Nietzsche attempted to demonstrate that in humanity ethics followed a dual evolution. Morality has two opposed origins and is born among the dominant and the slaves. There are two moralities, one noble and the other servile, for there are two human species, the one that rules and the other that obeys.

From a positive point of view, any appreciation of this genealogy of morals reveals that the dominant idea is justice. It is up to the investigator to determine which of today values, for the progress of the species, has the tendencies derived from the two original moralities, which have long been combined with the customs and opinions of our ancient civilization.

I wouldn't say that Nietzsche carried this investigation to its proper conclusion. Ultimately, his hot-headed temperament adopts a prejudice. He places his language on the scale, which weighs as heavily as a sword. Woe on the defeated! He sings the praise of the noble morality and at the same time curses the ancestral aspirations of the slaves who invented goodness, freedom, equality, piety, and peace. Feminization, weakness of souls, refuge of the weak. In truth, never has so profound a contempt—or so strong a diatribe—been thrown in the face of the "ideologues." Christianity, liberalism, socialism, anarchy, libertarian ideals, dreams of a humanity freed from the ugliness and suffering of oppression, petty ideas affirmed in the past by Jewish slaves and later by the uncouth Germans—the Reformation—later still by the French, rotted by Chrisman morality and sentimentality—the French Revolution— and today by the universal rule of the mediocre. These are the worst symptoms of decadence, the "twilight of man."

The new philosopher has only to associate himself with the men of decadence to accelerate his decomposition. The quicker this happens, morally and socially, the quicker life can be reconstructed on the rubble of the old world. If there is something that brings us close to Nietzsche it would be this point of view. Beyond the base "modern ideas" that must triumph, then immediately decompose, and finally cede their place to our eternal noble ideal, which will signal the resurrection of the vital forces of humanity, he nevertheless glimpses another ideal. Until today every elevation of the human type has been the work of an aristocratic society, and this will always be so: it is the labor of a society that has faith in long periods of time, in hierarchy, in the accentuation of differences between man and man and which needs slavery in one sense or another . . . The Gay Science.

It is not for me to refute the affirmations contained in this incantation. Nietzsche defends them with subtlety, stubbornly, resorting to a dialectic developed at the school of the German sophists, with all the fervor of passionate conviction. This is the way that he defends the authority bitterly fought against and dismembered by most thinkers. This problem of authority and freedom can be resolved by sociology. Élisée Reclus, Herbert Spencer, and Tylor, to name only the best of them, have concluded from the examination of the facts that the "human plant" can only grow in fresh air, under the sun. It will only possess all its potential beauty and produce its most beautiful fruits the day the shadows that imprison it dissipate.

The main error of this individualism of oppression is that it restores the ancient idea of freedom and great acts, which maintained that the exercise of authority increases the possibilities of pleasure and useful effort. This is only true in a restrictive sense, for the benefits that the dominant derive from the labor of slaves is certainly not worth the profound abdication of their best energies. The personality of the oppressor only asserts itself by deforming itself, and this professional deformation leads frequently to monstrous aberrations. Generally, the apparent victory in the realm of positive acts is hardly worth the inner defeat, the irreparable disaster into which the highest aspirations of the heart and mind fall. No man is as subject to slavery as he who owns slaves. He can neither flee nor free himself but rather must guard and defend his wealth, lose himself in servile labors. He can neither contemplate, nor love, nor dream, nor think, nor work freely. He is imprisoned by his interests. These necessities of daily combat, victorious or not, slowly but surely kill what is best in man.

And yet, "all light is within you." Doesn't Christ say that "having gained the world, he lost his soul"? I criticize the authoritarian individualism of Nietzsche for not having taken subjectivism into account. The individualist asserts himself through his own internal worth; through the domination of the self; through the cult of impartial reasoning; through generosity, disinterest, and the idealism that are the characteristics of higher egoism; and through the intense effort of fervent and judicious will, all of which is much closer to true nobility.

The ancient nobility, a result of victory, sometimes engendered beautiful types of humanity.

The French *seigneur* of the seventeenth century was so cultured, so courageous, so rich in honors, so full of abnegation for his king, so imbued with his superiority over the villein, that for him all human solidarity stopped at the borders of his caste. The *gentilhomme* was without any doubt the most civilized man the poor human species could produce at that moment of history. Later, the conditions for the realization of noble individuality completely changed. It would be mad to want to go back several centuries. The villeins, the *gentilshommes*, the nobles, these three estates have disappeared. The combats over money and for ideas as well as the works of the intelligence have created new conditions for existence. There are no more classes but rather distinctions. The supreme virtue is no longer authority but originality, independence, and the disdain of power.

The new nobilities, unlike the ancient ones, escape any stratification. They come from the immense anonymous mass and return there. For man there is no difference between servile races and proud races, such as we find among dogs between hunting races and guard races.

The noble man, the superior man of tomorrow will be a complete man: a clear intelligence, a heart capable of emotion, a virile energy. Neither toward himself nor toward others will he commit the crimes of obeying and commanding. He will be the guide, the example, the wise man, the hero, never the man with the whip. This new ideal is not only ours. The history of our civilization reveals the slow climb of the human herd toward the heights where this ideal will be born, subject to laws as certain and ineluctable as those that rule the fall of bodies. Our societies, despite the periods of regression to barbarism they pass through—such as our era—go from despotism to freedom, from the rule of the garrote and the sword to the rule of inner law, from the hierarchy of classes to individualism. Nothing can stop this evolution, which is connected to the same process as cosmic life. This, in any case, is what certain great minds concluded who Nietzsche detested.

Though we agree that Nietzsche's argument is strong and extremely seductive, in reality it rests on a prejudice. This intellectual had a brutal passion for active, exteriorized, and positive energies. We see in him the love of physical effort, of battle, as they were felt by our ancestors in the sixteenth century, for whom he demonstrates an unreserved admiration.

But from a philosophical point of view the passionate argument sins by excess, and even more when the attempt is made to give it a scientific appearance.

Nietzsche did not take into account that portion of the vitality and beauty of the revolutionary energies that have been active throughout the world since the beginning of last century. He acted as if the persecuted, the indomitable, the rebels, the idealists, and the desperate, in struggle against the old social order, hadn't testified to their existence among the lower classes, "the race of slaves," and as if they didn't have intellectual and moral resources as great as those of the more favored classes.

From the sole fact that it has given rise to revolts, to ideological ferment, to many attempts at realizing its goals, to socialism and anarchism, the revolutionary idea has asserted itself as a force for transformation that should not be deprecated. And Nietzsche, who admires all forms of force, didn't know how to do it justice. Nor did he know how to adapt his thought to the results of modern sociological investigations. He opposes simple assertions to the work of economists, psychologists, and sociologists, reconstituting step by step the stages of past progress in order to anticipate future progress. "The servitude of the greatest number is the condition for the progress of civilization": this is one of his preferred theses, one contradicted by scientific investigation. It is not because of servitude but despite it that man's forward march toward well-being has continued. One of the main factors of progress is precisely the ceaseless effort of the individual to free himself from what is imposed on him. We can even add that the very existence of injustice in society—which in itself already constitutes a disequilibrium—creates a danger for culture. A civilization that only belongs to some, whose best fruits only belong only to a minority, can be weakened or destroyed by the semibarbarian it has failed to value. The cities of antiquity decayed not only under the blows of the invader, but even more because of the indifference of the enslaved masses who didn't care to defend it. What did it matter to the million slaves of the seven hills that Alaric sacked the temples of marble, which had no value in their eyes?

Contrary to the Nietzschean postulate, the truth is that any elevation of the human type is the result of a liberation; that every culture is the fruit of many victorious activities against what is imposed on us, and that societies founded on violence and iniquity decay through violence and iniquity.

3. Nietzsche, Good German Imperialist

Current events cast a new light on the world of ideas. In this unhealthy glow we encounter appearances we didn't know of and which we didn't taken into account. And if stubborn wills, rights, and higher reasons don't weaken, illusions, on the contrary, vanish completely. We rule over the world from the valley. How many masks have fallen in the presence of those who know us; how many ideas denied, profaned, deformed, disguised without our having expected it, and how many faces veiled! And even the dead, whose labors seemed completed, are transformed. And after all this I catch a glimpse a new Nietzsche, the real one, the one who was a good German imperialist despite himself. "Since we see the black dawn break in the heavens of the mightiest" according to the beautiful verse of Victor Hugo; since the tables of the law upon which were inscribed the definitions of good and evil were smashed and only violence matters, the thinker who wrote *Dawn*, who wanted to situate the effort to live "beyond good and evil," the great amoralist appears to us to be a precursor. He preceded the existing imperialist Germany down the road that leads to the rubble of a civilization.

A contemporary German and a German imperialist: this is what Nietzsche appears to have been to his very marrow. From his Germanic and Protestant origins come his active temperament, his sense of realities, his passionate vigor so different from the insouciance of a French skeptic like Renan or Anatole France, or the reflexive Positivism of English free-thinkers, like Bain, Spencer, and Stuart Mill. Son of a Protestant pastor, he certainly owes to his profound Christian culture his ability to so pertinently understand the questions of morality and to free himself from accepted opinions. The author of *The Anti-Christ*, during the most tragic hours of his solitary existence, signed his letters "the Crucified" and gave one of his books a title whose cruel significance comes from an episode of evangelical history, *Ecce Homo*. From this we can judge to what extent his early Christian education contributed to forming his prodigious personality. I would like to point out that there does not exist today in any Latin country any religious group comparable in the seriousness of its faith, its customs, and its freedom of thought to German and English Protestantism.

At the very moment Nietzsche was writing, other thinkers in France and England pursued the same goal, inspired by the same scientific concept of the universe, applying, like him, the recent notions of determinism to the study of the most complex phenomena of human life. Spencer, who Nietzsche railed against in one of his most unjust pages, produced an enormous book on this matter. And to show the contrast between the temperament of the modern German imperialist and that of his rivals, we will cite Taine, who was also implacably logical, dedicating his entire life to the cult of thought, loving life with all his soul of a poet, and in life-loving Force; and Guyau who, studying ethics, founded anarchist morality in a definitive work, "Essay on a Morality without Obligation or Sanction"; and finally, Carlyle, "that semi-comic provocateur, that deceiver lacking in taste," according to Nietzsche, who, like him and a little before him, adored the creator of new values. Taine and Guyau, with their French method, their sovereign philosophical spirit, the harmony of their thought and language, formulated the same ideas but without violence, without impetuosity, and without the basis for life being modified in any way. It appears that Carlyle, animated by the flame of the descendants of the believers in inner light, also remained outside active life without realizing that every idea "is a force aiming to realize itself." Nietzsche's warrior temperament was necessary in order for determinism, atavism, and amoralism to succeed in being new reasons for action, new "reasons to live" in daily reality. In order to realize how different their characters were it is enough to open a book of Nietzsche's and compare one of his pages with one of Taine's. For example: "Write with blood and you will learn that the blood is spirit," said Zarathustra. His creator truly writes with his blood. He put his own life into this pulsating, swirling style, as feverish as it is intense, intoxicating, sprinkled with shouts and invective, filled with brilliant images, unique.

Let us point out here that this faculty of being impassioned by ideas, which is so rare among the humanists of today, coexists in Nietzsche with an extraordinary aptitude for abstract speculation. What is more, in our old Europe only the Germanic races seem to have inherited from the ancient Hindus the gift of metaphysical investigation. Only they have dared to dig down into the depths of the problems of Essence, of Primary Causes and Final Causes. From Leibniz to Nietzsche they have given the world several generations of philosophers and metaphysicians bold enough to attempt to understand the universe. France produced Auguste Comte, England Spencer, Germany Hegel, and today Haeckel, the most metaphysical of the scientifics. Nietzsche belongs to that great school as a disciple of Schopenhauer. Through this intellectual paternity he remains united to the prodigious Sophists, to the abstractors of quintessence, to the creators of cosmogonies that were Hegel, Fichte, Schelling, and Hartman. Only his fundamental prejudice is contrary to that of his old master. He wants not the extinction of the will to live through the renunciations of the sage but rather the exaltation of the will to power through the activity of the destroyer and the creator. He doesn't want to flee but rather to accept with joy the noble pain of living.

What characterizes the current German intellectual elite is a cult of intelligence and brute force, while for other peoples, especially among the Latins, culture is synonymous with refinement, the renunciation of violence, and the predominance of spiritual values. The contemporary

German imperialist is deeply in love with knowledge, is a poet and a speculative spirit, but places intelligence in the service of brute force. He seems to view victorious violence as the total realization of force. Perhaps we can define the most general law of his thought, that which provides all the others with their original structure, in this way: a cult of intelligence and a cult of force. From this flows imperialism, social organization, castes, honors, the aptitude for obeying and leading, the absence of moral scruples, the disdain for ideas, especially modern ideas, i.e., the Napoleonic contempt of ideologues. What remains of the concept of justice when the cannons boom?

If we were to judge the facts currently developing in a sequence in which no link has escaped our gaze, from the Bismarckian wars right up to the ongoing new destruction we would see that they are nothing but the translation of concepts that Nietzsche prophetically expressed when he wrote: "The hour returns, ever reborn, the hour in which the masses are disposed to sacrifice their lives, their fortune, their consciences, their virtue in order to procure that superior joy and to rule, a victorious and tyrannically arbitrary nation, over other nations. ("On Grand Politics," in *The Dawn*).

"We have entered the age of classical war, the scientific and at the same time popular war, of war made great through the methods, talents and discipline employed. All the coming centuries will look with envy and awe on this age of perfection."

"We stateless persons, 'good Europeans,' reflect on the need for a new order as well as a new slavery."

". . . because believe me, the secret to harvesting the most fertile of existences and the greatest joy is living dangerously. Be thieves and conquerors if you can't be dominators and possessors, you who seek knowledge" (*The Gay Science*).

Or when he exulted with the same fervor that must have guided the bad shepherds of the military nation: "You say that it is the good cause that sanctifies even war. I say to you, it is a good war that sanctifies every cause" (*Zarathustra*).

These aphorisms written twenty years ago take on a singular significance when we place them in parallel with the following ones:

The great sage Ostwald, who created energetics, wrote: "Germany wants to organize Europe . . . Here everything tends to draw a maximum of output from society . . . The stage of organization is a more elevated stage of civilization . . ." "Culture is a spiritual organization of the world" that doesn't exclude bloody savagery. "It is above morality, reason, society . . ." (Quotes taken from Romain Rolland in his book *Above the Fray*).

As we can already see, the spiritual son of Goethe, Hegel, Heine, and Schopenhauer, Nietzsche is manifestly of the race of Bismarck and Hindenburg, the race of predators.

Between his vision of the future and ours there is an abyss impossible to fill. Two ideals remain present in our poor destroyed humanity: imperialism and libertarianism. One asserts itself through fratricide, through victory by the knife and fire, oppression, the perpetual crucifixion of another species; the other points out a new path, the only one that can lead humanity toward a healthy perfection without bestiality; toward victories that aren't tarnished by descent into the dregs, blood, falsehood, mad hatred. and blindness.

These ideals support the struggle in all nations and, without any doubt, in all hearts. There is a libertarian Nietzsche, a libertarian Germany just as there is an imperialist England, France, and America. The two sensibilities, one inherited from an immemorial past of ancestral tortures and the other given rise to by the instinct for well-being, the lever for all progress, take turns predominating in any ethnic or national group. Contemporary Germany, in its most general tendencies and in Nietzsche's oeuvre, is the expression of conscious imperialism at its highest degree of development

We must remember the brilliant, rebellious idealism of the Germany of Schiller, of the admirable paganism of Goethe, of the invincible nihilist logic of Stirner, of the socialism of Lasalle and Marx, of Wagner's revolutionism; we must remember all this in order to know the *power of ideas*, we who have no other strength than that of the idea! The maleficent cult of violence has turned Germany into the horde we now see. Other ideas, other wills already active will regenerate it when it will finally understand that the liberation of the human animal, even though he is armed with science and logic, is not a means of access to the superhuman but rather a return to the prognathous anthropoid, the sub-man of the caves.

4. The Rebel: His Influence

I presented the imperialist Nietzsche who, through the realization of the superhuman, succeeds only in remaining "too human" and too actual in these troubled times. But every personality is multiple. It would be more correct to say that in each of us there are diverse potential or active personalities that successively dominate, making us adopt divergent or contradictory attitudes. It is thus that under the pressure of exceptional circumstances unexpected characteristics reveal themselves, incoherent and logical, paradoxical, and necessary.

All of Man is in every man, and the greater the vitality of an individual the more he must reconcile his inmost contradictions. The passionate authoritarian, feeling himself hemmed in on all sides, bothered by the thousand obstacles of society, which is made up of countless interests that are linked to each other and opposed to the development of predatory Man, suffering to see himself surrounded by mediocre creatures, by rotten institutions, by pettiness and misery, even this authoritarian rebels. This is the *impossibility to live* against which every man of thought and will, even if he is our enemy, must immediately raise his voice in protest. The entire difference between his act and ours resides in the awareness of motives and ends. He who wants to go freely toward the future with his brothers must rebel in the name of the shared suffering of which his is but an infinitesimal part. He who wants to be a Dominator and isn't able to become one must rebel against the obstacles that restrain his strength. Nietzsche was one of the latter, and magnificently so. A pamphleteer not simply of those who rise up against the tyrant of the moment, but of those who mark an entire society with the seal of their sarcastic contempt. He was satirical in the manner of Juvenal, of Aristophanes, or, closer to us, of Rivarol, who he appreciated; he was critical, and ironic, a sower of paradoxes and ideas that shook people out of their torpor. For rebellion opened the horizon for him, and it was this that in a strange way occasionally drew him closer to us! Contradictory and paroxystic, it is difficult when speaking of him not to imitate him, so disconcerting are the various aspects of his oeuvre. Is it true that it was the apostle of violence who, when writing of the way to reach true peace, said that a day will come when the most powerful people will willingly break its swords? "Sooner die than hate and fear, and sooner die twice than to allow oneself to be hated or feared. It is necessary that one day this exalted maxim become that of every established society" (*Dawn*).

Nietzsche glimpsed all the freedom, all the possibilities of life that were offered to the man of the future; to he who will come well after us, after the chains have fallen. At a moment of great serenity, when the imperious voices of primitive instincts became still within him, he understood which direction beauty leads us in order to pass through the darkness of today. And he asserted this in clear terms. I will quote but one of his most critical pages. Here is how he describes militarism.

> A drag upon culture.—When we are told that here men have no time for productive occupations, because military manoeuvres and processions take up their days, and the rest of the population must feed and clothe them, their dress, however, being striking, often gay and full of absurdities; that there only a few distinguished qualities are recognized, individuals resemble each other more than elsewhere, or at any rate are treated as equals, yet obedience is exacted and yielded without reasoning, for men command and make no attempt to convince; that here punishments are few, but these few cruel and likely to become the final and most terrible; that there treason ranks as the capital offence, and even the criticism of evils is only ventured on by the most audacious; that there, again, human life is cheap, and ambition often takes the form of setting life in danger—when we hear all this, we at once say, "This is a picture of a barbarous society that rests on a hazardous footing." One man perhaps will add, "It is a portrait of Sparta." But another will become meditative and declare that this is a description of our modern military system, as it exists in the midst of our altogether different culture and society, a living anachronism, the picture, as above said, of a community resting on a hazardous footing; a posthumous work of the past, which can only act as a drag upon the wheels of the present.—Yet at times even a drag upon culture is vitally necessary—that is to say, when culture is advancing too rapidly downhill or (as perhaps in this case) *uphill*. ("The Wanderer and His Shadow," in *Human, All Too Human*)

With glee he wrote: "We stateless individuals, good Europeans . . ." On the credit side of his grand concepts we must place that of the European, son not of a nation or a race, and even less of a society founded on egoism, the sum of petty aims—a state—but rather of all the races that have mixed together their customs, their blood, and their sap on the ancient land of Europe in order to produce the complex generations of today, heirs, in truth, of all human effort. And how indigent, according to this author, are all the petty ambitious fatherlands! We understand Zarathustra when he says: "What of fatherland! *Thither* striveth our helm where our *children's land* is!"

"Follow your path and let the peoples and nations follow the dark paths in which no hope shines."

He placed thrones in the mire and was horrified by both the public square and the politicians who are its buzzing flies. He ridiculed moralists, whose virtues resemble the poppy seeds that "procure a good night's sleep."

"I am Zarathustra the impious who says; who is more impious than I that I may enjoy his teachings?"

One shouldn't find it strange to see him express in this way ideas that usually appear to be contradictory. The origin of his errors—and I think that is the word that that must be used—can be found in the very origin of the power that made him a great poet, a pamphleteer, and a new philosopher: the extraordinary intensity of his cerebral life, which raised an instinctive hyperesthesic vitality to consciousness. Having attempted almost everything, he could also understand everything and explain almost everything. And being too self-willed, loving excessively the fact of feeling himself live intensely, he didn't consent to bow before the logical systematizations of thought that end by imprisoning us. It's better to appear inconsistent. The essential thing is not to impose, in addition to the current admiration of men, a new dogmatism but rather that we awaken them, since they are asleep in the bed of old beliefs. We must make them live and, above all, they should be made able to live intensely on their own, to contemplate, to understand, to create.

This, without a shadow of a doubt, was his idea as well as ours, and I believe that we should regret not that he was frequently paradoxical or inconsistent, but that he was only *apparently* so.

A higher logic guided him. In him the rebel and the bold investigator never ceased obeying the injunctions of the philosopher of authority and violence. States, fatherlands, armies, churches, the family, morality, modern ideas, decrepit authorities undermined by the decadents who want goodness, justice, equality, and peace because they cause degeneration: these people wear out the springs of great acts. They are diminished men, and since in this society humanism grows by making the healthy forms of impious and bellicose life retreat, it is necessary to speed up the collapse of this world in free fall.

"Man must be the best of predators."

"Smash, smash the good and the just."

We have already seen the weaknesses and errors at the heart of this thesis. He believed in it with all his soul and always explained and defended it as a passionate dialectician, and *this* was the reason for his revolts.

There is an interesting study to be done of the affinity of contraries and their psychological influences. People have not always been fair to Nietzsche. All things considered, he expressed himself quite clearly and brutally. One must truly work at it to see in him something other than a rebel and a critic. How then can one explain, other than by the affinity of contraries, his immense influence on groups with diametrically imposed mentalities? A good German imperialist, he found many disciples in France. An authoritarian aristocrat, he was so appreciated by the anarchists that it seems there are some who call themselves Nietzscheans.

I will hazard two explanations: I love his overflowing vitality, contagious to all who approach it: such is the prestige of his life. We are all tired of colorless philosophies, verbiage, worn out words, hypocritical expressions, teachings lacking in sincerity and passion. It all ends up lost obscurity. Oh the dull ideas that vegetate in this bloodless life, the official speeches, the poor little lies, the minuscule ideas of Lilliputians. One wants to cover one's ears and shout, "Enough!" Sleep is better than this decadence of the soul. Welcome, let him enter, the man—from wherever he might come—who loves and hates, whose sincere speech says to us: *"I desire! Make room or I'll clear the road despite you."*

This man, even though he is our enemy, sets an example and brings us something of great value: his truth, a precious truth.

The second explanation would be this: knowing our various insufficiencies we all aspire to perfect ourselves. And so we are attracted to precisely those who have qualities the opposite of our own. Being gentle, we love the violent; being rational, we deliberately seek the instinctive; sentimental, the rough please us. This is the call of forces other than those we hear within us, and we continually head toward unknown potentialities.

Let us return to the facts. Whatever the cause, Nietzsche's influence in the Latin world and in libertarian circles was great. Naturally, his teachings were deformed. It can be said of his disciples that they never understood him very well. "Every truthful word, if it is heard by too

many men, is transformed into a lie because of those who are superficial, the calculating, the charlatans," wrote another individualist, our
anarchist Han Ryner. Since there was nothing but truth in Nietzsche's
word, we note that it was misunderstood and systematically deformed
by some in order to render it anarchist, and by others to justify through
arguments extracted from his works, their bourgeois spirit, their ambition, and their vulgar egoism that he would have disdained as the most
grotesque of things too grotesquely human.

But this is the luck of all teachings. Petty things pass, but the oeuvre
remains. The seeds that Nietzsche spread also fell on better lands, where
they proliferated. They produced a vast intellectual movement. I won't
have the temerity to carry out a complete examination, but instead will
only mention certain names that testify to Nietzscheism's importance
in French culture. There is absolutely no question that his influence was
enormous, particularly during the contemporary era, and perhaps in
France more than elsewhere.

Henri Albert and Lichtenberger have with great care translated his
thought in order to make its most subtle nuances felt. Daniel Halévy
dedicated a biography to him that was as pious as it was complete. Jules
de Gaultier, one of the most original speculative minds of our time,
commented on him and explicated his thought in several valuable works.
Georges Palante, sociologist and critic, was largely inspired by his work,
along with Dr. Élie Faure in his studies of art, and Georges Sorel in his
works of sociology, among them *Reflections on Violence*.

In the anarchist world only the individualist tendency has felt this
influence, and this very profoundly. And yet my impression is that generally there was a misunderstanding due to the ignorance of the entirety
of Nietzsche's ideas. Certain Russian anarchists qualified themselves as
Nietzscheans. In the United States the newspaper *Nihil* represented this
tendency. To various degrees we find the same influence in the work of
Libero Tancredi in Italy, in the review *El Unico* published in Panama, in
l'anarchie" in Paris and in the French individualist organ *Par-delà la Mêlée*.

But is this influence a good one? I don't dare answer in the affirmative. The workers who form the majority of our groups generally don't
have sufficient education to confront the energetic seduction of the passionate imperialist with a critical spirit. It often occurs that they don't
understand him or that they follow him immediately, almost blindly.
And following him means abandoning us. It also happens, and this is
perhaps worse, that in wanting to follow his ideal of the superman,

so disproportionate in relation to the forces fighting against a terribly mediocre reality, a kind of childish pride seizes hold of our comrade and isolates him in a sterile and limited "cult of the self."

Despite these reservations, one can't help but see in him an initiator. He causes us to think and to live. And for those who, thanks to the development of their critical spirit, know how to remain faithful to themselves, there are so many fertile riches in his oeuvre.

Applied to social problems his philosophy all in all is not very original. It is nothing but Social Darwinism expressed with a singular quality of thought and style. And what was sometimes called by this name is nothing but a well-worn theory proper to the old society, in which man exploits his fellow man, a concept Darwin never formulated, quite the contrary.

"Man is wolf to man," Hobbes said in the seventeenth century. It has been repeated in our time by transposing to the social realm the principle of the struggle for life and natural selection—the survival of the fittest—and by the idea that the inequalities and miseries produced by the unavoidable and beneficent natural laws were the conditions for all forms of progress. Kropotkin wrote his decisive book *Mutual Aid: A Factor of Evolution* in order to contest this thesis, supported in England by Huxley. Here is his demonstration: It is not through internecine struggle that species progress, but through association in the struggle against nature. Darwin himself wrote: "There is no struggle between individuals of the same species, except in cases of penury or sexual competition." And even in the latter case the struggle often assumes aspects of emulation that exclude any recourse to violence, because it is useless and deceptive. Wolves, tigers, and sharks only devour each in cases where hunger has them in its grip, because if this were to happen they would disappear from the face of the earth to make room for other species more capable of fraternity and peace.

If man was able to leave his cave, where he would pass the night for fear of beasts, it is because men mutually daily assisted each other over the course of many centuries. It is for this same reason that civilization survived stupidly criminal wars and progress was able to resume. Fratricidal struggles periodically devastate humanity. Tomorrow the latter will come out of the current tragedy ill, impoverished, convalescent, and sluggish, but assembling the men who will take up life again;

take up the good and healthy struggle to make themselves better and happier. The immense crime that is currently being committed will not testify against the law of mutual aid, like madness against reason. Imperialism remains refuted by the facts, and this should not be forgotten, whatever the prestige in our eyes of the poet who defends it.

5. Dionysus—Conclusion

Men have always loved symbols. When they conceive the grandeur and the potential beauty of their lives they love to imagine perfect forms that are so alive that they immediately surpass mediocre reality. This ceaselessly renewed creation of their eternal divinities occurs in the most clear-sighted individuals. How can one not incarnate in dream images love, joy, hope, the victory of living, and life itself with its many sidereal, terrestrial, human riches? But the people who "abound in allegories," in the highest symbols, in poets erect immaculate and primitive statues that express man's ideal in a simple fashion. Nietzsche constructed his own, ancient but rejuvenated by the gift of his fervently modern spirit and called it, in Greek, Dionysus.

The greatest of all lovers of life had to choose among the ancient gods, who will never completely die, for below mystical lies and deformations they incarnate aspects of nature in human, though heroic, figures. We might say that he had to choose the one among them who was the personification of the healthy joy in existing. In opposition to the cults that disdained and condemned physical life, Dionysus exalted it without impoverishing it, with nobility and harmony. We can imagine him as a mocking athlete who, in one of those gardens where Epicurus invited his young friends, surrounded by naked young women, poets, and sages, raises a cup of tasty wine through a ray of sunlight. And this wine of Dionysus is the juice of all the fruits of the earth, the pleasure offered to all, which it is necessary to wholeheartedly accept. Dionysus taught the beauty of carnal love, of footraces and wrestling, of dancing and singing, of epic adventure and silent meditation. Be complete, live fully, don't be afraid to suffer in order to enjoy completely and you will be like Dionysus, the man-god who laughs and gives without measure, free under the liberated skies.

The beautiful, victorious human beast, intelligent, destined for the original springs of the harsh and tonic life nature grants the strong, this is what the superman will be. And after all, is it important that Nietzsche misunderstood some essential philosophical truths, that he sometimes erred concerning means and ends, that he was passionately unjust? Now that critics have distinguished between retrograde and true idealism in his oeuvre, we have no need fear being seduced by his errors. Let us stop before the statue of Dionysus and think about the teachings he left to us and which must remain . . .

Be free . . . "A free life remains open to great souls,"

Be willful . . . "O Will, thou change of every need MY needfulness! Spare me for one great victory!" Yea, something invulnerable, unburiable is with me, something that would rend rocks asunder; it is called MY WILL. Silently doth it proceed, and unchanged throughout the years."

Be generous! Be harsh toward yourselves in order to strengthen yourselves and to later give yourself without measure. "I believe you capable of all wickedness and for this I ask you to be good."

Enjoy life! With pride, with beauty. Love elevated life; savor it intensely. "Sensual pleasure is, for free hearts, something innocent, like the song of terrestrial joy; it's the overflowing recognition of the future by the present." "The desire for domination that rises in the pure and the solitary, attracting them to the heights of their own satisfaction, ardent like a love that will trace in the heavens seductive and dazzling joys." Oh, who will find the true name with which to baptize and honor such a desire? "A virtue that gives; it is thus that Zarathustra one day named this inexpressible abstraction."

Be egoists! Zarathustra "praised egoism, the good and healthy egoism born of a powerful soul, united with a svelte, beautiful, victorious and comforting body around which everything is a reflection. The agile body that persuades, the dancer whose symbol and expression is the souls happy with itself. The selfish pleasure of such bodies, of such souls, is called virtue.

"With what this egoist pleasure says of good and evil, it protects itself as if it surrounded itself with a sacred forest, with the words of its speech it repudiates far from him everything that has no value."

Certainly, such an egoism has nothing base about it and is so powerful and healthy that its fruits will necessarily be great goodness, the fraternal instinct, and profound love capable of sacrifice. Since it always seeks its own satisfaction, this is the very principle of the inevitable egoism that it is necessary to fully know. But while the man without strength only encounters satisfaction in the jealous defense of the limits of his mediocrity, the superior man finds it in the disinterested gift of his power. Christ allowed himself to be crucified, since his soul's highest satisfaction was in absolute sacrifice.

Such a desire cannot be confused with that of the wretches who, not dominating themselves, think they can rule by the whip. A will like this one demands full freedom for all. A generosity like this one cannot accept servitude.

If Nietzsche, led by his passionate temperament to extremes through the abuse of his exalted dialectic, didn't want this to be the case, it is up to us, free investigators, to approach his oeuvre and retain for our edification only those teachings that are worthwhile.

He was our enemy. So be it. He himself said to us: "Desire perfect enemies."

The struggle with them is more beautiful, more fertile. One can fraternize with "perfect" enemies. "You should have nothing but enemies worthy of hatred and not of scorn; it is necessary that you be proud of your enemies."

He was the philosopher of violence and authority, but like us he felt an immense love for life and knowledge, the invincible desire to fight for his cause, disgust for the current social order and the rule of the mediocre to which we are descending. He felt the need to destroy old ideas and things, to assist in destroying what is collapsing so that we can then be reborn.

In addition to the example of his boldness as a thinker, he taught us the horror of the mediocre life, the pride in suffering nobly, the cult of will and joy.

His prodigious talent for expression often vivified the ideas we serve. He was sincere and powerful. At times he was our fellow-traveler, and perhaps at those moments the best of his soul revealed itself to be too varied and complicated. His life's path was painful. Rare are the thinkers who suffered such a curse. Misunderstood, unrecognized, alone, isolated in his thought as in his daily existence and sick, sometimes despairing, but always able to master himself. For ten years he wandered around a deserted Europe, where he saw *nothing* worthy of being loved or served. His voice, which would later be greeted as that of a prophet, was lost with no echoes. No one paid attention to this great walker with his broad forehead who *was nothing more than a thinker.*

After those ten years of being uprooted, madness ruled him in his isolation. And ironically, he who wrote such magnificent pages on *voluntary death* survived his intelligence by ten years. In truth, he wrote with his blood.

For his oeuvre, so powerful in these times of pale mediocrity; for his absolute sincerity in these times of hypocrisy; for his passion in these times of cowardice; through his originality in these times of uniformity; for his sad end as a thinker; for his sad end as a madman, I love him. And I listen to and am largely inspired by his oeuvre. But I don't follow him. Imitating his example as a critic and free-thinker I only ask him for assistance in finding *my truth.*

I have no illusions concerning the value of his prejudices and I don't close my eyes to his errors. He looked men and things in the eye with a rebel's insolence and lack of respect. And how he would have despised the blindness of those who today want to set up a vain cult to him, because this master wanted no disciples.

In ending, I recall the words of Zarathustra to those who thought they understood him: "Now I order you to abandon me and to find yourselves."

(Originally appeared in *Tierra y Libertad* 359–69, August–December 1917)

Letter from a Man behind Walls

For Pierre Chardon

DECEMBER 29, 1918

Here, dear comrade, is my final "Letter from a Man behind Walls," since after a total of sixty months of imprisonment I am going to be FREE in that place where so many living ideas, so many wishes, so many high hopes attract me: Russia.

I am called on to (voluntarily) leave at the beginning of January in a convoy that will be handed over to the Soviets.

And so, until the reestablishment of postal communication, I can no longer take any interest in any way in your efforts. But as soon as it's possible I promise to send you news and, however far away I may be, to assist you in your labors as much as I can.

I can't find the words to express my joy at going to take part in the sufferings and labors of all those in Russia who are continuing the immense enterprise of social transformation. I think they'll be great workers for progress and that they will beautifully expand the human horizon.

For my part I go toward the uncertain and the unknown with confidence. The harshest trials have done nothing but confirm and solidify my ideas, my understanding of life. I remain faithful to clear ideas, happy to soon be able to serve and realize them through all my activities.

I have wonderful memories of my stay in Spain among our valiant and so-idealistic friends there. Unfortunately, it's impossible for me to write to them. Nor can I personally thank the various comrades who more or less helped me to live during these gloomy months of imprisonment. I'm unable to tell our good friend Armand one more time: "Hang in there!"

Dear Chardon, please transmit my fraternal greetings to all. I remain with you in my heart and I cordially shake your hand.

Le Rétif

(*La Mêlée*, February 1, 1919)

Bakunin's Confession

Our comrade Victor Serge, who has for some time been subjected to the insults of French anarchists, who do not forgive his loyal and sincere adherence to communism, was recently attacked with slanders and insults under the following evil pretext:

Victor Serge wrote an article on November 7, 1919, concerning the "Confession of Bakunin," a document unknown to the public to this day and whose existence we only know of through the allusions made to it by James Guillaume in his biographical notice (volume II of the Oeuvres de Michel Bakounine, Paris, 1907). Victor Serge's commentaries, respectful to the memory of Bakunin and historical truth alike, in no way presented the sacrilegious or iconoclastic character that unworthy adversaries later attributed to them, as the reader now, thanks to us, can judge.

Under what circumstances was this article translated, deformed, denatured, and reproduced in Germany? Victor Serge is unaware of this, as are we. I will not hide the painful surprise I experienced in learning that the Herzog's Forum had published a fiddled text. I am not going to linger over the successive alterations the article suffered in the various translations, retranslations, and reproductions in Switzerland and Italy. The essential fact is that Victor Serge's thoughts and expression were falsified against his will.

None of this was necessary to provide his adversaries with a pretext for defamations that I would blush to discuss. The only deplorable fact is that our respected friend Séverine was led into error by the campaign carried out against Victor Serge and published statements about him that are occasionally unjust. This is why, in order to put an end to all tendentious interpretations and malevolent deformations I think it necessary to publish here the authentic text of Victor Serge's article with the certainty that Séverine, that all readers will render our collaborator the justice he is due and the homage deserved by an upright writer, a disinterested revolutionary, a devoted and conscientious militant. Victor Serge addressed a response to Séverine that I hope the Journal du Peuple *will publish.*

—Boris Souvarine

THE SECRET ARCHIVES OF THE RUSSIAN POLICE CERTAINLY CONTAIN MANY documents of the greatest interest. We must count among them Bakunin's *Confession*, whose publication will unquestionably sadden a great number of comrades. According to all those who read this "confession," to which Professor Illinsky dedicated an article in the *Viestnik Literatoury* of Petrograd (no. 10, 1919), it casts a new, unexpected, and painful light in Bakunin's personality.

After his participation in the revolutionary movement in Russia, France, and Germany (1848–49) Bakunin was imprisoned in the Tsar's jails, first in the Peter and Paul Fortress, then at Schlüsselbourg. Later exiled to Siberia, he was only able to escape from there in 1861.

The documents brought to light in the archives of the Russian police deal with the period of his life passed in Siberia and in the dungeons of the autocrat of all the Russias. The man of steel, the irreconcilable revolutionary who was briefly the dictator of insurgent Dresden, who'd been chained to the wall in the citadel of Olmütz, whose head was disputed by two dictators, and who until the final day of his life was to remain the initiator and inspirer of an elite of rebels: this spiritual father of anarchism seems to have passed through a terrible moral crisis that he didn't come through unharmed. It was perhaps a near thing that the oak wasn't uprooted and didn't fall. Some—he still has so many enemies, even though he's been dead for fifty years—will even speak of "Bakunin's fall" with a wicked glee.

Bakunin wrote several letters from Siberia to his friends Alexander Herzen and Ogarev in which we find brief allusions to his *Confession*. Nicolas I, via Count Orlov, had proposed to him that he write to him "in the way a spiritual son writes to his spiritual father." (The Emperor, it must be noted, was entirely within his role in proposing this to his prisoner. Leader of the Orthodox Church, he considers himself the spiritual father of his subjects.) Bakunin writes: "Having given some thought to the matter, I thought that in front of a jury during a public trial I would play my role to the bitter end. But imprisoned behind four walls, in the power of the Bear, I could without any shame, round off the rough edges . . ."

"Round off the rough edges" looks to a reader of the *Confession* (and other documents) like a euphemism. In this notebook of ninety-six pages of tiny handwriting found in the archives of the Third Section of the ministry of the interior (department of police) Bakunin boasts of laying out for the Emperor "his entire life, all his thoughts, all his feelings." He writes to the Bear: "I will confess to you as to a spiritual father, from whom a man awaits pardon not in this world, but in the other."

And from the pen of the atheist these lines take on a strange meaning.

He describes his acts as fantastic projects, hopes devoid of any foundation, criminal plans. Recounting his life in foreign lands he declares that he has only "knowingly sinned" since 1846. The tone of the entire confession is that of someone who has been defeated, who humiliates himself, and who finds a bitter pleasure in flagellating himself.

"I was both fooler and fooled; I misled others and was myself misled, as if I did violence to my own spirit and the good sense of my listeners; a situation that was against nature, inconceivable, in which I placed myself and which at times obliged me to be a charlatan despite myself. There has always been much Don-Quixotism about me."

To be sure, it would be difficult for a man of conscience and action to speak of himself with more bitter harshness. Professor Illinsky, commenting on this passage, sees in it "the tragedy of a man of action who has arrived at doubting his work and becoming aware of his insincerity." But isn't the last phrase, which is justified by the quoted text, fundamentally unjust? Can't we oppose his entire tumultuous rebel life— both before and after this *Confession*—to these lines that Bakunin wrote in the grave in which he was buried alive? A man of action, and even more a leader—and Bakunin was truly a leader—is often forced to exaggerate. Going too far, exaggerating, accentuating, inflating some acts to the detriment of others, are the psychological necessities of all propaganda, augmented by the passion of the militant, augmented precisely because he is sincere. Later, in the gloomy meditation of the prison, in the depression of defeat, his severity toward himself perhaps imputed a lack of sincerity to what was simply his having been carried away by quotidian thoughts and deeds. Alas, we are forced to defend Bakunin against himself!

It seems that on each page of the *Confession* reasoning of this kind is needed if we're not to be dismayed. Bakunin is disenchanted with himself alone. The entire European movement in which he took so stormy a part now seems to him pathetic and vain. "All of Europe lives on lies," he says. He is "disgusted, nauseated," with the Germans. The revolution of 1848 demonstrated to him the "impotence of secret societies." "None of the current social theories (in England, in France, in Belgium) is capable of standing up to the test of three days of existence." He only remains truly faithful to his pan-Slavism. The Slavic peoples, in contrast to the degenerate nations of Western Europe, are the only ones to have remained healthy, the only ones who are communist by origin and temperament. Uniting them would produce a magnificent power, a new "Empire of the East" whose capital would be Constantinople. In order for Russia to be able to place itself at the head of the pan-Slavic movement and fulfill its mission, it requires a profound transformation. And here Bakunin again becomes a revolutionary confronting the Tsar, dreaming, perhaps despite himself, of a new revolutionary autocrat in whom the genius of Peter the Great would be reborn. At the current moment certain lines of the *Confession* are especially interesting. There is no question that Bakunin profoundly loved, knew, and understood Russia. He was farsighted about its destiny; he prophetically understood what history had determined was necessary for it.

> Representative, constitutional power, parliamentary aristocracy, and the so-called balance of powers in which the forces are so skillfully divided up that none of them can act: in a word, this entire narrow, crafty, indecisive catechism of European liberals has never inspired in me either veneration, profound interest, or even respect. I thought that in Russia more than anywhere else a powerful dictatorial power would be necessary that would occupy itself exclusively with enlightening the masses and elevating their moral level. What is needed is an authority free in its aspirations and sprit, but without parliamentary forms, which would publish free works but without freedom of the press; that would be surrounded with men of conviction and guided by their counsels, strengthened by their freely given assistance that no one and nothing can limit.

This is truly prophetic. Lenin couldn't describe the proletarian dictatorship any better and contrast it to the democracy of French and English radicals with any greater scorn. This unlimited power, dictatorial and libertarian, supported by men with fervent convictions, exists: it is called the Republic of the Soviets. In 1848 Bakunin already predicted Bolshevism, and shortly thereafter he advised Nicolas I about these methods. The ironies of history!

And so, when it comes to his intelligence, his *Confession* is in no way humiliating. Aren't the pages in which he expresses doubt compensated for by those where he prophesies with astounding lucidity? We can't contest the value of methods and acts; we can't contest that Bakunin saw things amazingly clearly.

The general tone of the "confession" is clearly defined in the following lines:

> Having lost the right to describe myself as a faithful subject of Your Imperial Majesty I sign with a sincere heart, "the repentant sinner, Mikhail Bakunin."
>
> More than the Tsar-judge, I stand now before the Tsar-confessor and I must open to him the most secret sanctuaries of my thought . . .
>
> I did not deserve this grace [that of writing this confession] and I blush at the thought of all I dared write and say of Your Imperial Majesty's severity.

If we attribute the tone and appearance of the *Confession* to a period of depression and crisis, to a period of despair, to the fact that this man of exceptional energy was imprisoned, isolated, condemned to death; was living face-to-face with the thought of imminent death and felt useless and worn, then how could we explain certain of his entreaties sent from Siberia, where he lived in relative freedom and whose tone, as a person who studied them said, is servile? It's certain that Bakunin suffered under a great torture. "Every day," he said, "one feels oneself becoming more stupid." In entreaties like this one all that can be heard is the cry of a man being tortured: "Don't allow me to die imprisoned for life. Imprisoned all you can do is remember, remember without cease and without fruit. Thought and memory become unspeakable tortures. One lives a long time despite oneself and, not dying, one feels oneself dying a bit every day in distress and idleness."

He humiliated himself, he weakened, to be sure, but he didn't betray. On one point he was unshakeable and this, in the eyes of Nicolas I, was essential. He wrote: "Don't demand that I confess the sins of others . . . I saved little in this shipwreck: my honor, and the knowledge that I never eased my lot through a betrayal."

When this painful book is finally published, studied line by line, and placed in context in the critical biography of the great anarchist, we will be able to draft a new judgment of Bakunin's personality. According to Professor Illinsky, who expresses himself with the greatest moderation, his character as a revolutionary will come out of this "diminished." Bakunin, wrote to the Siberian authorities applying for a post as a civil servant and hid this fact from his friend Herzen by engaging is a falsehood. "Without my consent . . ." he wrote, "Hasfor, the governor of Siberia, obtained the authorization for my assuming the post . . ."

During the first disputes between the socialists and anarchists in the International, the episode of the slanders against Bakunin by some of Marx's overzealous friends and which, according to some, Marx himself was not a stranger to, was a sad one. Rumors circulated concerning vague relations between Bakunin and the Tsar, between Bakunin and the Tsar's police. The discovery of the "confession" casts light on this subject. The slanders must have been rooted in the intentional semi-revelations of the imperial police of the confidential document the Tsar had filed in its archives. The Russian government even planned to publish it in order to discredit its adversary who, having escaped, had once again become its irreconcilable enemy.

If it was a question of an ordinary man, of an obscure revolutionary militant, then this crisis, Olmütz, Peter-and-Paul, Schlüsselbourg, the death penalty, isolation, and Siberia would suffice to explain it. But Chernyshevsky imprisoned and exiled for twenty years, constantly skirting madness, didn't weaken. But Vera Figner and Morozov, who left Schlüsselbourg after twenty years, didn't "repent" in this way. But all those, famous or unknown, who went mad or who died in the Tsar's jails, even if they suffered a passion a thousand times longer than that of Christ, even if they sometimes doubted themselves and their work, even if they sometimes faltered, remained silent, and their executioners knew nothing about it. To these people and those who inherited their spirit, Bakunin's *Confession* will cause pain. At that moment of his life Bakunin stumbled. He wasn't superhuman. More energetic, more impetuous, more ardent, more clear-sighted, more imaginative than most, he was nevertheless not unshakeable. Just as he dominated his generation, he still dominates ours, but we would have preferred that he be inflexible so that his legend would later be more noble, for he is among those who leave behind a legend. This recently discovered human document teaches us that, like almost every man, he had his moments of defeat and that, greater than most, he was also more broken.

Victor SERGE
Petrograd, November 7, 1919

(*Bulletin Communiste* 56, December 22, 1921)

The Anarchists in Russia

Victor-Serge (Kibalchich), one of the best known anarchist individualist militants, who rallied to communism during the proletarian revolution, addressed a letter to his anarchist comrades in France which they refused to publish. We reproduce it here according to our confrere the Soviet, which published the complete text.

To the comrades of *Le Libertaire*, the Fédération Anarchiste, and anarchist militants of various tendencies

AUGUST 30, 1920

Dear Comrades,

During my eighteen months in Moscow and Petrograd I greatly deplored the absolute impossibility of my corresponding with you. Several times I tried to send you brief letters by whatever means I could, but I have reason to believe they never reached you.

I finally have the opportunity to write you today, and I have so many things to tell you, important things related to our ideas and action, that I feel a great embarrassment.

This letter will thus be a bit disjointed and incomplete, but I hope it will soon be possible for us to correspond more or less regularly. And I place myself at your complete disposal to provide you with information, to answer all your questions, to provide you with all the documents you would like to have concerning the situation in Russia.

In France I was primarily active in anarchist individualist groups, but this is addressed to all the anarchist and communist comrades in France. Each tendency has its role; in the movement, each represents a facet of our truth, which is libertarian life or the aspiration for it. And

I believe that among ourselves, even when at times we find ourselves adversaries, we can remain comrades and fraternally assist each other in the search for truth.

Expelled from France, released from a concentration camp, I arrived in Russia—escorted by Senegalais as far as Finland and from there by white executioners—in the winter of 1919. I've already lived there for two winters, which were horrible. The blockade, foreign and civil war falling fiercely on this poor, exhausted country, where only a tiny minority of revolutionaries stood firm despite it all, this is the at times atrocious reality that I saw. I saw the population of Petrograd hold out with rations of 100 grams of black bread per day, plus a few dried fish per month in the heart of winter at a time when homes had no heat, no light, no water, naturally, and no toilets. Finland threatened us, Estonia attacked us, intellectuals sabotaged or conspired, the petite bourgeoisie every day hoped that tomorrow would bring the collapse and massacre of the Bolsheviks, officers and engineers of the Red Army betrayed us, and wherever the fighting was going on the Whites took no prisoners. There was the systematic slaughter of Jews, communists, and often of workers. All of the conscious working class and revolutionary forces being at the front, industry, which was in any case lacking in primary materials and combustibles, lay idle. I don't know how these things should be written about, for the reality of it was frightful. Any revolutionary who lived through this survived a test. For him, ideas will henceforth have a more profound meaning than they previously did.

It was during the first winter that, seeing that in all of the immense Russia there was only one force—one heroic and unshakeable—alive and capable of defending the revolution at a time when no one saw clearly and even many old militants despaired, I thought it was my duty to rally to it, and I joined the Russian Communist Party as an anarchist, without in any way abdicating my ideas, except for what was utopian about it in contact with reality.

I soon realized that this attitude imposed real sacrifices on me from the point of view of my freedom of individual action, and important concessions on principles. With complete clarity of mind I still to consent to this. Sacrifices and concessions are imposed on the anarchist militant (if he joins the CP or not) not before a doctrine or an organization, but in the face of the revolution itself, whose interests are the supreme law. For the revolution it's a question strictly of living and winning. Our personalities and individual ideas don't weigh much in the balance, and the revolutionary must have the stoicism required to acknowledge this. Those comrades who've gone to Russia and saw what is happening there will surely understand or approve me.

I summarized, in a study I'm sending you with this same post and which I request you publish, my understanding of the revolutionary experience from an anarchist point of view. These pages are too brief and incomplete, but such as they are I hope they will serve as the basis for useful discussion. The ideas I lay out there are obviously personal, but as a whole are in agreement with those of a great number of anarchists. To be precise I will name among the comrades who have joined the Russian CP: Alfa (of Borevestnik, etc.), Krasnostchekov (currently president of the Far Eastern Republic), Novomirsky, Bianchi (former secretary of the Union of Russian Workers of America), and among those active outside the CP the group from *Golos Truda*, the Anarchist-Universalist group of Moscow, and comrades Shapiro, Rochtchin, William Shatov, Alexander Ghe, and Vietrov, to name only the well-known militants.

As I briefly explain in the articles in question, most Russian anarchists nevertheless occupy a position that is more or less hostile to the Communist Party, which they have sometimes been in conflict with. Nevertheless, the immense majority of them are Sovietist and consider that any action that would result in disuniting the revolutionary forces would be harmful at the present time. They believe that even criticism will only be fruitful when the existence of the Russia of the Soviets will no longer be in immediate danger. This point of view, in fact, is that of Kropotkin, who lives not far from Moscow in the small town of Dmiterievo, where he devotes himself to major projects (a book on anarchist ethics), and that of comrades Karelin and the brothers Gordin, etc.

In Ukraine the conflict between anarchists and Bolsheviks has taken on a character that is often tragic and has ended in an armed fight. Comrade Voline (Eichenbaum), who lived for a long time in Paris, and who is at present imprisoned in Moscow, was the initiator of a powerful and active libertarian communist movement but which in the chaos of the civil war in Ukraine collided with the vast authoritarian-communist organization and was smashed. I don't know very much about the facts in this case. I do know that on both sides there were occasionally bloody excesses and that both sides demonstrated intolerance and ferocity. The rebellious peasants, led by an anarchist (Makhno), occupied entire provinces of Ukraine. Unfortunately, the anarchists in these regions didn't know how to avoid resorting to authority, violence, terror, and the abuses that necessarily flow from all this. In the battle that was engaged between these groups and the Communist Party people were executed on both sides. This distressing fight has had repercussions in Moscow itself.

I think it should none of this should cause us to lose sight of the higher interests of the revolution. As far as I have been informed, the Ukrainian anarchists have themselves avoided none of the errors for which they reproach the Bolsheviks. I have no doubt that had their movement been able to develop without hindrance it would have produced noble fruits and that this would have been infinitely fortunate and useful. But when it comes to making war I can't help but consider Trotsky a better organizer than Makhno, and the Red Army as a weapon to which the bands of Ukrainian partisans—who are often heroic—can in no way be compared. The Ukrainian partisans speculated on the spirit of small land-ownership of the peasants, on their nationalism, even on anti-Semitism, all of which had dreadful consequences.

In general, it seems to me that the lack of a practical program for action—their utopianism—and their lack of organization have killed the anarchist movement in Russia which has expended a prodigious amount of energy in service to the revolution. Among the comrades fallen at the front last year I will mention Anatole Yelazniakov and Justin Zhouk.

At the present time I see no possibility for a vast anarchist movement in Russia. The harsh needs of the revolution leave us no choice as to means. Everything they imposed was done by the Communist Party, who *one must be with* under penalty of being against it and with reaction. As soon as peace is made, as soon as we can seriously set to work on the task of social reorganization, I am sure that the anarchist spirit will be powerful in Russia. And I even think that among the most conscious and tested communists it will find its most living expression.

Alexander Berkman and Emma Goldman, expelled from America, have been in Russia since last December. At present they are carrying out a long trip in Ukraine for the Petrograd Museum of the Revolution. The sixteen years he spent in prison haven't caused Berkman to lose his moral vigor.

Allow me now, comrades, to speak about the French movement and the situation in France. A few months ago I had the opportunity to, by chance, receive five or six issues of *Le Libertaire*. They were interesting, to be sure, but they could easily have been published in 1912, that is, before the war and the Russian Revolution. I have the impression that the anarchists in France have not yet carried out the necessary revision of their ideas in the face of these historic experiences and limit themselves to preserving anarchist traditions. Under these conditions it seems that some sooner or later risk, in becoming communists, ceasing to be anarchists (and I see a great danger in this); while others, lacking a clear understanding of the revolution, remain without influence and at times will be saddened to see that through force of circumstance they are neighbors of Bourtzev and Hervé.

In order to correctly pose the great questions vital for the entire revolutionary world it is important before all else that you be informed of the Russian experience, that you enter into contact with the social revolution accomplished here. This can only be correctly done in one way: *send us good militants who'll work here for a time.* And try to remain in contact.

There is something stupefying in the indifference of the French masses at a moment when events of an unimaginable import are taking place. The enthusiasm nevertheless inspired by the Russian Revolution among the working-class elite could very well, if you don't intervene, be channeled, used, led astray by "socialist" or CGT politicians. The habits of inaction that they will eloquently sustain may hold back for a few more years the issue of the fight in Russia. It is certainly not possible for you to imagine what terrible repercussions your failures might have on the revolution. Remember that it was the failure of the general strike of July 21 in France that allowed the strangling of the Hungarian Soviet Republic and the coming of White Terror. The Polish aggression, which also delays peace for the Russian Revolution would perhaps not have happened if the French workers had truly demonstrated revolutionary will and vetoed the intrigues of the Quai d'Orsay. Know, comrades, that as long as you remain inactive blood will flow here daily, and we won't be able to begin the task of organization and liberation desired by all sincere communists, be they Marxist or anarchist.

Everything that could humanly be done for the triumph of the social revolution has been done in Russia, despite the errors and sometimes despite the crimes inevitable in the course of such social turbulence. Hunger, cold, daily worries, horrific material, and moral misfortunes, the deaths of the weakest, the terror, daily sacrifices, revolutionary

Russia has consented to all of them. This fact alone imposes great obligations on those foreign militants who understand this.

Fraternally,
Victor Serge
August 30, 1920

(*Bulletin Communiste*, 4 [second year] January 27, 1921)

Letter from Russia

PETROGRAD, SEPTEMBER 1, 1921

Petrograd on a beautiful August day. On Michael's Square, under the windows of a palace and a theater that is packed every night, three strange carriages are stopped. They're low carts, covered with tarps and pulled by small horses whose ribs sorrowfully stick out under their taut, dusty skin, worn out with sweat. The weary drivers, old bearded muzhiks, ask the way. All around there's the coming and going of trams, the dual river of (in fact) well-dressed passersby of the great city. Under the tarps, upon which a river of sun falls, there are tiny tousled blond heads and the grimy old faces of the sick consumed by hunger.

"Where are you from, little father?"

"From Samara."

From the country of hunger. And they've traveled more than a thousand kilometers, driven by the desire to live, to live despite it all, while there their entire people seems to be condemned.

Two little girls standing in the cart look without surprise on the crowd and the city. They have tired blue eyes, hollow cheeks gray from dust and anemia. They've already passed through so many inhospitable cities that even this one doesn't surprise them.

This is how they arrive in all the cities of immense Russia, the bravest and luckiest of those fleeing the Volga. They bring with them the dead and the dying, sometimes little wrinkled corpses, deformed beings with their bellies bloated by foul food, by illness. They pass through cities whose suffering counts for little compared to theirs, like savages of another race. The people of the city, dressed *à la euro- péenne*, often with a remainder of elegance, stop at the edge of the sidewalk to watch them pass. The best of them sigh. The others, the imbeciles, say, "The worse things are the better: the Bolsheviks won't pull through this time!"

Will they find asylum and bread in our great devastated city, where life is so harsh? I look out on the crowd on the square and I almost have my doubts. All the passersby have the look and clothing of the *ancien régime*. Workers, revolutionaries, some are dead, others vaguely carry out difficult tasks and are poorly dressed, ill-nourished and have nothing left to give. And yet a café and a confectionary have opened a hundred meters from here where the passing petit bourgeois spend in ten minutes three or four months' wages of a communist working woman. And suddenly, poor starving people, there comes the clear impression that you have nothing to hope for from these shopkeepers, from their customers, from the revolting petite bourgeoisie of the capitals that in your lack of consciousness you have so often supported. You have only to have hope in those—the exhausted proletarians, the communist escapees from the civil war—who are almost as poor as you.

We pass in front of shining new displays, both opulent and pitiful. Here one can eat a gastronomic feast, on condition that one is one of the big embezzlers of the stock of the Commune that the Cheka still executes when they catch them in the act. I enter.

Three gentlemen are there speaking with the owner of the establishment, an old, bespectacled antique merchant. The room is decorated with engravings, with miniatures, with porcelains the product of excellent deals made by a connoisseur. This tiny things represent millions of rubles. Through the window I can see moving off into the distance the miserable carriages of the starving. I wonder by what miracle the exhausted animals that pull them are able to remain standing.

And I heard a gentleman speak who had laid his wallet of a well-paid technician on a fluted chair: "The Americans, English capital . . . That would be an excellent affair . . . Yes, really a good one . . . A concession? No, not yet . . . Seventeen million you say? In valuta that comes to very little. Nineteen million . . . the Americans."

Snatches of words reach me. And then others:

"The famine . . . the political consequences of the famine . . . they're screwed . . . screwed."

And again:

"English capital . . . The Americans . . ." A thin young woman brings them café au lait and cookies. The owner-antique dealer shows off a miniature that they whisperingly estimate in rubles of the tsar, of the Duma, of the Soviets, in francs, in marks, in dollars . . .

I recall the Whites of 1919. This morning I read that a new plot has been uncovered. It's not yet the truest one, the most dangerous one.

There are already men who imagine that tomorrow they can carve up the dead revolution . . .

During the afternoon a young Jewish student from Kharkov came to my house. Quite simply, without realizing that he was recounting horrific events, that he was taking us back, we who were gathered together in 1921 in one of the great capitals of the civilized world, to the time of Merovingian killings, he told us as he sipped his tea how many times he was nearly killed because he was a Jew. Five or six times in eighteen months. How did he survive? The same slightly disconcerting chance that allows soldiers to survive five or six attacks spared him. Each in their turn the Whites, Petliura's band of murderers, the Makhnovtsi, and other whose political color was unknown wanted to kill him. His misfortune was to have the look of his race.

"Yid? Don't say no or watch out!

The first person he saw on the tumultuous night of pogrom, interrogated him in this way on the street, in a wagon, in his house. The rifle butts are raised over his head.

"Yes, a Jew."

"Against the wall! Move it!"

He moves peacefully (he had seen so many murdered since they'd killed his brother). He offers cigarettes to his executioner, who in a friendly way abruptly tells him: "Get lost!"

Another time the Makhnovtsi captured him. He declared that he knew a friend of the *batko*. And the *batko* himself pardoned him.

Yet another time an illiterate took his student booklet for the membership booklet of the Communist party and wanted to bash in his head.

And finally, another time, the murderers having brought him to a hedgerow to kill him, decided to shoot at him in flight by throwing him over the hedges. These killers, a little drunk, were clumsy . . .

This student finds these things simple, normal. Having come here to get some books he will return from whence he came with the hope of living despite it all. He's not a communist but sympathizes with the Reds: wherever they establish themselves, the pogroms cease.

During the evening I met a "revolutionary" enemy of the communists. We didn't fail to exchange more or less harsh words in passing.

Gesturing toward the street where the petite bourgeoisie seem, with the freedom of small scale commerce, to have odiously regained a foothold, he mockingly—and quite obviously with satisfaction—asked me: "Now do you deny the defeat?"

They shouldn't have done this . . . They shouldn't have done that . . . It's the party's fault . . . They should have listened to the far-sighted Mensheviks . . . Maybe they shouldn't have made a revolution at all . . . They should have left power to the Social Revolutionaries . . . They should have turned the unions into a Republic of Labor . . . They should have dissolved the state, decentralized, established anarchy . . .

The dissident and malcontent "revolutionaries" we meet conclude their invariable indictment in accordance with the label they wear on their caps . . . During the war, in the bars, it was in this way that good men carried out military criticism and strategy.

But I listen to the "comrade." And I realize that he feels a bitter satisfaction in noting what immense danger surrounds "the revolution of the others"; in saying "For my part, I wash my hands of it; I would have done better than Lenin"; in thinking that if everything collapses in a bloodbath by horrible reaction, he can proclaim with joy, shouting with impunity, "It's the Bolsheviks' fault!"

But he's never requisitioned bread in the countryside. He never carried out a house search. He didn't fight against Kronstadt. He never arrested anyone. He isn't a commissar. He never carries out any of the dirty work of the class war. He is clean, he is pure, he is an idealist.

He will triumph if the revolution perishes.

I know that this revolution has earned many criticisms, but I don't know who has earned the right to make them. It is so easy to criticize the transgressions of those who have attempted to master this formidable social tempest in which a world perishes, where, whatever is said and done, another world is born. But is this the time for criticism?

Is this the time when our New Economic Policy—which no one can doubt is necessary—is turning out to be a truce with the most tenacious and determined enemy of the revolution of the poor, with the petite bourgeoisie that rotted our institutions, pillaged (sometimes legally) our storehouses, survived every Red terror through obsequiousness and adores nothing but profit? When in the Volga region thirty million peasants—three-quarters of the total population of France— die of hunger? When millions of children and the weak are going to perish this winter, whatever we might do to assist them?

And doesn't it require a strange mental aberration to not understand that there are many and profound causes for the immense suffering of the Russians, for which the actions of leaders and parties count for little? Let us recall: four years of imperialist war and then four years of civil war; foreign intervention on seven fronts; endless conspiracies; the blockade; sabotage by technicians; the ignorance and narrowmindedness of the peasantry; the death of the best. All this in a country in which formerly there were the fewest railroads and the greatest number of illiterates in the world.

Four times the war passed and re-passed over the regions today suffering from famine following what was before the drought a still primitive agriculture. It is there that the Entente stirred up the Czechoslovaks in 1918. There that the Constituent wanted to govern. There that Kolchak returned. There that the Whites decimated in the cruelest fashion, through terror, an entire population. Now the land is dead. Who killed it?

It seems to me that every thing, every voice, every step taken on the street of a Russian city attests today more than ever to the fact that the Russian Revolution has, above all, been the magnificent sacrifice of a young elite people that is the future of the world.

(*Bulletin Communiste* 42–43 [second year], October 6 and 13, 1921)

New Tendencies in Russian Anarchism

SEPTEMBER 4, 1921

We know that the Russian Revolution was the cause, first within the Russian socialist parties and then the international ones, of a definitive split. In the face of the reality of the social revolution, men used to calling themselves revolutionaries had to takes sides for or against violence, for or against the immediate expropriation of the rich, for or against dictatorship. And the old Russian Social Democracy founded by Plekhanov had an abyss dug within it between the Mensheviks and the Bolsheviks. The Social-Revolutionaries divided into a categorically reactionary right and a Sovietist left. The Russian Jewish parties evolved in the same way. As for the anarchists . . .

The anarchists constituted a scattered, varied movement divided into poorly delineated and short-lived movements. And yet, from March to October 1917 it demonstrated great activity and great vitality. But as a result of the diffuse character of their movement there was no clear split in the movement. From the first moment most of them adhered to the October Revolution, which, along with the Bolsheviks, they had prepared and desired. It was only much later that the revolution would divide them into two opposed tendencies. Symptomatic indications nevertheless show that during the October Revolution there were currents among the anarchists who were against the latter. On the eve of events the *Golos Truda* (anarcho-syndicalist) published a declaration in which, responding to questions from its readers, it specified that it didn't want to support the movement that was being prepared and was only disposed to follow it if the masses did. This was how the most widely distributed anarchist organ among the Petrograd workers expressed itself on October 23, 1917. And the day after the battles of the revolution in Moscow Dr. Atbekian, an old friend of Kropotkin's, bitterly reproached the Bolsheviks for having unleashed a civil war.[1] But I repeat, this only indicates the weakest tendency. Most Russian anarchist militants didn't share the hesitations of *Golos Truda* or the scruples of the humanitarian philosopher. And I only cite these facts because they appear to me to mark the departure point of the divisions that are growing among the Russian anarchists, forced daily to declare themselves for or against the revolution (the reality-revolution, quite different from the theory-revolution, and even more from the ideal-revolution).

Today this division is so sharp that there are a great number of anarchists who are members of the Russian Communist Party and other anarchists imprisoned by the Extraordinary Commissions [the Cheka —ed.] which consider them, rightly or wrongly, the most formidable enemies of the Communist power. Apart from these extremes, all the Russian anarchist tendencies are subdivided into a left (bitterly hostile to communism) and a right (loyal to and sympathizing with communism), which, in these times of civil war, explains why former syndicalists are imprisoned by a regime in which other former syndicalists— sometimes friends of the former—occupy positions of responsibility. To be precise, I will point out that there are two groups of former syndicalists, that of *Golos Truda*, which was always legal, loyal, and whose members have never ceased to work within Soviet institutions, and the Anarcho-Syndicalist Confederation, irreducibly opposed to the Communist regime; that there are also two former Universalist groups, one with Bolshevik tendencies and the other hostile to Bolshevism; and that both these less sharply delineated nuances are in the Anarchist Communist Federation (for in Moscow there is a total of about ten anarchist organizations).

In summary, there are those who, having learned nothing from the revolution, maintain their traditional positions, and those who, seeing themselves left behind by events, strive mightily to summarize their experience and realize a synthesis from which a new anarchism will sooner or later be born.

In this article I will restrict myself to describing the efforts of the second group. The anarchists, open enemies of the Communist Party, have no legal press in Red Russia. Other libertarian elements, which I will qualify as Kropotkinist "centrists," whose opposition to the Communists is limited to the criticism of ideas, are currently

---

1   Alexander Moissievich Atabekian (1868–1933).

publishing the *Volnaya Zhizn*, organ of the Pan-Russian Federation of Anarchist Communists, A. Kareline,[2] editor, 1st House of the Soviets 219, Moscow), and the Potchin ("The Beginning," primarily dedicated to propaganda for cooperation, Moscow, Pan-Russian Federation of Anarchist Communists). These small papers, which unquestionably respond to a need, have nothing new to teach us. The new tendencies of Russian anarchism manifest themselves, on the contrary, with increasing distinctness, in the following reviews and documents, which I will briefly analyze:

1. Declaration of the Anarchist-Syndicalists (*Goloss-Truda*, June–July 1921);
2. *The Universal*, organ of the Pan-Russian Section of the Anarchist-Universalists, nos. 1–2, 3–4, February–May 1921;
3. *Through Socialism to Anarchism-Universalism*, organ of the Anarchist-Universalist Association (inter-individualist), nos. 1–3, Moscow, April, May, June 1921;
4. "Declaration of the Union of Russian Anarchists Repatriated from America" (revised and completed, Moscow, July 1921).

Aside from these documents, which are in a way official, I will also quote others of lesser value when they seem to me likely to put in relief a state of mind, a way of thinking.

"No dictatorship, but all power"

All discussions obviously gravitate around the problem of dictatorship.

After having remarked that the struggle for the emancipation of the laboring masses "inevitably leads to the destruction of the state, to the liquidation of authority"; that in every revolution the creative power of the masses must be developed, even against authority; that there is needed "as normal as possible a transition of power to anarchy" (yes, yes, but how?), the declaration of the anarchist syndicalists poses in principle that: "The productive energies of the country—the proletariat of the cities and countryside—unite not on a political basis but on that of class consciousness" (article 8) . . . and that the party or ideological organizations will "in no way intervene in the leadership and administration of economic and social life" (article 9).

---

2   Appolon Andreievich Kareline (1863–1926).

Various objections immediately come to mind. What do these organizations do? And if they refuse to abstain as they should, will they be forced to? By whom? And how? And finally, if the organized anarcho-syndicalists renounce intervening in the leadership and administration of a society in the process of revolutionary transformation in which they are only a minority, can they hope that that society, whose immense majority know nothing of the anarchist ideal, will attain it without their cooperation? That would be extremely optimistic.

I'll skip over the guarantee for all of a "maximum of freedom and well-being." We can guess what this maximum could, alas, be reduced to in a country blockaded and starved by a capitalist coalition, where revolution and reaction are engaged in a duel to the death. And I arrive (articles 15–16) at the song of praise to the October Revolution, "a true social revolution" from which was born the Russia of the Soviets, "a powerful lever for the emancipation of the proletariat of all countries." It is only after this preamble that there is any mention of the "usurpation of power by a political party" and of the "monstrous hypertrophy of state socialism" that was its consequence. This way of posing the question distances us considerably from these anarchists—and not the least well-known among them—according to whom there was no October Revolution. The real revolution was that of March; in October there was nothing but a political coup d'état. For there are Russian anarchists of this opinion.

But let me quote in its entirety article 18, which deals with the problem of dictatorship. It is remarkable:

> Art. 18—The dictatorship of the proletariat, as the expression of the domination of the organized class, leading to the dictatorship of one party and transforming the Soviet system itself into a bureaucratic, police, and primitive machine is inadmissible to the anarchist syndicalists. The slogan "dictatorship of the proletariat" in itself determines the destructive character of the revolution. We must oppose to it the creative and constructive slogan of "all power to the working class personified by its vanguard regiments."

Communists also condemn the harmful deformities and deviations of the dictatorship. But what is disconcerting here is to see *opposed* to the principle of the dictatorship exercised by a party that of *all power to the working class represented by its organized revolutionary vanguard* (the defective translation says it even better: by its regiments, which implies an idea of strict discipline.)

Let's not play with words: all power—the power to do everything—means a dictatorship; an organized revolutionary vanguard (even as a union) is the same as a party.

Moreover, we read further on: "Article 19—During the critical period of the revolution the anarchist syndicalists of the revolution consider admissible and sometimes inevitable the application of organized violent and repressive measures against the active defenders of the destroyed order."

Let us speak clearly: This means prison for the conscious or unconscious—it makes no difference—defenders of the bourgeoisie; death for the most fearsome among them; terror if necessary; and the organization, the systematization of all these measures by extraordinary commissions.

The positive part of this document is praiseworthy. The relations between the city and the countryside must be fraternal. To be sure. The "armed defense of the country" is organized by factory committees. Even though the experience of Red Hungary of a "union" army wasn't a happy one. One is allowed to hope that in other circumstances the factory committees will be able to form a Red Army.

The impression all this gives is quite clear: the Russian anarcho-syndicalists in realty only condemn the dictatorship of other revolutionaries. They know how to point out the errors of the latter, but in their criticism they don't know how to abstain from unpleasant exaggerations, (see in this regard article 23, a condemnation of "socialist imperialism" that no pacifist liberal would disavow). They note the material and moral exhaustion of the country, i.e., they don't share the illusions of certain Ukrainian anarchists concerning an imminent third revolution. They call for participation in the work of Soviet economic reconstruction (article 20). What are their guiding ideas? I see two.

"The productive energies of the country unite, not on a political basis, but on that of class consciousness." But isn't it necessary that within organizations based on a class consciousness that is developed to very different degrees, the revolutionaries endowed with the highest class consciousness and united by a community of ideals should come together, precisely to orient and lead events, to set an example of the sacrifices necessary, and also to crush the harmful tendencies within any workers' movement capable of asserting themselves during times of troubles? This grouping—be it anarchist syndicalist, if it calls itself "Federation" or "Confederation"—will it not, in fact, be political; will it not be the *party* that at the decisive moment will exercise dictatorship?

"The measures of revolutionary violence must in no case be set as a system of coercion" (article 19).

This is perhaps the most important point. The greatest danger of dictatorship is that it tends to firmly implant itself, that it creates permanent institutions that it wants neither to abdicate nor to die a natural death. In all of history there is no example of a dictatorship that died on its own. The necessary arm of the revolution of today, the dictatorship, when it will have replaced the best revolutionaries and corrupted the others, will it not become a formidable obstacle to communist progress? This is the problem to be faced by all revolutionary consciences. The anarcho-syndicalist declaration only sketches it and doesn't solve it. Revolutions have a certain duration. The convulsions of the French Revolution extended from 1789 to 1799. One doesn't transform a world in a few days. In these conditions repressive measures must be organically established as a system. No one will disagree that this period of transition and dictatorship should be a brief as possible. But experience doesn't allow us to conceive of it as lasting but a few days or even a few months. The most rapid phases of history are counted in years.

In the same order of ideas I have before me a proposed "Platform of Anarchism," written by a well-known Russian militant who incidentally belongs to no organization. This author also harshly condemns the state and the dictatorship of the party. He advocates that of the workers. "In the transitional period between the domination of capital and the triumph of labor, over the course of the revolutionary destruction of the organs of bourgeois violence and the construction of the free workers' society, the organized dictatorship of the workers is inevitable.

It must be exercised by the General Confederation of Labor and "any attempt by the parties and the soviets to deform the dictatorship of the proletariat must be mercilessly repressed."

We can fully understand the federal committee mercilessly repressing the most varied movements. But that this should be the application of a platform for anarchism is something less understandable.

The author speaks readily about the "Republic of Labor," which in the end is nothing but the CGT elevated to the power of a state and an army (by anarchists!) and an apparatus of coercion. But just because they are apolitical (?) do they offer more guarantees, more intelligence, more revolutionary devotion than the Communist Party and the CSR, that is, than the workers' minorities organized for the revolution on the basis of a doctrine of social emancipation? For my part, I am convinced of the contrary.

In the final section of this "Platform for Anarchism" I note an unexpected conclusion, that the author advocates the large-scale adherence of sympathizing organizations, of syndicalist organizations—inspired by the anarchists—to the Third International.

Such today is the ideology—a confused one, as we can see—of the Russian anarcho-syndicalists. Nevertheless, it attests to a remarkable evolution of anarchism toward new formulas that other Russian militants state much better.

"We want a strong organization"

Two issues of *The Universal*, organ of the Pan-Russian Section of the Anarchist-Universalists, appeared in February–March and April–May. Others are in preparation. This large format review has more than thirty-two pages of compact text in two columns, and so we can seek a complete and detailed expression of anarchist-universalism in its pages. Founded at the end of 1920, the Anarchist-Universalist Association initially adopted as its platform a manifesto written by Comrade Gordin.[3] There could be found in it the formal recognition of the principle of the dictatorship of the proletariat, of revolutionary and industrial centralization, the condemnation of traditional federalism, etc. But inflated by the influx of anarchist elements of a mentality completely different from that of the founders of the new movement, the organization soon passed through a crisis that ended in a stormy split. The minority, grouped around Gordin, who had launched the word "Universalist," was expelled by the majority. As in all old parties, the expulsion of the minority by the majority was accompanied—on both sides, it appears—by insults, defamation, and violence. Today the two groups, in excommunicating each other, exchange the most suggestive pleasantries. But let's move on. This simply proves that the anarchists as well are not equal to their ideas and that in the practice of organization, polemic, fraternity, and revolutionary tolerance they are in no way innovators.

---

3   Abba Gordin (1887–1964).

The best articles of the *The Universal* are signed by Comrade Askarov.[4] In issues 1–3 this comrade passes a severe and well-reasoned judgment on the recent past of Russian anarchism: "It's a mystery to no one," he says, "that since the October Revolution, for three years, the anarchists have manifested the most complete confusion in the work of social construction. . . . They have been inert." And "when the new state was formed they found themselves cast out of life."

Askarov considers the socialist state a fact. But in the face of this fact he stresses the resolution of the Universalists to *participate in the labor of constructing the new society* "which opens possibilities to us that we never had under the capitalist regime."

On the question of organization the Universalists are very clear: they "reject the old principles of anarchist organization," and this is fortunate! "Anarchist-Universalists, we consider necessary the creation of a single, coherent organization, bound by firm self-discipline and which places itself on a defined revolutionary platform" (no. 1, p. 10).

One would think one was listening to a communist develop the ideas so often defended by Zinoviev on international organization: "An organization of one sole bloc with iron discipline . . ." Here the expression is accentuated, categorical; there it is a bit ambiguous. The meaning is the same. Thus, in the matter of organization the revolution leads communists and anarchists to similar conclusions. In the same issue of "The Universal" another comrade opposes "the organized action of the masses to the traditional individualism of small groups." And this, too, is speaking like a communist.

The first Anarchist-Universalist Conference, according to the summary account in issues 2–3 of *The Universal*, signifies the "passing from anarchist Blanquism to the class struggle." It affirms that the Universalists need to participate in the Soviets, where they, incidentally, have several deputies (Askarov, Barmach,[5] Urovsky) and accepts the defense of the revolution by force of arms. On this subject I would like to recall that from their first steps the Anarchist-Universalists had greeted the first victories of the Red Army with joy . . .

"Taking into account the revolutionary importance of the Communist International in relation to the different countries, the Anarchist-Universalists declare that they have no desire to manifest

---

4   Germann Karlovich Askarov (1882–ca. 1935).
5   Vladimir Vladimirovich Barmach (1879–ca. 1938).

any hostility toward it." For the defense of the October Revolution they proclaim themselves disposed to form a bloc with the parties that continue it.

In the present situation, in regard to the New Economic Policy (freedom of small-scale commerce and middle industry) the Anarchist-Universalists (Askarov, *Universal*, issues 3–4) calls for the "preparation of the unions for the taking over of industry, the unionizing of the workers of the land, and economic reorganization through the free cooperation of workers and peasants," all of these excellent things that are in no way in disagreement with the communist program or its practice.

In summary, the Anarchist-Universalists defend the October Revolution, condemn the past errors of the Russian anarchist movement, advocate participation in the Soviets, recognize what the revolution owes the Red Army, don't want to demonstrate any hostility toward the Communist International, and seek practical, immediate, and peaceful methods of work within the socialist state.

These are undeniably indications of a tendency toward the revision of consecrated anarchist values. As for the present, the Universalists are particularly interested in the practical, but the consequences of their initiatives, if they were to develop, would be of a singular import in the realm of theory.

The timeliness of their initiative seems to be confirmed by their relative success. Despite extremely difficult conditions for existence, they have groups in Briansk, in the Urals, in Riazan, Minsk, and Samara. In Moscow they have a conference room, a bookstore, a club and a restaurant in the center of the city, and two clubs in the suburbs (in Krasnaya-Prennia and in Sokolniki).

"To anarchism through socialism"

Everything that is only in sketched by the "majoritarian" anarchist-universalists—to use a handy expression—everything among them that is confused, ambiguous, and indecisive can be found, though fully realized, in the form of a well-defined, original, and clear ideology among their "dissident" brothers, Gordin and his friends. For this reason the few issues that have appeared of their compact little review, edited by the latter, "Through Socialism to Anarchist-Universalism," are truly interesting. In order to distinguish themselves from other Universalists Gordin's friends, whose language is only too fertile in neologisms, have imagined a new term and call themselves "inter-individualists." Which does no harm.

The two Gordin brothers have played a key role in the Russian anarchist movement of these past few years. Tireless orators and propagandists, prolific writers, journalists, pamphleteers, and initiators of multiple enterprises, combatants at the barricades of July and October 1917, thanks to their ever-working imaginations they have greatly contributed to creating and sustaining both the life and the waste of this movement. In 1917 they founded the Association of the Five Oppressed ("the Proletariat, the Nationality, Femininity, Individuality, and [Youth]) and edited the anarchist daily of Petrograd, the *Bourevertnik*, which they had violently wrested from another tendency; they also dreamed up Pan-Anarchism, which was to multiply the "socio-technums" or centers of study and industrial practice. A delirious fantasy, a perpetual dream rising to the heights of lyricism, of healthy practical ideas, much energy, violence, and vehemence, all of it expressed in a language sprinkled with scientific-seeming barbaric neologisms. This is what is found in the literature of yesteryear of these Gordin brothers who, in 1917 and 1918, ceaselessly cast anathema on Lenin. Since then one of them, possessed by the *idée fixe* of a universal language of which he is the inventor and which is written in numbers, the language AO, has become—as he himself proclaims in Moscow through signs posted in his window on the Tverskaya—the "Beobi Man" and addresses lyrical messages to the Third International in cypher. The other, dominating his imagination, not allowing himself to become embittered by the avatars of his personal life, has progressively arrived at forging for himself an original doctrine, one undeniably viable and sane and which I will briefly examine.

"It is necessary that a new, healthy, and real anarchism succeed the destructive anarchism of Bakunin and mutualist anarchism of Kropotkin" (*Through Socialism* 2, May 1921, 41–42). This was Gordin's conclusion: "When the illusions of a vast anarchist movement lost its way amidst disorganization and chaos"; when they understood that destroying is not creating, remembering that at the most somber hours of the October Revolution the anarchist militants "were only able to foresee pillaging and sharing of the existing stock" they erected into a principle that "we must henceforth create and not destroy." "It is the creative spirit that is also a destructive spirit," but the opposite, Bakunin's old formula, is false. And Gordin asks (*Through Socialism* 2) if the necessary preconditions allowing for the formation of a libertarian society in Russia have currently been realized. No. At the height of the movement, "at a time when in certain milieux no one thought of repressing us, when they rather feared our repressions, we did not have a true movement because we lacked sufficient consciousness." In their critique of socialism the anarchists had to "either surrender themselves to a shameless demagogy or limit themselves to an abstract critique unintelligible to the masses." The fact is that in the current phase the revolutionary transformation of societies imposes a transition through socialism. Federalism, that is the division of power, the return to the localism of the Communes of the Middle Ages idealized by Kropotkin, a dogma of decentralization incompatible with the technical necessities of modern industry, an apolitical dogma: Gordin and his friends abandon all this baggage of old ideas, which in their eyes is outdated. They clearly say that they accept the dictatorship of the oppressed of yesterday over the oppressors of yesterday, the indispensable centralization of industry and revolutionary defense, and the organization corresponding to these new ends. They don't fear the nascent might of the socialist state, whose historically ineluctable mission most anarchists refuse to understand. Judging it with more lucidity than even certain of its founders, they hope for the state to reach its apogee. This must be the next stage of the revolution (or of evolution). The state that will come out of the class war and dictatorship will concentrate within it all the forces of social oppression against the individual. It will truly incarnate society, in this way assuming before the individual the responsibility for all the evil the collective can do. In this way, in the dialectic of history, "the state will dig its own grave, and all we have to do is hope for its victory" (Gordin, June 1921). And it's the individuality of the free man that will assume the succession of the state that died a masculine and normal death.

Gordin foresees and hopes for the victory of the Third International, whose goal is to create a federation of soviet republics. This stage, too, is necessary.

In truth, I see no contradiction between these ideas and those of communism. These anarchists have ended up as communists. And it is precisely this that some reproach them bitterly for. But what, it might be asked, distinguishes them as anarchists? By their philosophy of the personality. What is too often lacking in communist ideology is a philosophy of the individual for the individual's sake.

In issue number 3 of his review, Gordin lays out how and why he approves the New Economic Policy of the Soviet government. Revolutionary idealism, at first absolute, believes itself all-powerful.

It dares. It wants to dare. It believes it has victory in its grasp. But the battle forces it to become realistic by creating armies. The economic battle, difficult in another way, wrests from it other concessions. "Do people imagine that socialism could emerge victorious with one blow?"

Most often what Gordin writes—when it's not in verse—is well thought through and well expressed. I briefly and a bit broadly summarized his ideas. Gordin is the creator of a libertarian ideology contrary on many points to the traditions of the anarchist movement. It is odd to note that it is in perfect agreement with communism, even though it is the work of an adversary of communism who bitterly fought it from the first hour.

"We shouldn't be afraid to seize power"

At the end of 1920 the government of the United States decided to expel and deport en masse those revolutionary Russian workers whose pro-Soviet enthusiasm had become too turbulent. In one night their most militant organization was decimated by the police. Four to five thousand arrests carried out simultaneously broke the Union of Russian Workers of America, a federation of anarchist-leaning organizations that counted somewhere between seven and ten thousand members. After having imprisoned a certain number, and after killing some as a result of brutality, more than two hundred militants considered the leaders of foreign Bolshevism in America were put on ships for Russia. And yet most were anarchists. Notably, among them were found the members of the Committee of Russian Workers of America, whose former secretary now belongs to the Russian Communist Party. Upon contact with the harsh realities of the revolution many of these comrades found themselves completely disoriented. Some of them, after numerous intellectual experiences, nevertheless managed to conclude. Along with Comrade Perkus, a young theoretician and initiator in America of the movement of Soviet emigrants, they founded the Union of Russian Anarchist Workers Repatriated from America, whose platform has already been published overseas.

Without reticence they accept the principle of the revolutionary dictatorship. The even think that the anarchists must, if need be, exercise it. In fact, we read in their platform:

Concerning the attitude of the anarchists of Europe and America before the revolution and when the latter occurs, we think that they must not fear seizing power or dictatorship or the use, during the period of revolutionary transition from slavery to freedom, of both constraint and persuasion, if they don't want to remain outside of and dragging behind the movement, and if, on the contrary, they want to lead it.

The lines that follow this state that the forms of revolutionary dictatorship will obviously vary with the degree of intellectual and economic evolution of the different countries, the quantitative, and especially qualitative value of the organized masses.

If the anarchists, not understanding this, fail in their task, "it will be necessary for other groups, perhaps translating to a lesser degree the aspirations of the masses, to accomplish this task, as happened in Russia."

The principle of dictatorship must be accepted because "organized violence is much more rational that chaotic and arbitrary violence"; because in social revolutions, which are above all the work of "united, convinced, conscious, energetic, and advanced revolutionary minorities" there is no other final recourse than violence. "Precursors of a superior society, the anarchists, in the period of humanity's great revolutionary struggles, must adopt a realistic and positive attitude."

The realization of the anarchist ideal being conditioned by two factors, the intellectual and moral development of the masses and the technical development of industry, "it is essential to substitute for small-scale private industry a vast economy based on collective labor and to reeducate the worker."

In other words, anarchy, these anarchists say, will not be the fruit of chaotic violence. After the revolution—victorious through organized violence—it will be based on economic development and intellectual and moral culture.

"In this critical moment of history we must not have a hostile, but only a critical, attitude toward the extreme artisans of collectivism, the Communist-Bolsheviks."

For my part, I do not admit, despite a few deplorable exaggerations, that communism desires the absorption of the individual by the collective being. On the contrary, I am only a communist—of libertarian philosophy and ethics—because I see no possibility for the future liberation of the individual outside of a communism called on to evolve a great deal (once it has emerged victorious). To claim that communist ideology leaves no room for the individual thus seems to me to be inexact, though there are unquestionably communists who understand it in this way.

In fact, the Russian Anarchist Workers Repatriated from America feel themselves to be so close to the Communists that they feel the need to explain, at the end of their manifesto, why they don't join the party.

It is "in order not to lose our personality, and because Marxism only admits material economic forces, while our thought is also founded on the awareness of the personality, on individualism."

I understand that under the current forceful organization of the Russian Communist Party, a party in power, a party of the mobilized that we can fairly compare to a vast army of volunteers in service to the revolution and led by intransigent Marxists, these comrades fear they can't assert themselves as much as they'd like. I will only remark here that the question should rather be posed in this way: Is it preferable, for the salvation of the revolution, that the personalities of the militants be affirmed to the detriment of cohesion, of the whole, of the unity in action of the movement, or that a sacrifice be sweepingly made of them to the organization? History has answered this question (contrary to our past hopes) by necessitating the formation of a powerful party organization. What is more, the American comrades present us with a narrow Marxism. G. Sorel, B. Croce, K. Liebknecht, who I think delved far deeper into Marxism, understand it completely differently. I could also quote a speech of Trotsky's, given at the Third Congress of the Communist International, where he spoke of the value of personalities and the importance of the will to win. Perhaps there are indeed Marxists whose intelligent doctrine is the one revealed to us by the Russian anarchists of America. But thank God, it is not those Marxists who are making and will make communism.

Become communists de facto, the anarchists would surely find it easier to preserve their autonomy by remaining outside the party. I am not arguing this. I merely state the weakness of the reproaches they addressed to their Marxist brethren.

The platform of the Russian Anarchists Repatriated from America is signed by seven militants: Perkus, Oradovsky,[6] Derkatch, Lessiga,[7] Feinland, Bukhanov, and Ryoukov.

---

6   Markus Naumovich Oradovsky (ca. 1895–?).
7   Arthur Lessiga (ca. 1889–?).

Conclusion

And so, Russian anarchists, after four years of revolutionary experiences, say:

"No dictatorship, but all power!"

"We want a strong organization!"

"The road to anarchy passes through socialism."

"We shouldn't be afraid to seize power."

And the most remarkable thing is that the men who express themselves in this way are men belonging to different groups, divided among themselves by questions of principle, and who are often enemies. Coincidence? In sociology there are neither coincidences nor chance. The life of ideas has its own logic. *Le Libertaire* of Paris and the *Réveil* can stick to their old formulas. The Russian anarchists all more or less clearly feel that they must find something else. Through the quotations brought together in these articles we have seen that their current thought, when it will be better known overseas, will greatly surprise those who think they share their ideas.

The tendencies I have studied, however different they might be, have various common characteristics:

1. They agree in noting the organizational and creative incapacity of the Russian anarchists, of their practical insufficiencies in 1917–18, i.e., at a decisive historical moment;

2. They are deliberately undertaking a veritable revision of anarchism. In order to appreciate the importance of this we should refer to the discussions on organization and syndicalism at the International Anarchist Conference of Amsterdam. Among the Russians I quoted, almost nothing remains of the dogmas of the time;

3. They recognize the need for a serious organization;

4. In principle, they admit the principle of revolutionary dictatorship.

These are the starting points of an evolution.

But this is proving itself to be difficult. Too many old things, I mean things of the old world, hinder those Russian anarchists who want to advance at the same pace as life. In the publications I quoted entire columns are, alas, given over to sometimes lyrical, sometimes metaphysical extravagances in both prose and in poetry. Universalism, interindvidualism, bioximism (there is actually a bioximism!)—how many superfluous "-isms." Other columns are dedicated to the mutual praise of members of the same chapel, and a third to the merciless denigration of the excommunicated belonging to the chapel next door. Old, old customs that are as little anarchist as possible. We would like to see the anarchists, the free-thinkers par excellence, practice a little tolerance in their little groups, admit their opponent's good faith, and not supplement arguments with major excommunications. It is true that this mainly concerns the press of the two Universalist groups, both busy raining down invective on each other.

The sectarian spirit that betrays itself among the most "advanced"— if I can use the term—Russian anarchists can only hider the evolution of nuclei already weak and isolated.

Will they succeed in creating movement of some importance in the near future? I don't think so. It is too late. Events are unfurling in Russia without the anarchists, totally outside an influence they were able to either exercise or sustain. They will only be able to think of reconquering it when they will have competed their internal transformation.

But the impulsive, the embittered, the unpolished rebels who want anarchy immediately, and who are as ready to suffer martyrdom for that cause as to exchange blows or shots, form an incoherent, scattered anarchist majority that it is difficult to stand up to, given that, as it is dominated by feelings and instincts, it is pretty much unamenable to education. I don't think that the best elements of the movement will soon succeed in swimming against this current.

When we see the disaster of Russian anarchism during the revolution, the birth of these tendencies nevertheless appears to be something that is cause for joy. Sooner or later there will be—or at least I hope there will be—a new anarchism, one renewed and freed, thanks to its contact with the experience of the revolution, from its elementary utopianism and equipped with a practical and concrete program that will form organizations capable of assuming responsibilities and pursuing well-thought-out actions. This anarchism will doubtless be very close to Marxist communism. In any case it is its ally before and during the revolution, and at other moments its fraternal adversary. Knowing that in the aftermath of the revolution the libertarian spirit must be a grand, beneficent social force, it will understand that during the Civil War the anarchists must not be strictly a disorganizing element, strictly rebellious, demanding the absolute, but on the contrary must assume, even at the price of a few concessions to reality, the task of educating and organizing the masses that falls to them in the vast communist movement.

Moscow, September 4, 1921

(*Bulletin Communiste* 48–49, November 3, 1921)

Call for an Alliance with the Anarchists in Spain

(Editor's note: This letter was sent to the International Secretariat of the Fourth international via Trotsky's son, Leon Sedov. It was never acted on.)

AUGUST 8, 1936

Dear L.L. [Sedov]

This letter is addressed to the IS [International Secretariat]

At this moment a serious conflict is in preparation in Spain between anarchists, syndicalists, and Marxists. The first group has enormous influence over half the Spanish working class (the most active half) and has a considerable superiority in Catalonia, a region with a decisive strategic importance.

The persecution of the anarchists in the USSR, the fact that for some time they—as well as the syndicalists—have been deprived of any freedom of thought and even of existence, has created a poisoned psychology in the Spanish anarchists and syndicalists. Many of them are firmly determined to rapidly carry out armed struggle against the Marxists rather than allow them to accede to power.

In fact, this fight has already begun (the assassination of the socialist Desiderio Trillon, etc.). It could become the suicide of the revolution. I think that this must be prevented by all means. I think that the Fourth International must and can take the first step in reconciliation and an alliance with the anarchists. With this goal, I propose that the International Secretariat as soon as possible write an appeal to the anarchists and syndicalists containing a series of firm proposals and commitments.

They are:

1. Declaring that we, revolutionary Marxists, considering revolutionary discipline indispensable for the victory of the working class, accept responsibility for the measures taken during the Russian Revolution against the anarchist who placed the revolution in danger; we recall that many Russian anarchists understood and even approved these measures at the time, but we declare at the same time that that we consider as incompatible with the Soviet system and in general with the interests of the proletarian revolution the stifling of the anarchist and syndicalist currents of the revolutionary movement—with whom we want to cooperate in the fight against the common enemy—and depriving them of the right to existence. We want to vie with them in the organizing of a new society while carrying out against them an implacable ideological struggle, never forgetting we are class brothers.

2. On these bases we propose to the anarchist and syndicalist brothers a fraternal alliance and union.

3. We take a solemn vow to fight for the establishing of a true workers' democracy, for true freedom of thought and organization in the ranks of the revolution, joined to a true discipline in combat and production. We remember that the dictatorship of the proletariat is a dictatorship against the bourgeoisie and freedom for the workers.

I think that a brief and clearly written statement in this spirit would be something completely new in the current atmosphere in Spain, where it would bring a breath of fresh air and, taken as a veritable charter for action, would play a considerable positive role, even more so in that neither the Socialists nor the Stalinists know how to or are able to speak in this way. Given that the conflict has already broken out there is no time to waste.

(I learned from a private source that the Communist and Socialist militias aren't allowing anarchists to enter Spain. They cross the border at their own crossing points and a mobilization if anarchist forces to fight the Marxists has already occurred, with the following watchword: "We won't allow what happened to Russia to happen here. If necessary we will kill them all first.")

Please acknowledge receipt.
I shake your hand
VS

The petty squabbles of the French groups produce an extremely painful impression. They make me sick to my stomach.

Once More: Kronstadt

(Editor's note: This article was written in April 1938 and appeared in the July 1938 issue of the magazine New International, *then published by the Socialist Workers Party.)*

I receive your review with great pleasure. It is obviously the best revolutionary Marxian organ today. Believe me that all my sympathies are with you and that if it is possible for me to be of service to you, it will be most willingly rendered.

I shall someday reply to the articles of Wright and L.D. Trotsky on Kronstadt. This great subject merits being taken up again thoroughly and the two studies that you have published are far, very far, from exhausting it. In the very first place, I am surprised to see our comrades Wright and L.D. Trotsky employ a reasoning which, it seems to me, we ought to beware of and refrain from. They record that the drama of Kronstadt, 1921, is evoking commentaries at once from the Social Revolutionists, the Mensheviks, the anarchists, and others; and from this fact, natural in an epoch of ideological confusion, of the revision of values, of the battles of sects, they deduce a sort of amalgam. Let us be distrustful of amalgams and of such mechanical reasoning. They have been too greatly abused in the Russian Revolution and we see where it leads. Bourgeois liberals, Mensheviks, anarchists, revolutionary Marxists consider the drama of Kronstadt from different standpoints and for different reasons, which it is well and necessary to bear in mind, instead of lumping all the critical minds under a single heading and imputing to all of them the same hostility toward Bolshevism.

The problem is, in truth, much vaster than the event of Kronstadt, which was only an episode. Wright and L.D. Trotsky support a highly simple thesis: that the Kronstadt uprising was objectively counterrevolutionary and that the policy of Lenin's and Trotsky's Central Committee at that time was correct before, during and after. Correct this policy was, on a historic and moreover grandiose scale, which permitted it to be tragically and dangerously false, erroneous, in various specific circumstances. That is what it would be useful and courageous to recognize today instead of affirming the infallibility of a general line of 1917–1923. There remains broadly the fact that the uprisings of Kronstadt and other localities signified to the party the absolute impossibility of persevering on the road of War Communism. The country was dying of bitter-end state-ification. Who then was right? The Central Committee which clung to a road without issue or the masses driven to extremities by famine? It seems to me undeniable that Lenin at that time committed the greatest mistake of his life. Need we recall that a few weeks before the establishment of the NEP, Bukharin published a work on economics showing that the system in operation was indeed the first phase of socialism? For having advocated, in his letters to Lenin, measures of reconciliation with the peasants, the historian Rozhkov had just been deported to Pskov. Once Kronstadt rebelled, it had to be subdued, no doubt. But what was done to forestall the insurrection? Why was the mediation of the Petrograd anarchists rejected? Can one, finally, justify the insensate and, I repeat, abominable massacre of the vanquished of Kronstadt who were still being shot in batches in the Petrograd prison three months after the end of the uprising?

They were men of the Russian people, backward perhaps, but who belonged to the masses of the revolution itself.

L.D. Trotsky emphasizes that the sailors and soldiers of the Kronstadt of 1921 were no longer the same, with regard to revolutionary consciousness, as those of 1918. That is true. But the party of 1921—was it the same as that of 1918? Was it not already suffering from a bureaucratic befoulment which often detached it from the masses and rendered it inhuman toward them? It would be well to reread in this connection the criticisms against the bureaucratic regime formulated long ago by the Workers' Opposition; and also to remember the evil practices that made their appearance during the discussion on the trade unions in 1920. For my part, I was outraged to see the maneuvers which the majority employed in Petrograd to stifle the voice of the Trotskyists and the Workers' Opposition (who defended diametrically opposed theses).

The question which dominates today the whole discussion is, in substance, this: When and how did Bolshevism begin to degenerate?

When and how did it begin to employ toward the toiling masses, whose energy and highest consciousness it expressed, nonsocialist methods which must be condemned because they ended by assuring the victory of the bureaucracy over the proletariat?

This question posed, it can be seen that the first symptoms of the evil date far back. In 1920, the Menshevik social-democrats were falsely accused, in a communiqué of the Cheka, of intelligence with the enemy, of sabotage, etc. This communiqué, monstrously false, served to outlaw them. In the same year, the anarchists were arrested throughout Russia, after a formal promise to legalize the movement and after the treaty of peace signed with Makhno had been deliberately torn up by the Central Committee which no longer needed the Black Army. The revolutionary correctness of the totality of a policy cannot justify, in my eyes, these baneful practices. And the facts that I cite are unfortunately far from being the only ones.

Let us go back still further. Has not the moment come to declare that the day of the glorious year of 1918 when the Central Committee of the party decided to permit the Extraordinary Commissions to apply the death penalty *on the basis of secret procedure, without hearing the accused who could not defend themselves*, is a black day? That day the Central Committee was in a position to restore or not restore an Inquisitional procedure forgotten by European civilization. In any case, it committed a mistake. It did not necessarily behoove a victorious socialist party to commit that mistake. The revolution could have defended itself better without that.

We would indeed be wrong to conceal from ourselves today that the whole historical acquisition of the Russian Revolution is being called into question. Out of the vast experience of Bolshevism, the revolutionary Marxists will save what is essential, durable, only by taking up all the problems again from the bottom, with a genuine freedom of mind, without party vanity, without irreducible hostility (above all in the field of historical investigation) toward the other tendencies of the labor movement. On the contrary, by not recognizing old errors, whose gravity history has not ceased to bring out in relief, the risk is run of compromising the whole acquisition of Bolshevism. The Kronstadt episode simultaneously poses the questions of the relations between the party of the proletariat and the masses, of the internal regime of the party (the Workers' Opposition was smashed), of socialist ethics (all Petrograd was deceived by the announcement of a *White* movement in Kronstadt), of humaneness in the class struggle and above all in the struggle within our classes. Finally it puts us to the test of our self-critical capacity.

Unable to reply more thoroughly for the moment to comrades Wright and L.D. Trotsky, I hope you will be good enough to submit this letter to the readers of the *New International*. It will perhaps contribute toward priming a discussion which we ought to know how to bring to a successful issue in a spirit of healthy revolutionary comradeship.

Paris, April 28, 1938

(*New International* 4, no. 7, July 1938)

Kronstadt 1921
Trotsky's Defense, Response to Trotsky

In a note published in America at the end of July, Leon Trotsky has finally spelled out his responsibilities in the Kronstadt episode. The political responsibility, as he has always affirmed, belongs to the Central Committee of the Russian CP, which took the decision to "reduce the rebellion by force of arms if the fortress couldn't be brought to surrender first by peaceful negotiations, and later by an ultimatum." Trotsky adds: "I never spoke of that question [Kronstadt 1921], not that I have anything to hide but, on the contrary, precisely because I have nothing to say.... Personally I didn't participate at all in the crushing of the rebellion, nor in the repression that followed."

Trotsky recalls the differences that separated him from that time on with Zinoviev, the chairman of the Petrograd Soviet. "I remained," he writes, "completely and demonstrably apart from this affair."

It would be only fair to stand by this explanation, after certain personal attacks aimed at Trotsky through bad faith, ignorance, or sectarian spirit. For in history there is room to distinguish between general political responsibility and immediate personal responsibility.[1]

"I don't know," Trotsky writes again, "if there were unnecessary victims. I believe Dzerzhinsky more than his after-the-fact critics ... The conclusions of Victor Serge on this point—third-hand ones—are devoid of all value in my eyes ..." Those of Dzerzhinsky are, for their part, seventh or ninth hand, for the chief of the Cheka didn't go to Petrograd at

---

[1]   Since certain of the attacks to which I allude have come from the anarchist press, permit me here to spell out my ideas with the help of a recent example. The comrades of POUM and the CNT having been persecuted and murdered with impunity in the Spanish Republic, at a time when the CNT participated in various ways in a bourgeois government, the CNT obviously bears a part of political responsibility for these crimes against the working class movement, for which it would nevertheless be unfair to hold its leaders *personally* responsible [Note by Serge in the original].

that time and was only informed through hierarchical channels, about which there would be much to say (and Trotsky knows this better than anyone). As for myself, living in Petrograd I lived among the leaders of the city. I know through eyewitnesses what the repression was. I visited anarchist comrades at the Chpalernaya Prison, imprisoned, by the way, against all good sense, who every night watched the defeated of Kronstadt leave for the polygon. I repeat, the repression was atrocious. According to Soviet historians insurgent Kronstadt had at its disposal around sixteen thousand combatants. A few thousand succeeded in reaching Finland over the ice. The others were massacred in the hundreds, and more likely in the thousands, at the end of the combat or later. Where Dzerzhinsky's statistics, and what are they worth if they exist? The sole fact that Trotsky, at the height of power, didn't feel the need to inform himself with precision concerning this repression of an insurrectionary workers movement, the sole fact that Trotsky didn't know what all ranking communists knew: that they had just committed through inhumanity *a pointless crime* against the proletariat and the peasants—this sole fact, I say, is gravely significant. It is in fact in the realm of repression that the Central Committee of the Bolshevik Party committed, from the very beginning of the revolution, the gravest errors, those which were to most dangerously contribute on one hand to the bureaucratization of the party and the state, and on the other to disarming the masses and, more particularly, the revolutionaries. It is about time that we realized this.

(*La Révolution Prolétarienne*, October 25, 1938)

Anarchist Thought

The Origins: The Industrial Revolution of the Nineteenth Century
The most profound revolution of modern times, carried out in Europe in the first half of the nineteenth century, is almost unnoticed by historians. The French Revolution cleared its path, and the political upheavals that for the most part occurred during the period between 1800 and 1850 contributed to hastening it. The significance of the historic development of that period can be clearly seen: a new mode of production was established equipped with a new technique. In truth, the Industrial Revolution under the First Empire began with the first steam machinery. The locomotive dates from 1830. Looms, which appeared at the beginning of the century, had already led to the formation of an industrial proletariat in centers like Lyon. In a few decades the bourgeoisie, armed with machinery, transformed—often literally—the surface of the globe. Factories were added to manufactories, changing the physiognomy of cities, giving rise to unprecedented growth. Railroads and steamboats modified the notions of time and space that had remained stable since antiquity. With brutal clarity we can see the outlines of new social classes and the bitter struggles that break out between them. The "live working or die fighting" of the Canutes of Lyon signified the appearance of the Fourth Estate, born of despair. Less than twenty years later two young thinkers, known to just a few circles of revolutionaries, would affirm, as Sieyès had for the bourgeoisie in the past, that being nothing the proletariat must be everything, for such is the meaning of the *Communist Manifesto* that Karl Marx and Engels completed in 1847 in Paris and Brussels in wretched hotel rooms.

Europe prepared for the storm of 1848. This world, rich in experience, quietly and violently molded by the consequences of the bourgeois revolution (1789–93 through 1800 . . .) in its political status, radically changed by machinery and the modifications in social structure it accelerates, lived on the conflict of ideas that make one think of the combat of Titans. Germany, Italy, Central Europe, cut up into semifeudal states, had only just entered the path of national unity, as a result of which social aspirations became complicated by Young Italian, Young German, and Young Czech idealism. Russia, which had entered European life during the wars of the First Empire, which brought Alexander I and his Cossacks to Paris, remained an absolute monarchy founded on serfdom. England, on the other hand, where the Industrial Revolution had reached its highest point, was a crowned republic, in which bourgeois millionaires had no less sovereignty than the landlords. In France the traditions of 1789–93 continued to motivate the movements that made that country the laboratory of revolutions. The complexity, the dynamism, and the varied aspects of this time must be taken into account so we can see in it the birth of ours.

Karl Marx and Engels, having come to Paris from Germany, sought to realize the synthesis of German philosophy, the revolutionary experience of France, and the industrial progress of England. In doing so they laid the foundations for scientific socialism. In order to do so they had to refute the individualist assertions of another Young Hegelian, Max Stirner, the author of *The Ego and His Own*, which was a well-reasoned treatise on anarchist individualism. With all his physical frailty, no one better then Max Stirner, who lived and died in obscurity in the Prussian countryside, cultivating his field, alone and misunderstood, even by his wife, and who depicted the Unique becoming conscious of himself in order to resist the social machine. It was in opposing Stirner's ideas that his work helped Marx and Engels, who criticized him in *The German Ideology* by posing the problem of social man. In Paris they met two other founders of anarchism, Proudhon and Bakunin. We can thus see, and this is no real surprise, that the creators of all of revolutionary thought matured in the same combats, were formed by the same sometimes contradictory hopes, rubbed shoulders, understood, esteemed, and enlightened each other before going their separate ways; each obeying his internal law—the reflection of other, more general laws—in order to carry out his own mission.

At this time on ideas became fixed. Stirner's individualist doctrine, if it has few followers, eighty years later doesn't seem susceptible to revision or amending: in the abstract, it is definitive. The doctrine of the *Communist Manifesto* remains today the basis of socialism. Anarchism's gestation period would be longer, since it only reached its contemporary formulation considerably later with Kropotkin, Élisée Reclus, and Malatesta, after 1870 and the end of Bakuninism properly speaking. But the essential lines were laid out by the mid-nineteenth century. How can we not see, in this excerpt from a letter from Proudhon to Karl Marx, dated Lyon, May 17, 1846, one of the first affirmations of the anarchist spirit on the march to socialism:

> If you'd like, let us seek together the laws of society, the ways these laws are realized, and the progress that allows us to discover them. But for God's sake, after having demolished all dogmatisms *a priori*, let us not think in our turn of indoctrinating the people. Let's not fall into the tradition of your compatriot Martin Luther, who, after having overturned Catholic theology, with the use of excommunications and anathemas founded a Protestant theology. Germany has spent three centuries doing nothing but destroying Luther's replastering; let's not set humankind another task through new bungling. With all my heart I applaud your idea of one day examining all opinions. Let's carry out a good and honest polemic. Let's give the world an example of a scholarly and far-sighted tolerance, but because we are at the head of the movement let's not make ourselves the leaders of a new intolerance; let's not set ourselves up as the apostles of a new religion, even if it's a religion of logic and reason. Let us welcome and encourage all protests; let us condemn all exclusions, all mysticisms. We must never look upon a questions as settled, and when we have used our final argument let us start over if necessary, with eloquence and irony. Under these conditions I will enter your association with pleasure; if not, no.

Proudhon, Bakunin, and Marx

Proudhon's *What Is Property?* dates from 1840; *The Philosophy of Poverty* from 1846 (Marx will respond to it with his *Poverty of Philosophy*). With the legalistic but also the practical spirit of the French small artisan, Proudhon defines property as theft, notes in the clearest tones the antagonism between owners and exploited wage earners and deduces from this the need for a social revolution, but immediately seeks refuge in mutualism. Marx would say of him that "the petit bourgeois is a living contradiction," and Blanqui that "Proudhon is only socialist because the illegitimacy of interest." Kropotkin would justify him in these terms: "What did he seek in his mutualist system if not to render capital less offensive despite the maintaining of private property, which he despised with all his heart but considered necessary as a guarantee for the individual against the state." "The revolution that remains to be made," wrote Proudhon, "consists in substituting the economic or industrial regime for the governmental, feudal, and military regime." Most of the arguments that fed the polemic between Marx and Proudhon can still be found in the current arsenal of Marxists and anarchists. The anarchists' aversion for political action, seen as superfluous compared to economic action, the only one of any value, dates from Proudhon. Like many of today's syndicalists, who started out as anarchists and revolutionaries before settling into reformism, Proudhon, in the system he lays out, arrives at a number of reforms aimed at protecting the individual producer that are deduced, not from the study of social development, but from abstract principles based on feelings and morality. Despite himself, this leads the great revolutionary moralist to become a conservative despite himself. "After having shaken up the social system and proclaimed the imminence of the revolution, he ended by safeguarding the current mechanism in a more or less attenuated form. If because of his critique he is classed among the socialists, he remains a petit-bourgeois conservative in the realm of practice." The father of anarchism is also that of reformism.

At the very beginning of his career, Marx refuted Stirner and fought against Proudhon. During the final years of his life he made use of them within the First International to combat Bakunin, another incarnation, one totally indomitable, of the anarchist spirit. Of the minor Russian nobility, an officer in the army of Tsar Nicholas I, sustained by despotism to the point that he could only live for the revolution; a combatant in 1848 in Dresden and Prague; chained to the wall of his cell in Olmütz; turned over to the Tsar and imprisoned in Peter and Paul Fortress and Schlüsselbourg, while he was there wrote a *Confession* addressed to Nicholas I full of prophetic passages; deported to Siberia, from which he escaped; resuming again throughout the West, his life of a revolutionary; disciple and translator of Marx; irreconcilable adversary of Marx; founder of a secret International within the First International; rejected, bitterly fought against, sometimes defamed; in his final years a rioter in Lyon and a conspirator in Bologna, he would only renounce action in the final moments of his life, as he was dying. He changed often, though with a powerful fidelity to himself. This is his definition of anarchy, as he gave it in God and the State: "We reject all forms of legislation, all forms of authority and every privileged, licensed, official, and legal influence, even if it issues from universal suffrage, convinced that it can only be turned to the profit of the dominant and exploiting minority against the interests of the immense enslaved majority."

Let us quote here his little-known opinions concerning Marx and Proudhon. Bakunin writes to Marx in December 1868: "My dear friend. I understand now more than ever that you are right to follow the great path of economic revolution and to urge us to take it as well, detesting those who lose their way in the side street of sometimes nationalist, sometimes political escapades. I am now doing what you have done for the past twenty years . . . My fatherland is henceforth the International, of which you are one of the founders. And so, my dear friend, I am your disciple and proud to be so."

Franz Mehring, in his biography of Marx, quotes the following texts of Bakunin:

> Marx is a serious and profound economic thinker. His immense superiority over Proudhon comes from the fact that he is authentically materialist. Proudhon, despite all his efforts to free himself from the traditions of classical idealism nevertheless remained throughout his life an impenitent idealist falling first under the influence of the Bible and then of Roman law, as I told him six months before his death. And he was always a metaphysician to the tips of his toes. . . . Marx, as a thinker, is on the right path. He established— and this is his essential thesis—that the religious, political, and juridical phenomena of history are not the causes but the consequences of economic development. . . . On the other hand, Proudhon understood and had a better feeling for freedom than did Marx. When he wasn't allowing himself to be seduced by theories and fantasies Proudhon had the instincts of a true revolutionary. He adored Satan and preached anarchy. It is quite possible that Marx will manage to raise himself to a system of freedom more reasonable than that of Proudhon, but he doesn't have the spontaneous power of the latter.

Bakunin was himself sometimes called the incarnation of Satan by his contemporaries. Through all the dissensions, the intrigues, the polemics and maneuvers where no one came off looking good, and which led the International to its destruction, a bit before and a bit after the defeat of the Paris Commune anarchist ideas and sentiments were clarified. Bakunin's influence carried the day over Marx in Spain, Italy, Russia, the Swiss Romande, and partially in Belgium.

To Marx's "authoritarian socialism" Bakunin, with his secret organizations, opposed his "antiauthoritarian socialism," which lays the groundwork for an immediate and direct social revolution. "We refuse to associate ourselves with any political movement that does not have as its immediate and direct goal the total emancipation of the workers." This is also the quarrel between revolutionary romanticism and the nascent workers' movement. While Marx and Engels sought to build a vast international organization of the workers, called upon to progress step-by-step and finally become the most effective instrument of the class struggle, to intervene in political life, and finally to move with irresistible force toward the conquest of power, instituting the dictatorship of the proletariat (a dictatorship against the defeated owning classes and, its other face, broad democracy for the workers), the Bakuninists intended to provoke in the short term the subversion of capitalism from the simple unleashing of popular forces. They believed both in the revolutionary spontaneity of the backward, i.e., unorganized, masses, and the energetic action of minorities. They condemned political action, whose deceit they denounce, by opposing insurrectionary action to it. They denounce as an evil equal to capital the state and the principle of authority from which it proceeds. To state centralization Bakunin opposed federalism (not without centralizing their own organization). Finally, Bakunin, who seems to have never truly understood Marx, in certain regards was unable to shake specifically Russian ideas concerning the role of the underworld in the coming revolution of the underworld, the déclassés, of outlaws and bandits. He attributes a useful and important function to them. In fact, in vast, peasant Russia banditry was often a sporadic form of revolutionary protest against despotism. And the déclassés, nobles, and petits-bourgeois that had gone over to the people's cause began to form a revolutionary intelligentsia. Marx, on the contrary, learning from the experience of the industrial countries, knew that the lumpenproletariat, the subproletariat in rags that constituted the rabble of the big cities, far from being by nature a revolutionary factor, is infinitely corruptible and unstable, i.e., inclined to serve reaction. He based his hopes on the organized working classes and not on the unleashing of the mob. In The State and Anarchy Bakunin was indignant that the "peasant population which . . . doesn't enjoy the sympathy of the Marxists and finds itself at the lowest level of culture," according to Marx's schema of revolution would "probably [be] governed by the proletariat of the cities and factories." In absolutist and semifeudal Russia the poorest peasantry is, in fact a factor for revolution, one whose capacities Bakunin overestimates. And since there was hardly a proletariat, we can understand the anarchist's error. Marx, on the other hand, commenting on these lines, rightly observes that in Western Europe the small-holding peasantry "causes every workers' revolution to fail, as they've done to the present day in France," and will in the future impose government policy on it. "Bakunin would like," he notes, "for the European social revolution, based on capitalist production, to be accomplished at the level of the agriculture of the pastoral Russian and Slavic people."

It should be noted that Bakuninist anarchism only took root in agricultural countries, where there was no real proletariat: Russia, Spain, and Italy. He was equally influential at a few points where, having ideas similar to those of the libertarian and mutualist ideas of Proudhon, it became the ideology of small-scale artisans in Paris, the Swiss Romande, and in Belgium. As soon as industrial development became more marked in these countries anarchism surrendered its preeminence in the revolutionary movement to Marxist workers' socialism.

Kropotkin, Reclus, Malatesta

Bakunin died in 1876. The three heads that would rethink the problem anew are already ready to assume his succession. Prince Peter Kropotkin, officer, traveler, and geographer connected with Russian revolutionary circles, fell under the Bakuninist influence, and studied Fourier, Saint-Simon and Chernyshevsky. He escaped from the Peter and Paul Fortress to which, under the police state of the Russian Empire, any disinterested ideas inevitably lead. Élisée Reclus, a young scientist with a passion for knowledge about the earth, passed through the battalions of the Commune, saw Duval executed, and marched, a dusty-faced prisoner, along the road to Versailles. Errico Malatesta was an Italian worker. With them anarchist communism at the end of the century achieves an astounding intellectual clarity, a shining moral height. The workers' movement was weighed down with scoria and stuck in the mud in a capitalist society in a period of expansion. Vast union organizations and powerful mass parties, of which German Social Democracy is the best example, in reality became part of a regime they claimed to combat. Socialism became bourgeois, even in its ideas, which deliberately suppressed Marx's revolutionary predictions. It installed itself in capitalist prosperity during the blessed era when the dividing up of the world—that is, the countries that produce primary matter and markets—not having been completed, commerce and finance could believe that they were destined for endless progress. The working-class aristocracies and the political and union bureaucracies set the tone for working-class demands that were either toned down or reduced to a purely verbal revolutionism. It was a time of nothing but opportunism, parliamentarism, reformism, Bernstein's revision of socialism, Millerand's ministerialism, and political schemes. Jaurès's generous intelligence didn't prevent him from accepting the presence in Waldeck-Rousseau's cabinet of the socialist Millerand alongside the executioner of the Commune, General Marquis de Gallifet. Doctrinal intransigence, when it manifests itself in a Kautsky or a Guesde, isn't able to swim against the current; it remains theoretical. And even more, off-putting, for the profound life *manqué* has its formulas. Moreover, these abstract formulations are repellent, since they are completely out of touch with the profundity of life. Imagine how this state of affairs would affect personal life: that counts more than is people usually think. The militant has given way to the functionary and the political man, and the political man is often nothing but a politician. This socialism that has lost its revolutionary soul—more than once having sold it for a plate of lentils served on a butter plate—can it satisfy the all of the working class?

The proletariat is made up of strata of poorly paid workers, manual laborers and socially deprived professions (on this subject there will even be outlined a theory of major and minor professions), immigrants come from industrially backward nations, the déclassés, and cultured artisans threatened with proletarianization. In short, many worried and dissatisfied people for whom there is no capitalist prosperity and who, as a result of this, must still confront, in all its harshness, the problem of revolution and, along with that, that of the life of revolutionaries. Kropotkin, Élisée Reclus, Malatesta (and soon Jean Grave, Sébastien Faure, Luigi Fabbri, and Max Nettlau) provide them with a virile ideology, whose unquestionable merit is that of being inseparable from personal life. Anarchism is as much as a doctrine of social emancipation, a rule of conduct. We see in this a profoundly healthy reaction to the corruption of socialism at the end of the nineteenth century.

No more than it can be considered in itself, detached from its social content, can an ideology be separated from its moral content, from what we would today call its mystique. The theory of communist anarchism, though Kropotkin and Reclus showed great care in tying it to science, proceeds less from knowledge, from the scientific spirit, than from an idealistic aspiration. It's a utopianism armed with knowledge, and of a knowledge of the mechanism of the modern world much less objective, less scientific than that of Marxism. It is also an optimism of desperate déclassés, as was attested to by the bombs of Émile Henry and Ravachol.

From the observing of social iniquity and the movement toward collective forms of property, Kropotkin (*The Conquest of Bread, Words of a Rebel*) deduced the need for revolution. The latter must be made against capital and the state; the society of tomorrow will be communist and federalist, a federation of free communes made up of multiple associations of free workers. In *Mutual Aid*, one of his most remarkable books, Kropotkin strives to demonstrate that throughout time solidarity was the basis of social life. The communes of the *belles époques* of the Middle Ages, which had no need of a state, appeared to him to prefigure the future communes of a decentralized, stateless society. How should one work for the revolution? Anarchist communism rejected political action and only after years of internal struggles would it accept union activity. More than to social classes, it appeals to men of good will, to the conscience more than to the economic interests of the masses. Living in accordance with their ideal of free and disinterested men, the anarchists will awaken the masses' spirit of revolt and solidarity and will give rise in them to a new consciousness, will unleash their creative forces, and the revolution will occur the day the masses will have understood . . .

Idealism
Their writings produce a strange impression of naïve intelligence, moral energy, faith, and, it must be said, blindness.

> In order to resolve the social problem for the benefit of all there is only one means: revolutionarily expel the government; revolutionarily expropriate the owners of social wealth; place everything at the disposal of all and see to it that all forces, all capacities, all good the will existing among men act to meet the needs of all (Malatesta, *Anarchy*).

I didn't arbitrarily cut up a text; there is no context. Affirmations of this kind are scattered throughout anarchist publications. As for how this is to be accomplished, there's not a word of explanation. Let's take a look at the *Anarchist Encyclopedia*, published in Paris a few years ago. On the first page:

> Well-being for all!
> Freedom for all!
> Nothing through constraint, everything through free agreement!
> This the ideal of the anarchists; there is no other that is more precise, more humane, more elevated!

Sébastien Faure's sociology proceeds from the following observations:

1. The individual seeks happiness
2. Society's goal is to obtain it for him.
3. The best form of society is that which is closest to this goal.

From this is deduced, through the simplest mechanism of logical reasoning, the doctrine of universal harmony. Grotius, Mably, Helvetius, Diderot, Morelly, Stuart Mill, Bentham, and Buchner are quoted, and it ends with Benoît Malon: "The happiness of the greatest number through science, justice, goodness, and moral improvement: No more vast or humane ethical purpose can be found."

No doubt, no doubt, one would be tempted to object, if we weren't disarmed by this passion for the public good, determined to draw from within itself an entire edifice of reasoning behind which reality would disappear; but again, how should we go about this?

Sébastien Faure's conclusion has a prophetic tone and nothing more:

> Absolutely everywhere the spirit of revolt is replacing the spirit of submission. The vivifying and pure breath of freedom has arisen; it is on the march and nothing will stop it. The moment approaches when, violent, impetuous, and terrible, it will blow like a hurricane and will carry away all authoritarian institutions like wisps of straw. This is the way evolution occurs. And it guides humanity toward anarchy.

The old militant wrote these lines at the end of a long life of combat, at a moment when totalitarian regimes were imposing themselves through both counterrevolution and socialist revolution; where it was no longer a question of economic plans, of guided economies, of democratic dictatorship and authoritarian democracy.

In fact as in theory, the anarchist is anti-religious, anti-capitalist (capitalism is the current historic phase of property), and anti-statist. It carries out a triple combat against authority; it spares blows against neither the state, nor property, nor religion. It want to suppress all three of them. We want to abolish not only all forms of authority, but we also want to destroy them all simultaneously, and we proclaim that this total and simultaneous destruction is indispensable.

From a scientific point of view this doctrine of agitation is a clear regression from the optimistic syntheses of Kropotkin and Élisée Reclus, which arrive at an ethics and a libertarian socialism founded on the knowledge of historic evolution. (Philosophical optimism, moreover, has no need for justification; it is an essential idea and well rooted in us.) We are witnessing a decline in anarchism which, since the World War, has not produced a single ideologue comparable to those of the older generation. The celebrated militants of today—Rudolf Rocker, Emma Goldman, Luigi Bertoni, Sébastien Faure, E. Armand, Max Nettlau, Voline, Vladimir Barnach, and Aron Baron—are men of the prewar period. Men of action have gone over to syndicalism.

Christian Anarchism, Individualism
Two particular forms of anarchist thought merit study, Christian anarchism and Individualism, which have a point in common: "Salvation lies within you." Tolstoy sometimes called himself a "Christian anarchist." The spirit of revolt against all injustice sometimes affirms itself as the nonviolent resistance to evil. All that's needed is a propitious social environment, like that of Russian or Dutch religious sects.

In the past I lived through the experience of French individualist anarchism, one similar to other analogous movements, notably in the United States where Italians, studying Stirner, quoting Ibsen, inspired by Josiah Warren, Benjamin Tucker and Émile Armand, published a grand paper with the proud title *Nihil*. Allow me to quote here a few notes I published on this subject in *Esprit*:

> Anarchism swept us away completely because it both demanded everything of us and offered us everything. There was no remotest corner of life that it failed to illumine; at least so it seemed to us. A man could be a Catholic, a Protestant, a Liberal, a Radical, a Socialist, even a syndicalist, without in any way changing his own

life, and therefore life in general. It was enough for him, after all, to read the appropriate newspaper; or, if he was strict, to frequent the café associated with whatever tendency claimed his allegiance. Shot through with contradictions, fragmented into varieties and sub-varieties, anarchism demanded, before anything else, harmony between deeds and words (which, in truth, is demanded by all forms of idealism, but which they all forget as they become complacent). That is why we adopted what was (at that moment) the extremest variety, which by vigorous dialectic had succeeded, through the logic of its revolutionism, in discarding the necessity for revolution. To a certain extent we were impelled in that direction by our disgust with a certain type of rather mellow, academic anarchism, whose Pope was Jean Grave in *Les Temps Nouveaux*. Individualism had just been armed by our hero Albert Libertad . . .

His teaching, which we adopted almost wholesale, was: "Don't wait for the revolution. Those who promise revolution are frauds just like the others. Make your own revolution, by being free men and living in comradeship." Obviously I am simplifying, but the idea itself had a beautiful simplicity. Its absolute commandment and rule of life was: "Let the old world go to blazes." From this position there were naturally many deviations. Some inferred that one should "live according to Reason and Science," and their impoverished worship of science, which invoked the mechanistic biology of Félix le Dantec, led them on to all sorts of tomfoolery, such as a saltless, vegetarian diet and fruitarianism and also, in certain cases, to tragic ends. We saw young vegetarians involved in pointless struggles against the whole of society. Others decided, "Let's be outsiders. The only place for us is the fringe of society." They did not stop to think that society has no fringe, that no one is ever outside it, even in the depth of dungeons, and that their "conscious egoism," sharing the life of the defeated, linked up from below with the most brutal bourgeois individualism.

Finally, others, including myself, sought to harness together personal transformation and revolutionary action, in accordance with the motto of Élisée Reclus: "As long as social injustice lasts we shall remain in a state of permanent revolution." (I am quoting this from memory.) Libertarian individualism gave us a hold over the most intense reality: ourselves. Be yourself. Only, it developed in another "city without escape"—Paris, an immense jungle where all relationships were dominated by a primitive individualism, dangerous in a different way from ours, that of a positively Darwinian struggle for existence. Having bid farewell to the humiliations of poverty, we found ourselves once again up against them. To be yourself would have been a precious commandment and perhaps a lofty achievement, if only it had been possible. It would only have begun to be possible once the most pressing needs of man, those that identify him more closely with the brutes than with his fellow humans, were satisfied. We had to win our food, lodging, and clothing by main force; and after that, to find time to read and think. The problem of the penniless youngster, uprooted or (as we used to say) "foaming at the bit" through irresistible idealism, confronted us in a form that was practically insoluble. Many comrades were soon to slide into what was called "illegalism," a way of life not so much on the fringe of society as on the fringe of morality "We refuse to be either exploiters or exploited," they declared, without perceiving that they were continuing to be both these and, what is more, becoming hunted men. When they knew that the game was up they chose to kill themselves rather than go to jail.

One of them, who never went out without his Browning revolver, told me, "Prison isn't worth living for! Six bullets for the sleuthhounds and the seventh for me! You know, I'm lighthearted." A light heart is a heavy burden. the principle of self-preservation that is in us all found its consequence, within the social jungle, in a battle of One against All.[1]

The social roots of this ideology of young people who've lost all hope can be seen. Some individualists died on the gallows, others in the penal colonies; some preferred to be killed while resisting the police, finding a final satisfaction in delivering the final combat against society on their own. They were made of the stuff of true revolutionaries, but that suffocation era was one of calm saturated with the electricity of the prewar period.

Anarchist thought is connected to bourgeois philosophy through the individualist error. We find two opposing sources in it: proletarian

---

1   This section was later used in a slightly different form in Serge's *Memoirs of a Revolutionary*. This passage is excerpted from Peter Sedgwick's translation (New York: NYRB Classics, 2012), 23–25.

idealism leading to libertarian socialism, and absolute individualism pushing to its ultimate consequences the Social Darwinism of capitalist competition. We can clearly see its connection with the "laissez-faire, laissez-passer," the antistatism, and the individualism of liberal economists, as well as with the Positivist philosophy of a Herbert Spencer (*The Individual against the State*). Bourgeois society lives on individualism until the moment when its disproportionately developed production mechanism ceases to be governable by individuals, trusts and cartels having killed free competition and the class struggle having put property in question. It is then that the masses are discovered, that the need is seen for a better organization of industry, viewed as a whole through central planning. The very notion of the individual or, more accurately, of the person is modified. Man appears to us more social than ever: shaped, enriched or impoverished, diminished or enlarged by his condition; unstable, complex, and even contradictory, for what was called his Self is above all the point of intersection of a multitude of lines of influence. Our notion of the individual is not weakened by this but renewed, placed again in its context. But the individualist anarchism of Émile Armand, behind the times by at least a quarter of a century, still proceeds from affirmations like this one:

> Despite all abstractions, all secular and religious entities, all herd ideals, at the base of all collectivities, societies, associations, and agglomerations; of all ethnic, territorial, moral and religious totalities is found the person-unit, the individual-cell. Without the latter the former would not exist. . . . It is obvious that the individual existed before groups. Society is the product of individual additions.

Nothing is less obvious than the preexistence of the individual in relation to the group: at the very least it is necessary that the family precede it. And we know that the family is gradually freeing itself from the primitive community. Everything leads us to believe that the animal species from which the human species was born were sociable. Society clearly preceded humanity; in any case it preceded the person and the very idea of the individual, just as being necessarily precedes consciousness, just as knowledge grows out of ignorance, and the completed work from the draft.

The individualist anarchism of today, living on outdated ideas, has renounced any revolutionary ambition, a resignation in which we can recognize an admission of weakness. This tendency confines itself to the organization of "outsiders" by paying close attention to the relations between the sexes.

The Test of Revolutions: Bakunin the Professional Revolutionary

Is it proper to judge a doctrine of total revolution by the test of revolution? Bakunin, for whom "the creative spirit is also a creative spirit," had brutally clear ideas about revolutionary practice. The Russian soil inspired an energy in him that nothing could diminish. With him we are far from the vague humanitarian and subversive rhetoric of the recent *Encyclopédie Anarchiste*. (On the other hand, we find something of him in the biography of Durruti.) Bakunin was motivated by the inextinguishable need to transform the world. No effective weapon was inadmissible. An antiauthoritarian, he had a passion for organization. Against and despite Marx, well before Lenin he worked relentlessly at constructing a vast organization of professional revolutionaries in the strict sense of the term: devoted, disciplined, obedient to the "invisible dictator," himself, in order to unleash the tempest. In the First International he invented infiltration, and this was the drama of his International Alliance of Social Democracy—backed up by a secret society—which was to play a decisive role in the collapse of the International (1872).

In studying him one is struck by the continuity of his thought and action. What revolution was he preparing the instrument for at the end of his life? For the one he conceived in 1848. Brupbacher sums up his ideas at that moment:

> For Bohemia he proposed a radical and decisive revolt which, even defeated, would have overturned everything. All the nobles would be driven out, all the ecclesiastics, and all the feudal lords; all domains would have been confiscated and on one hand they would have been divided among the poor peasants, and on the other hand used to cover the costs of the revolution. All the castles were to be destroyed, all the tribunals suppressed, all trials suspended, all mortgages and debts below 1,000 guldens canceled. Such a revolution would have rendered any attempt at restoration impossible, even if it were attempted by victorious reaction, and would also have served as an example to German revolutionaries. Bohemia was to be transformed into a revolutionary camp from which would set out the offensive unleashed by the revolution in all countries. . . .

In Prague they would have created a revolutionary government with unlimited dictatorial powers and assisted by a small number of specialists. Clubs, newspapers, and demonstrations would have been prohibited and revolutionary youth sent into the country-side to carry out agitation and create a military and revolutionary organization. All the unemployed were to be armed and enlisted in a "red" army commanded by former Polish and Austrian officers and non-commissioned officers.

In the "confession" he addressed from the fortress of Schlüsselbourg to Tsar Nicholas I, signed "the repentant sinner," (a few years later he would tell friends in London "I had to free myself from the claws of the bear") he painted a portrait of the future Russian Revolution where all that is missing are the words "dictatorship of the proletariat." He wrote:

> More than elsewhere, I think that in Russia a strong dictatorial power will be necessary, a power that will be exclusively concerned with the elevation and education of the masses. A power free in its leanings and spirit, but free of parliamentary forms; publishing books with free content but without freedom of the press; an authority surrounded by supporters, enlightened by their counsels, and strengthened by their free collaboration, but which is limited by nothing and no one.

We find even here a clear prefiguration of the theory of the withering away of the state that Lenin would formulate in 1917:

> I said that the difference between this dictatorship and monarchical power will consist solely in that the former, in keeping with the spirit of its principles, must aim to render its own existence superfluous, for it will have no other goal than the freedom, independence, and increased maturity of the people.

The Bakuninists in the Spanish Revolution of 1873–74
In Spain in 1873 the Bakuninists passed through a test of fire. Unfortunately, as usually occurs, the disciples weren't the equal of their master, paralyzed by their own slogans. King Amadeo fled and the Carlist insurrection broke out in the Basque region. In most cities spontaneous uprisings assured the intransigent republicans and the Bakuninists an easy victory. Seville, Cordoba, Grenada, Malaga, Cadiz, Alcoy, Valencia, Murcia, and Cartagena declared themselves free communes. The Commune

of Cartagena, or "sovereign canton," was to resist for more than five months, from late July 1873 until January 11, 1874. The revolutionary cantons were put down one after the other. Engels provided an analysis, perhaps partisan, but in any case convincing, of the causes of this defeat that would lead to a monarchic restoration. The Alliancistas—members of Bakunin's Democratic Alliance—rejected political action, abstaining from participation in elections to the Constituent Assembly, "in this way contributing to ensuring that it was almost exclusively bourgeois republicans who were elected." "As soon as events place the proletariat in the front ranks," Engels remarks, "abstention becomes an act of foolishness and the active intervention of the working class an unquestionable necessity." This was not the only act of foolishness. At the height of the struggle the Bakuninists of Barcelona, still averse to the political struggle, called on the workers only for a general strike: they didn't want to seize power. (Victory would have been more or less assured by Barcelona's support, but Barcelona didn't budge.) And *Solidaridad Revolucionario* wrote: "The revolution is on the public squares."

A skirmish forced the Bakuninists to seize power in the manufacturing city of Alcoy. They created a Committee of Public Safety, though their delegates at the Congress of Saint-Imier had decided shortly before this that, "any organization of a so-called provisional or revolutionary political power can only be a new form of deceit and would be as dangerous for the proletariat as the existing governments."

Heavily handicapped by their doctrine, what could they do? They did nothing. Bakunin had just declared himself for partisan warfare against military centralization (*Lettres à un français*, 1870). Each commune fought for itself. The gendarmerie—the Guardia Civil—was able to defeat them one by one. Andalucía was put down in a fortnight. Valencia resisted for two weeks. In all of this the division between Internacionalistas (Marxists) and Alliancistas (Bakuninists, the more numerous) played as baleful a role as the verbal intransigence of the republicans. Engels concluded, "The Bakuninists of Spain clearly showed us how not to make a revolution."

The Russian Revolution
The anarchist influence was often great in Russia at the beginning of the revolution, but events inexorably posed the sole capital question, one for which the anarchists have no response: that of power. The Tsar abdicated in the face of the working class and the insurgent garrison

of Petrograd. Who does power belong to? A Provisional (bourgeois) government is created alongside the workers' soviet. There are two powers. After the July riots Lenin, hidden in a shepherd's hut in Finland, addresses the problem of problems by writing *The State and Revolution*. The anarchist objections concern him every bit as much as the habitual authoritarianism of socialism. These are two fatal shoals. Lenin intends to render justice to the anarchists, formerly treated as bandits by Plekhanov and many other mandarins of international reformism. "Marxism degraded by the opportunists" understands nothing of the problem of the state. Nor does anarchism:

> On these two questions of concrete policy: must the old state machine be demolished and what should it be replaced with, anarchism has brought nothing even a little satisfying. . . . We do not after all differ with the anarchists on the question of the abolition of the state as the aim. We maintain that, to achieve this aim, we must temporarily make use of the instruments, resources, and methods of state power against the exploiters, just as the temporary dictatorship of the oppressed class is necessary for the abolition of classes. Marx chooses the sharpest and clearest way of stating his case against the anarchists: After overthrowing the yoke of the capitalists, should the workers "lay down their arms," or use them against the capitalists in order to crush their resistance? But what is the systematic use of arms by one class against another if not a "transient form" of state? the state?

For "revolution is the most authoritarian thing there is" (Engels). We know Lenin's solution: demolish the old state machine from top to bottom and immediately construct on the rubble a power—a state—radically different and new, one like there's never been, one that the Paris Commune of 1871 seemed to prefigure. A Commune-state with no caste of functionaries, without a police and army distinct from the nation, where the workers would exercise direct power through their local, federated councils. A state consequently decentralized and at the same time equipped with an active central mechanism. A democratic and libertarian state working to prepare its own absorption into the collectivity of labor, but exercising against the expropriated classes a veritable dictatorship in the interests of the proletariat. Lenin wasn't a utopian forging theories: he was inspired by what actually existed in order to draw the largest party toward what should be. This new state already existed alongside, beneath the old one, formed everywhere by the soviets. All that was needed was to consecrate it through the thrust of the final insurrection. All power to the soviets! If the libertarians were to join in with this movement wouldn't they be enormously useful tomorrow, when it will be necessary to protect society from bureaucratic sclerosis? But on the eve of the insurrection of November 7, 1917, the anarchists, whose *Goloss Truda* (*The Voice of Labor*, antisyndicalist organ) was the most widely distributed paper, remained faithful to their negative credo. Five days before the street battles they wrote: "We don't believe in the possibility of accomplishing the social revolution by political methods . . . by the seizing of power."

But what then is to be done? What is to be done? They say, in the same article, that it is necessary to "open new horizons to the masses, to humanity that are creators of the revolution."

Yes, but how? And in the first place, what are they themselves going to do, the Bolshevik insurrection being ready? The syndicalist anarchist group declared that it was adopting a "negative attitude" toward the political action being prepared, but is determined, "If the action of the masses is unleashed, to participate in it with the greatest energy."

At that moment the anarchist solutions, based on the "creative labor of the masses" of the moment, were worth nothing, but their revolutionary spirit didn't allow them to completely abdicate. They grudgingly followed the movement.

One of the most serious of them relates in these terms his impressions of the evening of the proletarian revolution:

Around 11:00 p.m. . . . . I found myself on one of the streets of Petrograd. It was dark and peaceful. In the distance sporadic gunfire could be heard. Suddenly, an armored vehicle sped past me. From within the vehicle a hand threw out a large packet of sheets of paper, which flew off in all directions. I bent down and picked one up. It was an appeal from the new government to the workers and peasants announcing the fall of Kerensky and, on the bottom, the list of the new government of "people's commissars," Lenin at its head. A complex feeling of sadness, of anger, of disgust and, at the same time, a kind of ironic satisfaction took hold of me. "These imbeciles, if they're not simply demagogic imposters," I thought. "They must think that they're carrying out a social revolution like this! Well, they'll see, and the masses are going to learn a good lesson."

"According to the anarchist thesis," Voline continues, "it was the working masses themselves who must by their broad and powerful action set themselves to solving the reconstructive problems of the social revolution."

All socialists are in agreement with this thesis, which is nothing but the paraphrase of their common slogan: the emancipation of the workers is the task of the workers themselves. But when is able to only formulate this general affirmation in a country that has been turned completely topsy-turvy, then one has reduced oneself to impotence. It's not enough to have needs and aspirations to transform society: one must have knowledge, clear ideas, the capacity to organize and sacrifice. Did the Russian masses as a whole have a sufficient degree of revolutionary consciousness and capacity? Anarchist theory, depending strictly on the spontaneity of the masses, would have been correct in a country so advanced that before even abolishing private ownership of the means of production the workers would have been penetrated with a socialist mentality and equipped with an education rendering them capable of administering production. But this was far from the case in Russia. The masses knew what they didn't want: despotism and exploitation. In broad terms they knew what they wanted: peace, land, bread, and freedom. But all the revolutionary parties combined (and there were no unions of any influence under the *ancien régime*), bringing together the most conscious, the most devoted, the most educated sectors of the population, formed only a tiny percentage. If we grant them a half a million members and sympathizers—of unequal value, for these parties grew vertiginously in a few months—represented an activist minority of about 0.3 percent. Without the Bolshevik organization it is extremely likely that the feeble revolutionary spontaneity of the masses would have been promptly repressed by another social minority, that of the counterrevolution led by the generals. The dictatorship of the proletariat saved Russia from a military dictatorship.

One would seek in vain in the abundant anarchist literature of the period for a single practical proposal. There are nothing there but lyrical affirmations and idealistic demands. How to ensure the functioning of the transport system, make sure the bakeries function, repress the officers' conspiracies? It was necessary to act immediately. A few anarchists, soon condemned by most of their comrades, entered the soviets, where their taste for freedom could be so useful. Most just pouted. When the peace of Brest-Litovsk had to be signed because the front had disintegrated, because the Tsar's peasant army no longer wanted to fight (here the spontaneity of the masses manifested itself with abundant clarity), because they had attempted the experiment called for by Trotsky of "neither peace nor war" and seen the Austro-Germans advance wherever they pleased without encountering any resistance, the anarcho-syndicalists of Petrograd—the *Goloss Truda*, with Voline—refused to recognize the odious treaty and preached partisan warfare. They even carried it out in the marshes of the west, abandoning their newspaper and their influence in the capital. They based all their hope on "the revolutionary spirit, the light of the world." The phrase is lovely. Except the revolutionary spirit, not being disincarnate, is nourished with bread and can't make war without artillery.

In their daily paper *Anarchy*, the Moscow anarchists, led by the Gordin brothers, professed an exclusively humanitarian faith. They had hundreds if not thousands of armed Black Guards who had clubs at their disposal that were veritable citadels. Organized in several groups without common discipline, in their press they denounced the actions of their irresponsible members, without succeeding in putting a halt to them. They declared themselves in principle "against the Soviets, being against all states," but in reality formed a small state within the state, turbulent and too well armed. They were disarmed by force, almost without combat, on the night of August 11–12, 1918, by order of Trotsky and Dzerzhinsky. The Black Guards disappeared; the press and the groups vegetated.

Nestor Makhno

Russian anarchism nevertheless demonstrated amazing vitality, but only far from the great industrial centers, particularly in the agricultural regions of Ukraine. It was there, between the Don and the Dnieper, in Gulai-Pole that in the summer of 1918 a former anarchist prisoner, Nestor Makhno formed one of the countless bands of insurgent peasants who carried out partisan warfare against the Austro-Germans. The entire Ukraine had risen up; the demobilization provided them with an abundance of arms, it had its wheat to defend and its freedom to conquer. Makhno also fought against the National Directorate of Symon Petliura. Defending the independence of the peasants he would soon fight against the Reds, that is, against the centralized power of the Soviets. Defending the revolution he relentlessly harassed the Whites, commanded by Denikin and then Wrangel. It must be said that his

Black Army rendered the Russian Revolution inestimable service. In 1919, while General Denikin, who had taken Orel, threatened Tula, the arsenal of the republic and the final stop before Moscow, Makhno cut his communications, disorganized his rear and caused his collapse. In 1919, while Frunze, Tukhashevsky, and Blucher seized Perekop, the key to the Crimea, and defeated Baron Wrangel, Semen Karetnik and Marchenko, Makhno's lieutenants, (Makhno remaining in Gulai-Pole, for he was rightly wary) forced the straits of Sivach over the ice, drove toward White Crimea and entered Simferopol.

The epic of the Ukrainian anarchist peasants was long, chaotic, and strewn with acts of heroism, excesses, crimes and outbursts of enthusiasm: it was magnificent and tragic. Nestor Makhno showed himself to be one of the most remarkable popular figures of the Russian Revolution: chief of the people of the land; organizer of a unique army; an anarchist though tremendously disciplined; in a way a dictator, but denouncing authority as the worst of evils; the creator of a bold strategy that allowed him to defeat one after the other the old, experienced generals who had been students at the old war colleges, as well as the young Red generals; and creator of a new technique of partisan warfare where the horse team, either cabriolet or cart—the *tatchanka* of the Russian countryside—bearing a machine gun, was one of the instruments. The anarchist confederation The Tocsin (Nabat), with Voline, Archinov, Aaron Baron and Rybine (Zonov) gave the movement its ideological impetus.

Makhno's Black Army was often accused of anti-Semitism. There were anti-Semitic excesses carried out by all parties in Ukraine, but not where the Blacks were truly masters of their movements, as Soviet authors were forced to recognize. In communist publications they denounced this as a movement of well-off peasants. This is not true. Conscientious research carried out under the aegis of the Historical Commission of the Communist Party of the USSR established that poor and middle peasants formed the majority of Makhno's troops. People reproached this movement for its disordered character and its excesses; it was characterized as "banditry." The same reproaches should just as correctly be addressed to all the movements that fought over Ukraine: not a single one was free of excesses.

It was a perfectly viable movement for peasant autonomy. The Bolshevik government committed the serious error of defeating it by resorting to betrayal. It's only fair to note that the psychological hostility was merciless on both sides. The Blacks considered the "dictatorship of the commissars" a new form of autocracy and dreamed of unleashing a Third Revolution against it, that of the anarchist people. The Reds considered the anarchist and anarchist-tending partisans as a source of disorganization within the socialist state aimed at serving the petit bourgeois—principally rural—counterrevolution. There were countless wrongs on both sides. Makhno rallied to the Reds against the Whites, was declared an outlaw, and then was recognized again by the Soviet power. The greatest wrongs, in any case, must be recognized as belonging to the strongest. And they were already on the slippery slope to an authoritarian state.

In a recent document Trotsky relates that he and Lenin thought of granting the anarchists an autonomous territory. The anarchist peasants of Gulai-Pole had the right to this equitable solution. They were promised it, but events took a different turn.

In the summer of 1920 the White Army of Baron Wrangel carried out a victorious offensive in the south of Ukraine. A delegation of the Central Committee of the Bolshevik Party offered to unite with Makhno against the common enemy. The accord was signed October 15, 1920. All the anarchists imprisoned on Soviet territory, "except those who fought the Soviet power, weapons in hands" were to be freed. They were assured full freedom of propaganda. The partisan army was incorporated into the Red forces while maintaining its own formation. For the Reds it was signed by Frunze, the commandant of the Southern Front and the members of the Revolutionary Councils of the front, Bela Kun, and Goussev. For the Blacks, Korilenko and Popov.

The united operations brought about a rapid victory over Wrangel. Makhno's people then understood that the accord would not last long. As soon as they learned in Gulai-Pole that Karetnik and his partisans in Crimea were marching on Simferopol, Gregor Vassilevski, a collaborator of Makhno's, shouted: "That's the end of the treaty! I guarantee the Bolsheviks are going to attack us in one week."

In fact, the anarchists, who had recently been released from prison and were preparing a congress in accordance with the agreement signed with Frunze, were suddenly arrested in November all across Russia. The Blacks, attacked in Crimea by the Reds, defended themselves. A few hundred of them, led by Marchenko, succeeded in breaking thorough the circle of fire and joined Makhno. "The leader of the partisan army, Karetnik, was invited by the Soviet command to go to Gulai-Pole and was treacherously arrested along the way. Gavrilenko, the head of the general staff on campaign, several members of the general staff and unit commanders were invited to a conference and arrested. All were executed."

On November 26 in Gulai-Pole, Nestor Makhno, with about 2,500 men, both cavalry and infantry, was surrounded by Red troops greatly outnumbering his own. The Soviet newspapers published an order from Frunze calling on him to join the Red Army and accusing him of rebellion, banditry, and connivance with Wrangel. Finally, Frunze's declared him an outlaw. Makhno succeeded in breaking through the Red lines and made a fighting retreat to the Dnieper. A division of Budenny's cavalry joined him. His leg broken, he commanded the troops while stretched out in a wagon. His peasants fought to the cry of "Live free or die fighting!" In the villages they distributed tracts on "the free Soviets." Hunted down by the Reds, fighting every day, the Blacks grew exhausted.

In a letter, Makhno describes the final moments of the struggle:

> What to do? I couldn't hold myself in the saddle or sit in the carriage, and a hundred meters behind me I saw indescribable cavalry fights. The men were being killed just so they could save me. The enemy was five or six times stronger than us. The five machine gunners, commanded by Micha of the village of Chernigovka, near Berdiansk, came up to me and said, "Batko, the cause of our peasant organization needs you. We're going to be killed, but we'll save you and those alongside you. Don't forget to tell this to our families." Several of them embraced me and I never saw them again. Leva Zinkovski carried me in his arms and laid me down in a peasant cart. I heard the crackling of the machine gun and the explosion of bombs. The machine gunners covered our retreat. We went about four kilometers and crossed a river. The machine gunners were killed.

Harassed by Budenny's cavalry, Makhno crossed the Dniester in August 1921 and sought refuge in Romania. After being imprisoned in Romania and Poland he was granted asylum in France, where he died in Paris, having spent his years there as a factory worker.

Who is responsible for the strangling of a profoundly revolutionary peasant movement that the central power had recently recognized in the Politburo of Lenin and Trotsky? The Soviet government of Ukraine, headed by Rakovsky? Frunze's army, where Bela Kun, known for his deceptiveness, could be found? All of them, probably, in measures that it would be good to know. But it was mainly due to the spirit of intolerance that increasingly gripped the Bolshevik Party from 1919; to the monopoly of power, the ideological monopoly, the dictatorship of the leaders of the party, already tending to substitute themselves for that of the soviets and even the party. Whatever the case, this perfidy was an enormous error mistake. From then on a chasm was dug between anarchists and Bolsheviks that would not be easy to fill. The synthesis of Marxism and libertarian socialism, so necessary and which could be so fertile, was rendered impossible for the indefinite future.

Anarchist Altruism

In reality, the rational value of a doctrine is not key to its effectiveness. Even today irrational doctrines that are hardly able to stand up to criticism have played a decisive role in history. Anarchism, despite the conscientious labors of Kropotkin and Reclus, who in any case were not far from Marxist socialism, puts forth a set of utopian and idealistic ideas that can be linked to the spirit of small-scale production that preceded modern large-scale industry. Buried deep beneath these ideas are affective and instinctive complexes that are the outgrowth of our historic past. The spirit of freedom, with all it implies of dignity, generosity, moral grandeur, and stimulus to action, constitutes anarchism's true value. This is far more important than the shaky and naively smug ideas of an unscientific school of thought.

Unlike the upholders of other ideologies—a few forms of religious thought and the ardent forms of communism excepted—the anarchists seek to live in accordance with their ideas. Anarchism remains, even in its most absolute negations, a lived morality. I knew young individualist illegalists, who confessed to having no conscious scruples, who in an act of solidarity allowed themselves to be killed in order not to abandon their pals. At the other pole of anarchism old Kropotkin ended his long life outside Moscow writing his *Ethics*. He asked at the very beginning of his revolutionary career: "Fighting for truth, for equality with the people: what in life is more beautiful?" The moral sources of Marxist revolutionary thought are in no way different. Compare Kropotkin's words to these lines from Trotsky: "Under fate's implacable blows I would be as happy as I was during the best days of my youth if I contributed to the triumph of the truth. For humanity's greatest happiness is not in the exploitation of the present day, but in the preparation of the future" (L. Trotsky in *Stalin's Crimes*). The anarchist ethic places its accent on the revolt of the individual; the Marxists ethic subordinates itself to the fulfillment of historical necessity. The former arrives at a kind of Personalism; the latter at a revolutionary technique.

The inner faith of anarchist rebels resembles the classic forms of altruism, but at the point of combat. And since it proceeds from moral and psychological complexes that wind tight all the springs of being, it has no difficulty in pushing itself as far as it can possibly go, rising above both defeat and personal misfortune. Let us excerpt a page from Élisée Reclus and a few lines from Vanzetti:

> I recall as if I were still living it a touching moment of my life when the profound joy of having acted in accordance with my heart and my ideas was mixed with the bitterness of defeat. It was twenty years ago. The Paris Commune was at war with the troops of Versailles and my battalion had been taken prisoner on the plateau of Chatillon. It was morning and a cordon of soldiers surrounded us, while mocking officers strutted before us. Several of them insulted us. One of them, who later became one of the most elegant pastors of the Assembly perorated on the folly of the Parisians, but we had other things to think about than listening to him. The officer I found most striking was a man of sober speech and a harsh gaze and the face of an ascetic; probably a country squire raised by the Jesuits. He slowly walked along the steep edge of the plateau, standing out in black like an evil shadow against the luminous backdrop of Paris. The sun's rays, just rising, spread in a layer of gold over the houses and domes. Never had the beautiful city, the city of resolutions appeared more beautiful to me! "You see your Paris!" the sinister man said, pointing his weapon at the dazzling tableau. "Well, not one stone of it will be left standing on another."

Vanzetti, sentenced along with Sacco to the electric chair, on April 9, 1927, responded to Judge Thayer:

> If it had not been for this thing, I might have lived out my life talking at street corners to scorning men. I might have died, unmarked, unknown, a failure. Now we are not a failure. This is our career and our triumph. Never in our full life can we hope to do such work for tolerance, justice, for man's understanding of man, as now we do by

accident. Our words—our lives—our pains—nothing! The taking of our lives—lives of a good shoemaker and a poor fish peddler—all! That last moment belong to us—that agony is our triumph.

This moral strength, whose social sources are profound, is not diminished by the intrinsic weakness of anarchist ideology. It offers little room for doctrinal criticism. It simply is. If, having learned from all we are living through the libertarian socialism it animates would be strong enough to assimilate the gains of scientific socialism, this synthesis would guarantee revolutionaries an incomparable effectiveness.

(*La Crapouillot*, January 1938)

Serge in English

FICTION

Men in Prison (*Les hommes dans la prison*, 1930). Translated and introduced by Richard Greeman. Garden City, NY: Doubleday & Co., 1969; London: Victor Gollancz Ltd., 1970; Middlesex: Penguin Books Ltd., 1972; London and New York: Writers and Readers, 1977; Oakland: PM Press, 2014. A searing personal experience transformed into a literary creation of general import.

Birth of Our Power (*Naissance de notre force*, 1931). Translated by Richard Greeman. Garden City, NY: Doubleday & Co., 1967; London: Victor Gollancz Ltd., 1968; Middlesex: Penguin Books Ltd., 1970; London and New York: Writers and Readers, 1977; Oakland: PM Press, 2015. From Barcelona to Petersburg, the conflagration of World War I ignites the spark of revolution, and poses a new problem for the revolutionaries' power.

Conquered City (*Ville conquise*, 1932). Translated and introduced by Richard Greeman. New York: NYRB Classics, 2009. Idealistic revolutionaries cope with the poison of power as the Red Terror and the White struggle for control of Petrograd during the Civil War.

Midnight in the Century (*S'il est minuit dans le siècle*, 1939). Translated and introduced by Richard Greeman. London and New York: Writers and Readers, 1981; New York, NYRB Classics, 2014. On the eve of the great Purges, convicted anti-Stalin oppositionists in deportation attempt to survive, resist the GPU, debate political solutions, ponder their fates, and fall in love.

The Long Dusk (Les derniers temps, 1946). Translated by Ralph Manheim. New York: Dial Press, 1946. The fall of Paris (1940), the exodus of the refugees to the Free Zone, the beginnings of the French Resistance.

The Case of Comrade Tulayev (L'Affaire Toulaèv, 1951). Translated by Willard Trask. Introduction by Susan Sontag. New York: NYRB Classics, 2007. A panorama of the USSR and Republican Spain during the Purges, with a cast of sharply etched characters from provincial policemen to Old Bolsheviks and the Chief himself.

Unforgiving Years (Les années sans pardon, posthumous, 1973). Translated and introduced by Richard Greeman. New York: NYRB Classics, 2010. Tormented Russian revolutionaries in Paris on the eve of World War II, Leningrad under siege, the last days of Berlin, and Mexico.

POETRY
Resistance: Poems by Victor Serge (Résistance, 1938). Translated by James Brook. Introduction by Richard Greeman. San Francisco: City Lights, 1972. Most of these poems were composed in deportation in Orenburg (1933–36), confiscated by the GPU, and reconstructed from memory in France.

PM Press plans to publish James Brook's new translation of Serge's complete poetry in 2016.

NONFICTION
Revolution in Danger: Writings from Russia 1919–1921. Translated by Ian Birchall. London: Redwords, 1997; Chicago: Haymarket Books, 2011. Serge's early reports from Russia were designed to win over his French anarchist comrades to the cause of the Soviets.

Witness to the German Revolution (1923). Translated by Ian Birchall. London: Redwords, 1997; Chicago: Haymarket Books, 2011. A collection of the articles Serge wrote in Berlin in 1923 under the pseudonym R. Albert.

What Every Militant Should Know about Repression (Les Coulisses d'une Sûreté Générale: Ce que tout révolutionnaire doit savoir sur la répression, 1925). Popular pamphlet reprinted in a dozen languages. Serge unmasks the secrets he discovered working in the archives the Czarist Secret Police, then explains how police provocateurs operate everywhere and gives practical advice on security to activists.

The Chinese Revolution (1927–1928), Online at http://www.marxists.org/archive/serge/1927/china/index.html.

Year One of the Russian Revolution (*L'an 1 de la révolution russe*, 1930) Translated by Peter Sedgwick. London: Pluto Press; Chicago, Haymarket Books. Written soon after Stalin's takeover in Russia, this history presents the Left Opposition's take on the October Revolution and early Bolshevism.

From Lenin to Stalin (*De Lénine à Staline*, 1937). Translated by Ralph Manheim. New York: Monad and Pathfinder Press, 1973. A brilliant, short primer, on the Russian Revolution and its degeneration, with close-ups of Lenin and Trotsky.

Russia Twenty Years After (*Destin d'une Revolution*, 1937). Translated by Max Shactman (Includes "Thirty Years After the Russian Revolution," 1947). Atlantic Highlands, NJ: Humanities Press, 1996. Descriptive panorama and analysis of bureaucratic tyranny and chaos in Russia under Stalin's Five-Year Plans, based on statistics and economic, sociological, and political analysis.

The Life and Death of Leon Trotsky (*Vie et Mort de Léon Trotski*, 1951), by Victor Serge and Natalia Sedova Trotsky. Translated by Arnold Pomerans. London: Wildwood, 1975; Chicago: Haymarket Books, forthcoming. Still the most concise, authentic, and well-written one-volume Trotsky biography, based on the two authors' intimate knowledge of the man and his times and on Trotsky's personal archives (before they were sealed up in Harvard).

Memoirs of a Revolutionary (*Mémoires d'un révolutionnaire*, 1901–1941) Paris: Éditions du Seuil, 1951. Translated by Peter Sedwick. New York: NYRB Classics, 2012. Originally titled "Souvenirs of Vanished Worlds," Serge's *Memoirs* are an eyewitness chronicle of the revolutionary movements of Belgium, France, Spain, Russia, and Germany studded with brilliant portraits of the people he knew. This is the first complete English translation and comes with a glossary.

The Serge-Trotsky Papers: Correspondence and Other Writings between Victor Serge and Leon Trotsky. D. Cotterill, ed. London, Pluto Press, 1994. Includes their personal letters and polemical articles as well as essays on Serge and Trotsky by various authors.

Collected Writings on Literature and Revolution. Translated and edited by Al Richardson. London: Francis Boutle, 2004. Includes Serge's reports on Soviet Cultural life in the 1920s (published in Paris in *Clarté*), studies of writers like Blok, Mayakovsky, Essenin, and Pilniak as well as his highly original contributions to the debate on "proletarian literature" in the 1930s.

Anarchists Never Surrender: Essays, Polemics, and Correspondence on Anarchism, 1908–1938. Oakland: PM Press, 2015. An original anthology of Serge's writing on anarchism translated, edited, and introduced by Mitchell Abidor. Foreword by Richard Greeman.

Notebooks, 1936–1947. Sketches and meditations on subjects ranging from the Stalinist terror, Gide, Giraudoux, and Trotsky to Mexican earthquakes, popular wrestling matches, and death. NYRB Classics plans to publish this in 2016. Translation by Mitch Abidor and Richard Greeman. Intro by Claudio Albertani.

UNTRANSLATED BOOKS IN FRENCH:

Le tropique et le nord. Montpellier: Maspero 1972; Paris: La Découverte, 2003. Four short stories: *Mer blanche* (1931), *L'Impasse St. Barnabé* (1936), *La folie d'Iouriev* [*L'Hôpital de Léningrad*, 1953] and *Le Séisme* [*San Juan Parangarcutiro*]

Retour à l'Ouest: Chroniques, juin 1936–mai 1940. Preface by Richard Greeman. Marseille: Agone, 2010. From the euphoria of Popular Front France in June 1936 to the defeat of the Spanish Republic, Serge's weekly columns for a trade union–owned independent daily in Belgium provide a lucid panorama of this confused and confusing period.

MANUSCRIPTS:

The Victor Serge Papers (1936–1947), Beinecke Library, Yale University. Twenty-seven boxes of correspondence, documents, and manuscripts (mostly unpublished) on a wide variety of subjects from politics to Mexican anthropology. Catalog online:

http://drs.library.yale.edu:8083/fedoragsearch/rest?filter=&operation=solrQuery&query=Victor+Serge+Papers.

The Life of Victor Serge

1890   Victor Lvovich Kibalchich (Victor Serge) born on December 30 in Brussels to a family of sympathizers with Narodnik terrorism who had fled from Russia after the assassination of Alexander II.

1908   Photographer's apprentice and member of the socialist *Jeunes-Gardes*. Spends a short period in an anarchist 'utopian' community in the Ardennes. Leaves for Paris.

1910–1911 Becomes editor of the French anarchist-individualist magazine, *l'anarchie*. Writes and agitates.

1912   Serge is implicated in the trial of the anarchist outlaws known as the Bonnot Gang. Despite arrest, he refuses to turn informer and is sentenced to five years in prison. Three of his co-defendants were guillotined.

1917–1918 Serge is released from prison and banned from France. Goes to Barcelona where he participates in the syndicalist uprising. Writes his first article signed Victor Serge. Leaves Barcelona to join the Russian army in France. Is detained for over a year in a French concentration camp as a Bolshevik suspect.

1919   Arrives in Red Petrograd at the height of the Civil War. Gets to work organizing the administration of the Communist International under Zinoviev.

1920–1922 Participates in Comintern Congresses. Edits various international journals. Exposes Tsarist secret-police archives and fights in the defense of the city.

1923–1926 Serves Comintern as a secret agent and editor of *Imprekor* in Berlin and Vienna. Returns to the Soviet Union to take part in the last stand of the Left Opposition.

1927	Series of articles on the Chinese Revolution in which he criticizes Stalin's complacence towards the Kuomintang and draws attention to the importance of Mao Zedong.
1928	Expelled from the Communist Party and relieved of all official functions.
1928–1933	Barred from all other work, Serge takes up writing. He sends his manuscripts to France, since publication in the Soviet Union is impossible. Apart from many articles, he produces *Year One of the Russian Revolution*, 1930; *Men in Prison*, 1930; *Birth of Our Power*, 1931; and *Conquered City*, 1932.
1933	Serge is arrested and deported to Orenburg in Central Asia, where he is joined by his young son, Vlady.
1935	Oppositionists raise the 'Case of Victor Serge' at the Congress for the Defense of Culture in Paris. Paris intellectuals campaign for his freedom.
1936	Serge is released from Orenburg and simultaneously deprived of Soviet citizenship. His manuscripts are confiscated and he is expelled from the USSR. He settles first in Brussels, then in Paris. His return to Europe is accompanied by a slander campaign in the Communist press.
1937	*From Lenin to Stalin* and *Destiny of a Revolution* appear in which Serge analyses the Stalinist counter-revolution. He is elected a councilor to the Spanish POUM (Independent Marxist Party) and campaigns against the Moscow trials.
1940	Serge leaves Paris just as the Nazis advance. In Marseilles, he struggles for months to obtain a visa. Finally finds refuge in Mexico.
1940–1947	Serge lives in isolation and poverty. Writes *The Case of Comrade Tulayev* and *Memoirs of a Revolutionary* for his "desk drawer," since publication was impossible.
1947	November 17: Serge dies and is buried as a "Spanish Republican" in the French section of the Mexico City cemetery.

Victor Serge (1890–1947) was born to Russian anti-Tsarist exiles living in Brussels. As a young anarchist firebrand, he was sentenced to five years in a French penitentiary in 1912. In 1919, Serge joined the Bolsheviks. An outspoken critic of Stalin, he was expelled from the Party and arrested in 1929. Nonetheless, he managed to complete three novels (*Men in Prison, Birth of Our Power*, and *Conquered City*) and a history (*Year One of the Russian Revolution*), published in Paris. Arrested again in Russia and deported to Central Asia in 1933, he was allowed to leave the USSR in 1936 after international protests by militants and prominent writers such as André Gide and Romain Rolland. Hounded by Stalinist agents, Serge lived in precarious exile in Brussels, Paris, Vichy France, and Mexico City, where he died in 1947.

Mitchell Abidor is the principal French translator for the Marxists Internet Archive and has also translated works from Italian, Spanish, Portuguese, and Esperanto. He has published two earlier collections of his translations: *The Great Anger: Ultra-Revolutionary Writing in France from the Atheist Priest to the Bonnot Gang* and *Communards: The Story of the Paris Commune of 1871 as Told by Those Who Fought for It*. Abidor recently translated Jean Jaurès's *Socialist History of the French Revolution* into English for the first time, and is editor and translator of several forthcoming books with PM Press, including *Voices of the Paris Commune*. He lives in Brooklyn.

ABOUT PM PRESS

PM Press was founded at the end of 2007
by a small collection of folks with decades of
publishing, media, and organizing experience.
PM Press co-conspirators have published and
distributed hundreds of books, pamphlets,
CDs, and DVDs. Members of PM have founded enduring book fairs,
spearheaded victorious tenant organizing campaigns, and worked closely
with bookstores, academic conferences, and even rock bands to deliver
political and challenging ideas to all walks of life. We're old enough to
know what we're doing and young enough to know what's at stake.

We seek to create radical and stimulating fiction and non-fiction books,
pamphlets, T-shirts, visual and audio materials to entertain, educate
and inspire you. We aim to distribute these through every available
channel with every available technology—whether that means you are
seeing anarchist classics at our bookfair stalls; reading our latest vegan
cookbook at the café; downloading geeky fiction e-books; or digging new
music and timely videos from our website.

PM Press is always on the lookout for talented and skilled volunteers,
artists, activists and writers to work with. If you have a great idea for a
project or can contribute in some way, please get in touch.

PM Press
PO Box 23912
Oakland, CA 94623
www.pmpress.org

FRIENDS OF PM PRESS

These are indisputably momentous times—the financial system is melting down globally and the Empire is stumbling. Now more than ever there is a vital need for radical ideas.

In the seven years since its founding—and on a mere shoestring—PM Press has risen to the formidable challenge of publishing and distributing knowledge and entertainment for the struggles ahead. With over 250 releases to date, we have published an impressive and stimulating array of literature, art, music, politics, and culture. Using every available medium, we've succeeded in connecting those hungry for ideas and information to those putting them into practice.

Friends of PM allows you to directly help impact, amplify, and revitalize the discourse and actions of radical writers, filmmakers, and artists. It provides us with a stable foundation from which we can build upon our early successes and provides a much-needed subsidy for the materials that can't necessarily pay their own way. You can help make that happen—and receive every new title automatically delivered to your door once a month—by joining as a Friend of PM Press. And, we'll throw in a free T-shirt when you sign up.

Here are your options:

- **$30 a month** Get all books and pamphlets plus 50% discount on all webstore purchases

- **$40 a month** Get all PM Press releases (including CDs and DVDs) plus 50% discount on all webstore purchases

- **$100 a month** Superstar—Everything plus PM merchandise, free downloads, and 50% discount on all webstore purchases

For those who can't afford $30 or more a month, we're introducing **Sustainer Rates** at $15, $10 and $5. Sustainers get a free PM Press T-shirt and a 50% discount on all purchases from our website.

Your Visa or Mastercard will be billed once a month, until you tell us to stop. Or until our efforts succeed in bringing the revolution around. Or the financial meltdown of Capital makes plastic redundant. Whichever comes first.

Birth of Our Power

Victor Serge

ISBN: 978-1-62963-030-4
$18.95   256 pages

Birth of Our Power is an epic novel set in Spain, France, and Russia during the heady revolutionary years 1917–1919. Serge's tale begins in the spring of 1917, the third year of mass slaughter in the blood-and-rain-soaked trenches of World War I, when the flames of revolution suddenly erupt in Russia and Spain. Europe is "burning at both ends." Although the Spanish uprising eventually fizzles, in Russia the workers, peasants, and common soldiers are able to take power and hold it. Serge's "tale of two cities" is constructed from the opposition between Barcelona, the city "we" could not take, and Petrograd, the starving capital of the Russian Revolution, besieged by counter-revolutionary Whites. Between the romanticism of radicalized workers awakening to their own power in a sun-drenched Spanish metropolis to the grim reality of workers clinging to power in Russia's dark, frozen revolutionary outpost. From "victory-in-defeat" to "defeat in victory."

"Nothing in it has dated… It is less an autobiography than a sustained, incandescent lyric (half-pantheist, half-surrealist) of rebellion and battle."
—*Times Literary Supplement*

"Surely one of the most moving accounts of revolutionary experience ever written."
—Neal Ascherson, *New York Review of Books*

"Probably the most remarkable of his novels… Of all the European writers who have taken revolution as their theme, Serge is second only to Conrad… Here is a writer with a magnificent eye for the panoramic sweep of historical events and an unsparingly precise moral insight."
—Francis King, *Sunday Telegraph*

"Intense, vivid, glowing with energy and power… A wonderful picture of revolution and revolutionaries… The power of the novel is in its portrayal of the men who are involved."
—*Manchester Evening News*

"Birth of Our Power is one of the finest romances of revolution ever written, and confirms Serge as an outstanding chronicler of his turbulent era… As an epic, Birth of Our Power has lost none of its strength."
—Lawrence M. Bensky, *New York Times*

Also from SPECTRE CLASSICS from PM Press

Men in Prison

Victor Serge
Introduction and Translation by
Richard Greeman

ISBN: 978-1-60486-736-7
$18.95   232 pages

"Everything in this book is fictional and
everything is true," wrote Victor Serge in the
epigraph to *Men in Prison*. "I have attempted,
through literary creation, to bring out the
general meaning and human content of a
personal experience."

The author of *Men in Prison* served five years in French penitentiaries
(1912–1917) for the crime of "criminal association"—in fact for his
courageous refusal to testify against his old comrades, the infamous
"Tragic Bandits" of French anarchism. "While I was still in prison," Serge
later recalled, "fighting off tuberculosis, insanity, depression, the spiritual
poverty of the men, the brutality of the regulations, I already saw one
kind of justification of that infernal voyage in the possibility of describing
it. Among the thousands who suffer and are crushed in prison—and how
few men really know that prison!—I was perhaps the only one who could
try one day to tell all . . . There is no novelist's hero in this novel, unless
that terrible machine, prison, is its real hero. It is not about 'me,' about a
few men, but about men, all men crushed in that dark corner of society."

Ironically, Serge returned to writing upon his release from a GPU prison
in Soviet Russia, where he was arrested as an anti-Stalinist subversive
in 1928. He completed *Men in Prison* (and two other novels) in "semicaptivity" before he was rearrested and deported to the Gulag in 1933.
Serge's classic prison novel has been compared to Dostoyevsky's *House
of the Dead*, Koestler's *Spanish Testament*, Genet's *Miracle of the Rose*,
and Solzhenitsyn's *One Day in the Life of Ivan Denisovitch* both for its
authenticity and its artistic achievement.

This edition features a substantial new introduction by translator Richard
Greeman, situating the work in Serge's life and times.

"No purer book about the hell of prison has ever been written."
—Martin Seymour-Smith, *Scotsman*

"There is nothing in any line or word of this fine novel which doesn't ring true."
—Publishers Weekly